Good
Housekeeping

PLANNING
THE
PERFECT
GARDEN

Good Housekeeping PLANNING THE PERFECT GARDEN

Ralph Bailey
EDITOR-IN-CHIEF

Elvin McDonald
EXECUTIVE EDITOR

Compiled under the auspices of the Editors of Good Housekeeping

BOOK DIVISION, HEARST MAGAZINES, NEW YORK

Table of Contents

About This Book

Arranging and growing plants with purpose is one of the most fascinating, challenging and potentially rewarding of all aspects of gardening. *Planning the Perfect Garden* is to garden planning what a good cookbook is to meal planning: There are sixty-four gardens illustrated in color, each faced by a planting diagram and a list of the plant materials needed to achieve the effect shown in the photograph. Following this 128-page color portfolio is the Plant Finder, an exhaustive compilation of plants grouped according to kind—for example, annual flowers, hedge plants and trees—that will help you locate specific answers to countless garden planning questions. Following the Plant Finder is an Index of Common Names which matches the popular names of plants with the specific Latin names. For the sake of clarity, Latin names have been used mostly throughout this book, but if some of these puzzle you a quick check of the Index of Common Names will give you the answers.

We have included as wide a range of gardens as possible—from a tub three feet in diameter, planned for flowers beginning in earliest spring and continuing until frost in autumn, to complete landscape designs for various properties and interests. The perfect garden for you may be any one of these, or a combination of several. If you have limited time and space, the tub garden may be exactly what you are looking for. On the other hand, if you want a complete landscape with areas for outdoor living, lawn games, vegetables, herbs and fruit trees, there is also a plan for you.

If you have limited time or energy for gardening, we suggest you plan a garden of size and content you can handle with pleasure. Gardening is one of the greatest of all pastimes, but it should always be an activity you enjoy and look forward to, never back-breaking drudgery. If you own a sizable property, it may be better to develop one perfect small garden, perhaps as a surround for your outdoor living area, instead of trying to plant and maintain extensive flower and shrubbery borders. After studying all of the photographs and planting plans here, you will be able to define more precisely the size and kind of garden that is just right for your own lifestyle. Any garden, whether small or large, requires a long-range commitment of time, energy and money. If you plan ahead, you can have a perfect garden without its being a burden.

In 1972 the 16-volume *Good Housekeeping Illustrated Encyclopedia of Gardening* was published, and from its more than 2500 pages, we have selected the sixty-four color plates included here and the Plant Finder. This single volume is a logical outgrowth from the 16 earlier books, for it shows in detail exactly how to use the countless plants included in the *Encyclopedia*. *Good Housekeeping Planning the Perfect Garden* was preceded in 1974 by *Good Housekeeping Basic Gardening Techniques*, a book that is to a gardener what a good dictionary is to a writer; it can make you a good gardener who doesn't always have to be dependent on an expert to answer every question that arises in day-to-day gardening.

Good Housekeeping Planning the Perfect Garden, like the 16-volume *Good Housekeeping Illustrated Encyclopedia of Gardening* and *Good Housekeeping Basic Gardening Techniques*, is a direct outgrowth of the life's work of the late Ralph Bailey, who was for more than a quarter of a century garden editor of two distinguished magazines, *House Beautiful* and *House and Garden*. He not only loved gardening but brought to it and to his editorial work an irreplaceable knowledge, a warm sense of humor and a brilliant talent for prose that made gardens bloom on paper and gardeners-at-heart of all his readers.

Unfinished at the time of Mr. Bailey's death, the earlier 16 volumes, *Basic Gardening Techniques*, and now *Planning the Perfect Garden*, have been completed and edited under the auspices of the *Good Housekeeping* staff, by Elvin McDonald, the Senior Editor and Garden Editor of *Good Housekeeping*'s sister publication, *House Beautiful*. Mr. McDonald has been an avid practicing gardener and garden writer since his early teens when he wrote articles published in virtually every gardening and home service magazine. In 1950 at age 14 he founded the America Gloxinia and Gesneriad Society. Today, as author of more than 40 books on the subject, he brings to *Planning the Perfect Garden* practical dirt-gardening experience on a ranch in arid western Oklahoma, suburban landscapes in Kansas City and Long Island and windswept terraces of New York's high-rise apartments. In his apartment alone there are more than 300 different plants growing at the windows and under fluorescent lights.

For sharing their expertise in specialized areas, the editors would like to acknowledge the contributions made by Betty Ajay, Mary Deputy Cattell, Jacqueline Heriteau Hunter and Bill Mulligan. The planting diagrams have been prepared by Dale Booher. The photographers whose work appears include Morley Baer, Wesley Balz, Feliciano, George de Gennaro, Gottlieb Hampfler, Leland Y. Lee, Elvin McDonald, Frank Lotz Miller, Ezra Stoller, Michel Tcherevkoff and Tom Wier.

The Editors
Good Housekeeping

INTRODUCTION

Planning Your Perfect Garden

A well-thought-out and carefully executed landscape design will give you grounds that are attractive to look at, comfortable to live in and easy to maintain. Today more and more family life is lived outdoors, so the size of your family, its hobbies, habits and general way of life will play a large part in landscaping plans. Other elements to take into account in planning your grounds are local climate, topography, the general style of the community and your own sense of style and taste.

A plan on paper makes it possible to avoid mistakes and to tie all these requirements into a pleasing and unified whole. It may be amateur or professional, but a drawing ought to exist. The necessity for a plan is most obvious on a brand-new property where everything is still to be done. It is just as valuable, however, where a garden is to be remodeled, either for a new owner or for a change in family size or way of life.

Advantages of Hiring Help

Professional advice is an economy in working out a long-range plan. There are parts of the country where landscape advice is not available; other owners feel they cannot afford the fee of a competent professional or mistakenly think their needs are too modest for such help. Actually, a small property may have greater need for the guidance of a landscape architect or landscape designer. The small spaces and low budget, intrusive neighboring houses and garages of the small lot make it more difficult to design to satisfy the need for beauty, comfort and efficiency. And any mistake here is more apparent and correcting it may take a discouraging amount of time and money.

The services of a professional landscape architect range from consultation only to the purchase of a complete set of plans, cost estimate and supervision of work. Fees depend on the type of plan and help required. On preliminary visits to the site, existing conditions will be evaluated. The trained designer takes into account the neighborhood in general, the architecture of the house, the existing plant material, soil conditions, prevailing wind at various seasons and views in all directions, either desirable or undesirable.

A survey of the property as it exists will be necessary. You can take these measurements yourself, or hire an engineer. Without an accurate plot plan or survey, accurate drawings are impossible. Include on the plot plan buildings, existing driveways, plant masses, trees, walks, fences, property lines and, if possible, the location of cesspools, septic tanks, electric and water lines and other utilities. For most newer properties there already exists a title survey made in small scale. It shows property lines and buildings. Photostated to a larger size, this makes a starting-point drawing on which other information can be traced by you or the professional surveyor.

Prepare a Questionnaire

If you have engaged a professional landscaper, this person will require additional information about you, the size of your family and its lifestyle. A professional may present a questionnaire that includes:

1. How many in the family—adults, children, and their ages?
2. Is it a year-round house? If not, what month or months is the family likely to be away?
3. How many cars are likely to be coming in and out daily—family or guest drivers?
4. What is the local provision for garbage and trash collections—daily, weekly or on infrequent order?
5. Is outdoor laundry-drying rare, daily, weekly; large or small?
6. Are most deliveries made by truck or by the family?
7. Is street traffic heavy and is street parking permissible?
8. Where are tools to be kept?
9. Is entertaining usually in small groups, large groups, frequent or infrequent, formal or informal?
10. Who furnishes the gardening labor—the family or hired gardener —how much time of either, or each, is available?
11. Are any special areas desired now or later for flower borders, a rock garden, a greenhouse, a vegetable garden, a play yard, a swimming pool, special game courts?

12. Has the client or have members of the family any particular preferences in materials, colors, styles, plants?

With an accurate survey and answers to these questions in hand, the professional landscape architect proceeds to make a general overall plan which shows paved areas, walks, general plant masses, service yard and the shape and size of all areas. While this plan is to scale, it can have very few details and is really only a picture of space allotment. From there the landscaper can go on to detailed working drawings either immediately, or as you are ready to commission or undertake the work yourself. A master or overall plan alone is helpful, but like any partial service it is only a start in the right direction.

Do-It-Yourself Planning

If you are not planning to have professional help, proceed in much the same way as the landscape architect. He or she does a survey or has it done, and fills out his or her own questionnaire before starting work. Without professional help, you must analyze your own problems, desires, necessities, assets and liabilities; the more exhaustive the analysis, the more likely is the final result to be both practical and interesting.

The problems of grading and drainage are the first considerations; they make or mar the beauty and the livability of a property. If the site is perfectly flat, there should be relatively few problems. If, however, it is rolling country or very steep hillside property, grading and drainage must be taken into account in placing the house and in designing or redesigning overall landscape and service areas. The sharper the slope, the more complex the problems and the more expensive the solutions. Also, the more interesting the layout in the long run.

In gently rolling property, it is often possible in initial planning to improve drainage and grading by accentuating existing grades, a solution that may also create interesting variations in levels. Such plans must be studied very carefully, however, to avoid a too man-made appearance. Steep banks, for instance, are more artificial-looking than long, gradual slopes. More-or-less flat areas, as garage courts, terraces and areas immediately adjoining the house, should be fitted into the landscape with as little disturbance to natural grades as possible.

In rolling land, the terraces, gardens and lawns can pitch at a rate of about 1 foot in 25. They will then look level in comparison with slightly steeper slopes nearby. If the garden slope is more gradual, it is likely to look tilted in the opposite direction or stick out of the landscape in an artificial fashion.

Problems of Hilly Land

On hilly land, grading is a major problem and must be planned with great care. An accurate topographical survey by an engineer is imperative, otherwise plans will be inaccurate, estimates impossible to get and the final results will have none of the drama and attractiveness such properties can afford. Careful preliminary planning can save hundreds of yards of fill or excavation, many feet of wall and a great proportion of the budget. On such properties, retaining walls are more economical than banks. The walls may be of concrete, brick or stone, according to the architecture of the house and the materials locally available. Retaining walls are particularly important on small properties, because a wall takes up a fraction of the space of a bank of the same height. Even a heavy stone wall takes up no more than a foot and a half of ground space, while a drop of four feet, if the bank is to be mowable, takes up twelve feet.

Good planning may cover mistakes in grading to a certain extent as far as appearance goes. However, good planning can't disguise the expense or irritation of water in the basement, water on the driveway and ice on the walks caused by faulty drainage. This is one area where professional design and labor are likely to be an economy in the long run.

The second step in landscape design is to work out successful solutions to the need for utility areas and good traffic patterns. The driveways, garage courts and entrance court are of first importance in comfortable daily living. Most of us begrudge the room that is necessary for paved surfaces that motor cars take up, yet no one factor can cause more irritation, more repair or correction than inefficiently planned motor approaches. The driveway must be planned so that access from the street is both comfortable and safe.

Planning Traffic Patterns

Where no street parking is permissible, room must be found on the property itself for parking two or three cars without completely blocking all other traffic. On a straight driveway, nothing less than 18 feet wide allows one car to park and another to pass. The all too common twelve-foot driveway is an extravagance. It is not wide enough for two cars and too wide for one. It spends unnecessary money to achieve no useful purpose. Where cars or trucks must turn on the property itself in order to get to the street, two or three feet in length can make all the difference between safe and comfortable maneuvering and encroachment on adjacent plantings, lawns, fences or buildings.

Family preference and climate may play a very large part in planning the driveway and entrance courts. In areas that can expect heavy snowfall, provision should be made for piling up snow as the plow comes through. Where there is a great deal of inclement weather or the family habits demand, the driveway may have to go directly to the front door, or at least to some door without exposure to the weather. If cars cannot reach the front door directly, their relation to it should be carefully studied; otherwise, the owner is likely to receive deliveries at the front door and guests in the kitchen.

The surface of the driveway may range from gravel or crushed stone to blacktop or paving. A garden texture such as mortared brick or stone is particularly good-looking and most effective if there is a front entrance court. Blacktop is probably the least gracious surface in country or informal surroundings. If gravel or crushed rock is chosen for the surfacing, it saves a great deal of subsequent raking and dulling of lawn-mower blades if it is bound into the road by a light coat of asphalt. The surface should be chosen in terms of the surroundings as a whole, the amount of traffic and, of course, the budget.

Planning Service Areas

The next most important area is the collection point for garbage and trash. The most attractive garden in the world does not gain from trash barrels, garbage pails or baskets awaiting disposal. In communities where there is no regular collection service, provision for disposal of these materials should be planned for on the property itself. This means an efficient incinerator or out-of-sight storage for trash that is called for infrequently or on special order. The truckman or the family station wagon should be able to get very close to the place of storage. Usually it is better to make provision for trash cans close to the kitchen door or service entrance where they are accessible from house and grounds and from the driveway. This can prove to be a design problem that affects all the surrounding area and should be solved in the planning stage.

Outdoor laundry also plays a role in landscaping design. Even with a dryer in the house, most families do some outdoor drying. It may be occasional hand laundry, wet bathing clothes or bedding. If the family does not hang out large laundries, the drying area can be reduced to a minimum. It may be only a portable clothes reel or a rack on the back of the garage. On many older properties, big clothes posts and lines exist because they have always been there. In such gardens, the owner should see how many hours a week laundry is hung outdoors and how many feet of line are in use. Frequently, there is twice as much drying yard as needed, taking up space that could be valuable for other purposes.

Outdoor Work Areas

Other utility areas that may be wanted include space for compost piles, cold frames and garden work areas. They depend on the gardening enthusiasm of the family. The compost pile need not be completely unpresentable, but neither it nor cold frames are objects of art. They should be in inconspicuous places, easy of access, but not featured. A small orchard, an ornamental hedge, a low stone wall, a specimen shrub are some of the landscape elements that can be used to camouflage these less-than-beautiful features.

Storage space for tools can prove to be a major problem later, if not provided for in the original plan of the property. Probably the most economical place to store them is in or near the garage. With a new garage it is a good idea to plan either additional length or width, so that there is plenty of room for large power tools and hand tools without cramping the cars. Doors leading directly from the grounds to the tool space make this storage area easy to get to and should be included if possible.

If the garage is already built, it may be tight for large-size present-day cars and will have to be enlarged if tools are to be stored in it. A low shed, either on the side or the end of the garage, may be preferable to in-garage storage. If the architecture or location of the garage does not permit this, a separate toolhouse or tool storage wall or fence may be the solution. Such structures can be inexpensive and will add greatly to ease of management and efficiency. It is almost an axiom that the more accessible the garden tools are, the more likely the grounds will be well-groomed and the tools well cared for.

Recreational Areas

When all the utilitarian spaces have been analyzed and at least partially planned, the outdoor living areas can be designed. They depend on the desires of the individual family, on the budget and on the climate. First, there must be access to all parts of the property with paved surfaces where there is to be either frequent foot traffic or a considerable amount of furniture and congregation of people. Direct and obvious access to the front door and the kitchen door is mandatory. Both of these entrance walks should be of some hard material, durable, easy to clean and more or less impervious to weather. Brick, flagstone or textured concrete is satisfactory. If other materials are used the house is likely to be tracked with mud or snow because the walks cannot be cleaned properly. It is important for the walk to the front door to be wide enough for two people to walk abreast —four feet at least. If the size of the garden allows, five feet is more comfortable. If grass is worn down along the sides of a walk, the walk is too narrow. A path worn into a shortcut indicates the walk is in the wrong place. The shortest distance between the point of arrival and the front door is usually the attractive and efficient place for an entrance walk. People will not detour along curves arbitrarily laid out for no apparent reason.

The next important paved areas are one or more terraces. Most families spend time outdoors and need surfaced living areas that are easy to maintain, attractive and convenient. The size, location and material of an outdoor living room are dictated by the architecture of the house and grounds and by the general landscape plan. Since outdoor furniture is larger in scale than indoor, it is wise in planning a terrace to err on the side of over-generosity. Sixteen feet minimum width is advisable for the main terrace and is particularly important if this terrace is raised above the level of the lawn. The outdoor living room should be adjacent to the living quarters of the house and accessible from one or two doors, preferably the living room and the kitchen or dining room. As far as space and layout permit, it adds greatly to family enjoyment of the outdoors if there are one large living terrace and two or three smaller ones where seasonal conditions of sun and wind can be used to advantage, terraces planned for the morning, the afternoon, or for spring, summer, fall or even for winter.

Surfacing Materials

The surfacing material of the paved area where there is to be furniture should be easy to clean and even enough for furniture to be level. Brick or flagstone can be laid without cement in the joints—it is more attractive that way. The joints, however, should be very tight so that there is no space for grass that will have to be clipped by hand, or for furniture or feet to catch. Concrete is usually less expensive and very easily maintained but gives an industrial feeling. It can be used in combination with brick, flagstone or wood. With careful addition of color and texture, it is particularly appropriate with contemporary houses.

As the plan of the garden develops, certain other areas may need to be paved. If there are big trees where neither ground covers nor grass will grow, it may be wise to have brick or stone set under the trees.

Most people think of landscape design only in terms of plant materials —lawns, shrubs, trees and flowers. These are important and integral elements of the overall design, but probably should be the last to be considered in detail. Certainly, nothing enhances the beauty of property more than a well-designed and well-cared-for lawn. Unfortunately, nothing can take a larger proportion of the budget of time and money and be more of a disappointment if it is not properly planted and executed. As a generalization, grass should be restricted to areas where it will grow well, usually in good sunlight, and should be as free as possible of edges that need hand-trimming. It is as important to design shape and boundaries of turf areas as to plan paving, flower gardens or any other defined area. Bits and pieces of grass, hard of access, not well unified, add nothing to the appearance of the landscape and demand a great deal in hours of upkeep needed. The test of a well-designed lawn is that it can be fertilized, mowed and raked with power machinery with a minimum of hard work of any sort. There are always times when lack of labor or time or bad weather leaves ragged edges, so that instead of being an asset, the lawn is a detriment. Reducing this to a minimum takes forethought.

Designing a Lawn

The lawn is undoubtedly the largest solid green area in the garden, so its pattern should be well proportioned and have pleasant lines. Where grass adjoins any sort of paved area (driveways, paved terraces, walks) there should be a definition created by steel curbing, brick, concrete, stone or other hard edges. Where turf is adjacent to shrub borders, flower borders or other plant masses, the same care should be given to establishing a pleasing curve or straight line that can be maintained. Without an edging, flowers grow over the margins of grass paths, shrub borders get to be scallops instead of free-flowing curves and the garden loses the quality of repose that is essential to good garden design.

Next in importance after lawn areas and flower borders are the woody plants—trees and shrubs. On small- or medium-sized property each mass of shrubs and each individual tree must serve two or three purposes. Plantings of evergreens and deciduous plants should provide a background to flower gardens, screen out a neighbor's house or garage and provide material for cutting for the house. One tree may have to shade some of the house windows, frame the house from the street and make a tall neighboring house less intrusive. Trees and shrubs are the most permanent of all the plantings and must be considered in terms of present and future effects. They should be selected to provide year-round beauty or effect, not just one season of bloom. They must be in proportion to the size of the house and the size of the property. In a spacious garden large shade trees such as linden, Norway maple and beech will be appropriate, while on the small property dogwood, flowering crab apple or a shade tree with high, light branches—a sycamore, for example—can give the same effect without taking up ground room.

When planning shrub borders good design includes plans not only for combinations of flowers but, more important, for combinations of texture, seasonal effect and growth habit. When vertical growth habit is combined with horizontal growth habit, small leaves with large, there is an interesting pattern throughout the year. Without this discrimination, shrub borders are likely to look monotonous and indeterminate, whether they are broadleaf evergreens for year-round effect or deciduous shrubs with no particular character except at flowering time.

Gardens with Mobility

Wheel in the dolly, roll out the garden. Outdoors or in, green-thumbing in today's style means growing an abundance of flowers, shrubs, trees and vines in portable containers. Dream your dream. Is it a carpet of flowers by the patio? Sudden greening at the door? Or a real tree casting its dappled shade in the living room? The magic lies in movable pots.

The spring bulb flowers shown opposite were rooted and brought to the bud stage in an out-of-the-way part of the garden, then placed on steps at the front door. The bulbs include purple crocus, pink and blue hyacinths and red and white tulips. Pots of spring-flowering bulbs in full bloom are nearly indispensable when dressing up the outdoor living area of a garden. Where winter temperatures stay above 25 degrees F., hardy bulbs can be planted in October in outdoor containers of all sizes and left to winter in any convenient area. In more severe climates you can plant directly in larger containers (minimum size, two feet in diameter by two feet deep). Keep bulbs four inches away from the edge. Push containers close to the side of a building for protection and cover with layers of newspaper and plastic or canvas. Keep moist at all times. Remove protective covering at the end of severe cold. It is also possible to plant in sizable clay pots and store these in a garage, cold frame or unheated cellar. When danger of freezing is over, then move outdoors. When buds are well along, move to display area. After flowers fade, transplant to garden.

Another way to enjoy the mobility of a container garden is suggested by the sketch: Sink pots to the rim wherever you want instant color in the garden. When the flowers are gone it is a simple matter to lift out the pots, return them to a utilitarian growing area and replace with something just coming into bloom.

This technique of sinking pots to the rim may be used for bulb flowers even in cold climates. Pot up and sink in the ground in October, or before winter freezes. After freezing, mulch heavily. In spring, remove mulch. When buds show color, remove pots, clean and place in display area.

Welcome Entries

The two door-yard gardens shown opposite suggest appropriate landscaping for a contemporary house *(upper)* and a traditional. The traditional uses red geraniums in the sun, pink impatiens in the shade, with dwarf junipers in the background and English ivy draping the walls. The contemporary, for which the plan is shown, depends almost entirely on low-upkeep evergreen shrubs and ground covers that present a similar appearance year 'round with welcome splashes of flower color in season. Trees pruned high create a natural arch over the area. The wood decking and two tailored trees in tubs are distinctive, stylish touches to please the eye and invite entry. 1. English ivy. 2. Rhododendron. 3. Ophiopogon. 4. English ivy. 5. Redbud tree. 6. Daffodils. 7. *Vinca minor.* 8. Japanese holly.

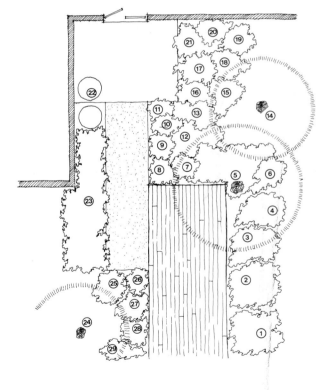

9. Dwarf juniper
10. *Pinus mugo*
    var. *pumilio*
11. Dwarf
    rhododendron
12. *Pieris*
    floribunda
13. *Viburnum*
    davidii
14. Oak tree
15. *Ajuga reptans*
16. *Skimmia japonica*
17. Ophiopogon
18. Japanese holly
19. *Ajuga reptans*
20. Ophiopogon
21. Dwarf
    rhododendron
22. Tree lilacs
    or roses
23. English ivy
24. Dogwood tree
25. Dwarf
    rhododendron
26. *Cotoneaster*
    dammeri
27. Rhododendron
28. Ophiopogon
29. *Vinca minor*

Pear Tree Dooryard Garden

Although the flower garden shown is in front of the owner's house, the plan is a good one for any sunny, flat site measuring approximately 20 by 30 feet. It is essentially a perennial border, designed to give flowers from earliest spring until cold weather in autumn. Everything can be planted in early spring excepting Oriental poppies, daffodils, iris and peonies which need to be planted in late summer or early fall. Although hybrid lilies are not indicated, they would make a welcome addition planted in clumps throughout the garden. Hardy asters and chrysanthemums might also be added for fall bloom; plant in the spring. The lower photograph shows English primroses. 1. *Iberis sempervirens*. 2. Snapdragon. 3. Delphinium. 4. Oriental poppy. 5. English primrose. 6. Snapdragon. 7. Delphinium. 8. Daffodil. 9. Oriental poppy. 10. *Iberis sempervirens*. 11. Freesia. 12. Delphinium. 13. Snapdragon. 14. Pansy. 15. English primrose. 16. Snapdragon. 17. *Iberis sempervirens*. 18. German iris. 19. Stock.

20. Dwarf pears
21. Azaleas
22. Everblooming roses
23. *Bellis perennis*
24. German iris
25. *Iberis sempervirens*
26. Spuria iris
27. Peony
28. German iris
29. Coreopsis
30. *Bellis perennis*
31. English primrose
32. Summer phlox
33. Peony
34. Foxglove
35. Lythrum
36. Spuria iris
37. Foxglove
38. Peony
39. *Bellis perennis*
40. Forget-me-not
41. Lily-of-the valley

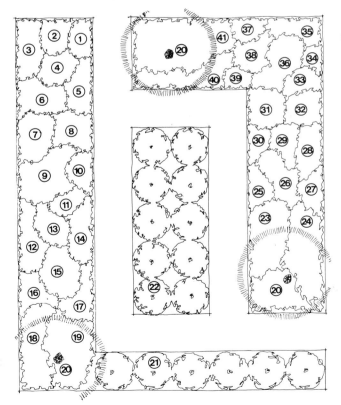

Low-upkeep Desert Garden

This plan suggests a minimum-maintenance treatment for an entryway garden in a hot, dry climate in full sun. Although an expanse of lawn is the traditional welcoming mat, this flower-covered ground cover requires much less upkeep, even less water and fertilizer than healthy grass would need. Only items 1, 3, 9 and 10 have to be planted annually in the spring. The rest are hardy perennials and shrubs. Spring-flowering bulbs such as tulips, daffodils, hyacinths, crocus and grape-hyacinths might be underplanted throughout the areas covered by items 1, 3, 9 and 10; plant in autumn, just before winter freeze-up. To keep petunias and sweet-alyssum blooming over a long season, clip back the plants after a period of heavy flowering. This prevents the formation of seeds and encourages stocky new basal growth.

1. Chrysanthemum. 2. Hypericum. 3. White petunia. 4. Potentilla. 5. *Oenothera trichocalyx*. 6. *Oenothera missouriensis*. 7. *Hypericum polyphyllum*. 8. Ceanothus. 9. Carpet of Snow sweet-alyssum. 10. Rosie O'Day sweet-alyssum. 11. *Sedum acre*. 12. Prostrate rosemary. 13. English lavender.

No-sweat Garden for a Circular Drive

The island often created by a circular driveway to the front door presents various landscape problems—and opportunities—depending on the climate and individual site. Here the owners wanted sturdy, carefree perennials and shrubs that could withstand long summers of full sun and hot, dry weather, with a minimum of maintenance. The plants used are 1. *Sedum acre*, 2. *Cotoneaster dammeri*, 3. English lavender and 4. *Juniperus horizontalis* Webberi (a matlike spreading juniper with bluish green foliage). In a similar situation that receives a half day or more of shade in the summer from surrounding tall trees, the plant materials used might be: 1. *Vinca minor* (myrtle or periwinkle), 2. *Euonymus fortunei* Emerald 'n Gold, 3. hardy ferns and 4. *Ilex cornuta* Carissa (a dwarf holly with glossy green leaves). The smaller, inset photograph shows a closeup of *Sedum acre*.

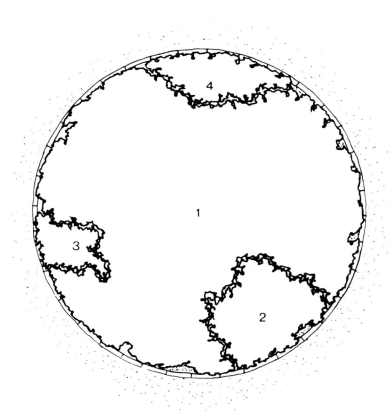

Oriental Entry Garden

Using a minimum of construction and plant materials, this entryway garden suggests Japanese landscaping, but with subtlety. Redwood sunk into the ground and allowed to age its natural gray divides the two kinds and colors of mulch, water-polished charcoal stones on the right, reddish brown bark chips on the left. Red impatiens bloom profusely in the dappled shade beneath the tree, and a young staghorn fern hangs on its trunk in warm weather. Fall-planted daffodil bulbs might be put in under the tree in order to have early spring bloom. Impatiens plants set out at the beginning of warm weather will hide the ripening daffodil foliage and provide a long season of bloom. Tuberous-rooted begonias might be used instead of, or along with, the impatiens. A prostrate juniper grows next to a rock on the right.

1. Prostrate juniper
2. Impatiens
3. Redmond linden

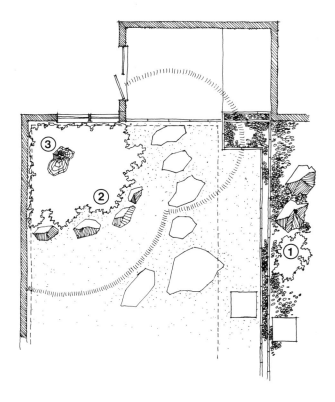

Formal City Garden

What you see here and on pages 30-31 and 32-33 are three city gardens designed to escape the metropolis. Each owner of these San Francisco townhouse gardens, situated side by side and sharing common walls, began with a narrow, sloping space 18 by 52 feet. The finished gardens all give privacy and a place of beauty from any vantage point (all may be enjoyed from upper floors in the houses). All have different levels and disappearing paths. Shelves, benches and steps give places to display containers of flowering plants and choice foliage. For beauty without upkeep *(opposite)*, Landscape Architect K. C. Kawamoto combined flagstones and mellowed bricks in classic design. City garden surrounded by overlooking apartments has surprising feeling of seclusion, created by backdrop planting around fountain. In dining area near house, plants are espaliered on treillage. Geraniums and pink hydrangea are in bloom. Nandina, Japanese maple and purpleleaf plum offer contrasting textures and colors. Unobtrusive fixtures provide after-dark lighting. Creeping thyme spreads its mossy-green mat between some of the flagstones. The splash of the fountain helps mask the industrial hum of the city surround.

1. Ceanothus
2. Wild strawberry
3. Nandina
4. Cutleaf maple
5. Agapanthus
6. Purpleleaf plum
7. Yew
8. Boxwood
9. White azalea
10. *Ficus retusa nitida* standards
11. White geranium
12. Creeping thyme

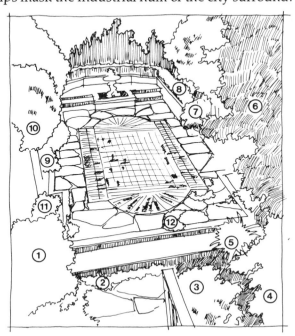

Architecturally Sophisticated City Garden

Geometrics order this garden, designed by Landscape Architect Thomas Church, and like the ones on pages 28-29 and 32-33, it began as a narrow, sloping space 18 by 52 feet, behind a San Francisco townhouse. In little space, Church makes a bold statement: plants selected, placed and trained with purpose. Deck, seating, steps and gravel are practical at ground level, a work of art from above. Ivy carpets the ground and traces free-form designs on walls. For ornamentation with restraint: Japanese maple bonsai, sculptured globes of boxwood and yew in pots. White geraniums edge deck. Instead of boxwood and yew, the topiaries might also be rosemary, myrtle or even the fast-growing annual dwarf bush basil. One of the beauties of this garden is that it requires very little upkeep in order to maintain its restrained perfection. In a few hours after work, or on the weekend, one or two persons could easily do all of the gardening necessary—with pleasure.

1. White geraniums
2. Crassula (jade)
3. English ivy
4. Agapanthus
5. Clipped yew
6. Cactus bowl garden
7. English ivy
8. Clump of thornless honey-locust trees
9. English ivy
10. Boston ivy
11. Clipped boxwood
12. Potted myrtle
13. Japanese maple bonsai

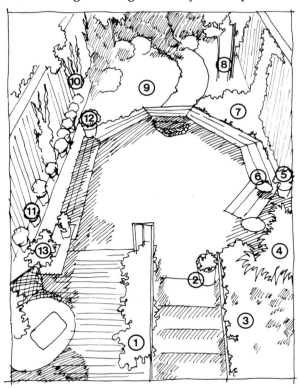

Gardener's City Garden

Swatch from a botanical garden, remarkably achieved by Landscape Architect Thomas Church in small space: Primroses, pansies, cinerarias, roses, azaleas and camellias have burst into bloom. This garden, like the two preceding on pages 28-29 and 30-31, began as a narrow, sloping space 18 by 52 feet. Now a dining terrace, an octagonal deck and an airy gazebo exist at three levels. Large pots of blue felicia and white Boston daisies are moved on occasion for bouquets at close range. Creeping thyme outlines the flagstones. Steps lead to tiny patio at first-floor level, a private retreat. Although situated behind a townhouse in San Francisco, this space succeeds in being a true gardener's garden stuffed with horticultural treasures and at least a few blooms nearly every day of the year. Restraint is the key here— the discipline needed to refrain from planting anything too large or too quick-growing to be in scale—plus a commitment to keeping every spent bloom promptly picked and any wayward growth tucked in place or clipped off. Spent seasonal bloomers, cinerarias for example, are replaced with annuals.

1. Boston daisy
2. Felicia
3. Mazus
4. White geranium
5. Pieris
6. Confederate-jasmine (espaliered)
7. Potted nandina
8. Assorted dwarf annual flowers
9. Pansies, cinerarias, primroses, ferns
10. Roses
11. Weeping cherry surrounded by dwarf annual flowers
12. Assorted annual and perennial flowers; camellia espalier

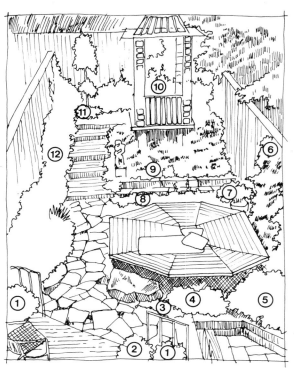

View from the Terrace

The owners of this terrace wanted flowers up close, but nothing large enough to block the view toward the valley and mountains beyond. They chose to limit the plantings in spring to two simple flower forms, daisy and pansy, and mostly two colors, yellow (gamolepis) and white (Boston daisy). The low, white retaining wall is wide enough to accommodate sizable terra-cotta tubs and has proved to be an effective way to display container plants in various combinations. The carpetlike brickwork of the terrace is framed by pebble-surface concrete. In summer, pink and white geraniums might be used for the larger containers and almost any bright-flowered, low-growing annual as the table centerpiece. In autumn, pots of chrysanthemums and hardy asters could be used as a welcome change. In mild-winter climates, the gamolepis and Boston daisies can follow; in climates where freezing occurs, the pots can be filled with cut evergreens if they are on view from the house in winter.

1. Boston daisy
2. Gamolepis
3. Viola

French Quarter Patio

From the sequestered patios of the French Quarter, like that shown here, to plantation pigeonniers and colonnaded summerhouses, the gardens of New Orleans are made for the pleasures of living outdoors. Mysteriously forbidding gates open from the streets to tranquil courtyard gardens protected by high walls draped in ivy and jasmine. Underfoot, worn paving wears the patina of age, and lichen-covered statuary reposes in the shade of giant magnolias and oaks. Ancient crape myrtles thrust bouquets of shimmery flowers to iron-galleried townhouses dating back to the 1790's. Canopies of bougainvillea bloom over shuttered windows and balconies and sweet-olive releases its all-pervading perfume. These gardens are rooted in the best of French and Spanish traditions, but as today's surrounds for entertaining and dining alfresco, they have a style that is strictly New Orleans. The plantings on the patio of this 1828 house in the Vieux Carré are cultivated in containers so that they can be moved around. A swimming pool has been added, about where the photographer stood to take the photograph. 1. Croton. 2. Caladium. 3. Strawberry jar. 4. Lily-turf. 5. Geraniums. 6. Ferns. 7. Oleander. 8. Philodendron. 9. Staghorn ferns. 10. Boston ferns. 11. *Begonia semperflorens.* 12. Myrtle. 13. Asparagus-fern. 14. *Ficus retusa nitida.*

City Terrace Get-away

Often the idea of a city terrace for dining and gardening is more glamorous than the reality. Unfortunately, polluted air, street noise and wind tend to prevent the space from being truly livable except on sunny, warm, lightly breezy holiday weekends when everyone else has fled to the country. Here the problem has been solved by adding a treillage shelter, open along the walls but covered with clear acrylic plastic which keeps out rain and shields some of the air-pollution residue. Plantings have been reduced to a few favorite seasonal flowers such as cineraria, calceolaria and chrysanthemum, with one potted rose for bloom over several months. Most of the hanging plants are choice herbs selected to provide fresh tastes in the kitchen, at the same time they lift some green into the city sky. These can be kept over winter indoors in a cool, sunny window. On bright days the palm is often moved into the archway to absorb its quota of sunlight. This tiny terrace illustrates both practical and esthetic reasons for exercising restraint when landscaping small spaces: Less can indeed be more. In this case the few plants are also easily cared for to achieve a perfect appearance.

1. Potted rose
2. Cineraria
3. Fairy primrose
4. Creeping thyme
5. Parsley
6. Chrysanthemum
7. Calceolaria
8. Dwarf bush basil
9. Cymbalaria (Kenilworth-ivy)
10. Aeschynanthus (lipstick vine)
11. Prostrate rosemary

Tea for Two—with a View

Hardly anything is nicer for a garden to have than a beautiful view—except possibly a comfortable place to sit and contemplate such a scene. Here a grayed redwood deck, attached to the house, provides comfortable seating for dining and lingering long to soak up the tranquility of gentle motion and changing light in the water pond and along its banks. High-upkeep plantings have been kept to a bare minimum, with salmon-pink geraniums in tubs on the deck providing most of the color. Pieris, azaleas and peonies in a small bed to the side all bring brief periods of bloom in early summer, and later the spuria irises will sway their white, blue and purple flowers among the grassy leaves at water's edge. At party time the ledge where the geranium tubs rest turns into seating for a sizable crowd.

1. Variegated vinca, geraniums and yucca
2. Spuria iris and cattails
3. Pieris japonica
4. Deciduous azaleas
5. Peonies

Medieval Flower and Herb Garden

When the snow melts into drifts of daffodils, Grecian tulips sway promising buds and fruit trees change overnight from bare branches to great bouquets, we can say with Gerard, the medieval herbalist, "Who would therefore looke dangerously up at Planets, that might safely looke down at Plants?" Our eyes are accustomed to dazzling spectaculars, but imagine the exhilaration that spring brought to man in the Middle Ages. Gardens as we know them were nonexistent, but inside the protective walls of the European monasteries there grew collections of treasured herbs and culinary plants. The plan shown is that of the medieval garden which grows today at The Cloisters in New York City. All of the plants are easily cultivated without benefit of a greenhouse or complicated planting procedures. 1. *Ruta graveolens.* 2. *Cheiranthus cheiri.* 3. *Rosa gallica* variety *versicolor.* 4. *Rosa eglanteria.* 5. *Allium schoenoprasum* (chives). 6. *Allium ascalonicum* (shallot). 7. *Artemisia abrotanum.* 8. *Artemisia dracunculus* (tarragon). 9. Sage. 10. *Dianthus seguieri.* 11. *Mentha pulegium.* 12. *Artemisia absinthium.* 13. *Iris pumila.* 14. Lavender. 15. Marjoram. 16. *Rosa alba.* 17. Caraway. 18. *Iris florentina* and *I. germanica* (white and blue). 19. *Rosa centifolia.* 20. Lemon balm. 21. Feverfew. 22. *Santolina virens.* 23. *Angelica archangelica.* 24. *Acanthus mollis.* 25. *Rosa damascena* variety *versicolor.* 26. *Satureja montana.*

27. Rosemary
28. *Cydonia oblonga* (quince)
29. *Rosa damascena* (damask rose)
30. *Aquilegia vulgaris* (columbine)
31. *Viola tricolor*
32. *Rosa canina* (dog rose)
33. *Fragaria vesca* (European strawberry)
34. *Santolina chamaecyparissus* (lavender-cotton)
35. *Mentha crispa* (curled mint)

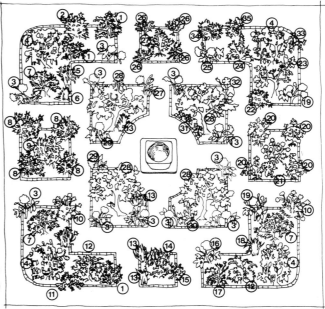

Dianthus plumarius

Centaurea montana

Dwarf pomegranate

Spanish squill

Rosa gallica variety *versicolor*

Quince

Seclusion from a Busy World

One of the major reasons for having a garden spot is to have a perfect retreat from the cares of the day. The little terrace shown is just that, with its brick walls, slate surface and beds of hyacinths, tulips, daffodils and azaleas in full bloom. Large clay pots hold roses close enough to the table for the fragrance to be enjoyed at tea time. The plan here suggests how to achieve privacy near a busy street where it might be thought impossible. 1. Russian olive tree underplanted with annuals. 2. Perennial border of chrysanthemums for fall, bulbs for spring. 3. Climbing roses or clematis. 4. Potted herbs. 5. Espaliered pyracantha or honeysuckle. 6. Bradford pear or Autumn Flame maple. 7. Double-flowered weeping peach. 8. Colorado blue spruce or Austrian pine. 9. Savins juniper or a Korean boxwood. 10. Andorra juniper, upright yew or Sarcoxie euonymus. 11. White birch or white flowering dogwood. 12. Spreading yew, potentilla or Emerald 'n Gold euonymus. 13. Pachysandra, vinca or English ivy. 14. Flowering crab apple tree.

15. Baltic ivy or crown-vetch
16. Green King hybrid elm or Norway maple
17. Redbud, Amur cork tree or Rubylace locust
18. Pachysandra, ajuga or a vegetable garden
19. Baltic ivy or *Vinca minor*
20. Flowering shrubs such as forsythia, smoke bush or viburnum
21. Lilac, weigela or mock-orange

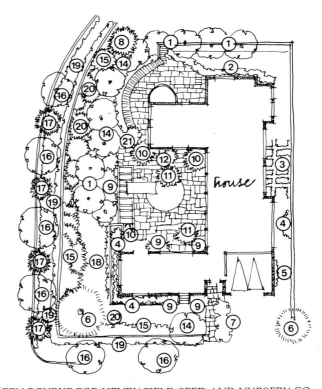

DESIGN BY KATHLEEN BOURKE FOR HENRY FIELD SEED AND NURSERY CO.

Swimming-pool Garden

Since warm weather centers attention on the swimming pool, the area immediately surrounding makes a great place to grow containers of flowers and perhaps, as the owner of this property has done, espalier some hybrid tomatoes along the fence. Quantities of small clay pots have been wisely kept in three major groupings around this pool so that en masse they not only yield a splash of flower color, but care is easier, especially at watering time. Pots of primroses, pansies, violas, forget-me-nots and English daisies might be enjoyed around the pool during the first chilly swims of the season, and pots of chrysanthemums and dwarf hardy asters could give bloom from August until winter freeze-up. The earth-colored concrete patio paving blocks blend naturally into the landscape and provide sure footing for wet bare feet. One of the finer points to remember when siting a swimming pool is that it's nice not to have to look down at the pool from inside the house during that part of the year when it is not in use.

1. *Begonia semperflorens*
2. Geranium
3. Chrysanthemum
4. Shrimp plant (beloperone)
5. Geranium
6. Dwarf feverfew
7. Dahlberg daisy (thymophylla)
8. *Dracaena deremensis* Warneckei
9. Assorted sunloving house plants
10. Tomatoes espaliered on fence
11. Clivia and geraniums
12. Tubbed ficus tree

City Garden San Francisco Style

Immediately beyond the ivy-espaliered wall of this tiny garden in San Francisco is a busy street, yet inside, all is serene. Landscape Architect Thomas Church has masterfully turned what might have been wasted space—because it was so cramped—into a real flower garden with space for reading and relaxing as well. In a less benign climate English ivy might be used for the espalier instead of *Hedera canariensis; Albizia julibrissin* kept pruned back ruthlessly instead of the tree-fern; mountain-laurel instead of ligustrum; dwarf rhododendron instead of pittosporum; a pink daylily instead of the agapanthus. The fatsia is not so easily duplicated in a cold climate, although annual castor beans would give a similar appearance—or an indoor fatsia three might be summered outdoors. The photographer's trick of adding containers of fresh-cut chrysanthemums in the foreground is worth remembering when you want instant bloom among plantings in the immediate outdoor living surround. The raised planting bed with ledge provides extra seating at cocktail-party time.

1. Cut chrysanthemums (white and yellow)
2. Impatiens
3. Agapanthus
4. *Cestrum nocturnum* (fragrant at night)
5. Ligustrum
6. Fatsia
7. *Hedera canariensis* espalier
8. Tree-fern
9. Tuberous-rooted begonias
10. Hydrangea
11. Echeveria and crassula
12. Ophiopogon (lily-turf)
13. Baby's-tears
14. Pittosporum

Landscaping in the Round

This garden, designed entirely with the comforts of outdoor living in mind, consists of three main areas, all round and all connected by circular stepping stones, one for dining, one for relaxing and sunbathing and one a swimming pool. The pebble mulch and pachysandra ground cover reduces the amount of lawn maintenance. Although the shrubbery plantings beyond the pool give some flowers in spring and summer, most bloom is concentrated in the yellow and orange patio containers, shown here in early autumn with chrysanthemums. Pansies or primroses might be used in spring, followed by marigolds or petunias in summer. Although undergrowth was removed from the woodland setting at the time of constructing this garden, most major trees were saved simply by careful design and planning ahead, even to the point of paving around the trunk in the foreground. The dappled sunlight or light shade provided by trees growing as these are is an excellent place to naturalize ferns, daffodils and wild flowers.

1. Pachysandra
2. Chrysanthemum
3. Pampas grass
4. *Euonymus alatus*
5. Scotch broom
6. Lilac
7. Assorted shrubs for spring and summer bloom, some berries in autumn.

Courtyard Viewing Garden

This courtyard garden, surrounded by a contemporary house, is a patio in the original sense of the word since it is surrounded by four walls and open to the sky. The design, plantings and upkeep of a garden situated as this one is are crucial points since the landscape is always on view from within the house. On the other hand, a garden like this can be the delight of all, literally a work of art that changes constantly, every hour of the day, every day of the year. The owner of this property has kept plantings to a minimum to reduce upkeep and create a restful, open, uncluttered picture. The swatch of green ground cover leading from the house to the pink-flowering rhododendron turns a darker shade in winter but remains an encouraging color, as do all of the shrubs. Before frost, the ferns (1) are brought indoors and an assortment of hardy spring-flowering bulbs planted in their place, then mulched with pine needles. By the time they have finished flowering in the spring, the weather is warm enough to bring out the ferns. Summer color is provided by tubs of geraniums in the sun and hanging tuberous-rooted begonias in the shade. In cold winter climates, a patio garden like this one often has a slightly warmer microclimate which makes possible the successful cultivation of plants that normally could not survive, camellias and amaryllis, for example. 1. Nephrolepis and Polypodium ferns. 2. *Ceratostigma plumbaginoides*. 3. Native maples; dogwood, redbud or clump birch would also be excellent choices. 4. Rhododendron. 5. Primroses in spring, geraniums in summer-fall. 6. Violets. 7. Lily-of-the-valley. 8. Daffodils. 9. *Iberis sempervirens*. 10. Aucuba. 11. Columbine. 12. Bleeding-heart. 13. Hanging tuberous-rooted begonias. 14. Hosta.

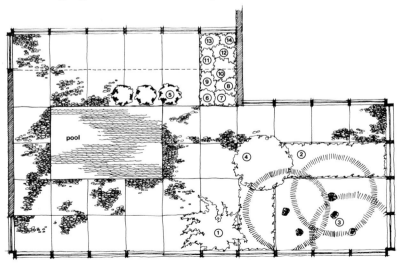

Rock-wall Garden

Before landscaping, this garden space was a steep incline, virtually unin-
habitable by plants or people. Boulders and large rocks on the site were left
in place and used in formulating plans for adding the waterfall which
splashes into a reflecting pool; a pump re-circulates the water. Native
stones were brought in to complete the dry-wall construction (no mortar
was used). As each layer of stones was positioned, rich topsoil mixed with
well-rotted compost and peat moss was added behind and between. On
completion of the stonework, plants were tucked into planting pockets of
soil, both in vertical and horizontal positions. Plants for a dry-wall rock
garden like this one can be selected to give a burst of bloom all in one
season, or to give patches of color from earliest spring until frost. If the
garden is fairly sunny in early spring but partially shaded in summer by tall
deciduous trees, as is the one pictured, most of the spring-flowering hardy
bulbs make good choices—species tulips, daffodils and crocus. 1. Hepatica.
2. Lily-turf. 3. *Euphorbia myrsinites*. 4. Epimedium. 5. Asperula.

6. *Juniperus chinensis*
7. *Nepeta mussinii*
8. Primrose
9. *Linaria alpina*
10. Aethionema
11. Azalea
12. *Phlox subulata*
13. Arabis
14. *Aurinia saxatilis* (basket-of-gold alyssum)
15. Mazus
16. Heuchera
17. Cerastium
18. *Pellaea atropurpurea*
19. Erodium
20. Sedum
21. Sempervivum
22. Camptosorus
23. *Ceratostigma plumbaginoides*
24. Polemonium

Landscaping in the Tradition of Japan

Using plant materials that grow almost universally, Landscape Architect Warren Waltz worked with the owner of this hillside acre in Bel Air, California, to create a tranquil escape from the metropolis of Los Angeles. The garden, which grew out of the owner's travels to Japan and his collection of Oriental objects, is on direct view from the house. Stroll paths through mosslike tufts of sagina, a member of the pink family, lead to two sitting and dining areas, and a shaded, fern-planted retreat under an old oak. Each pine tree is an exquisite piece of sculpture, the result of patient trimming and training over a period of years. Portions of the city have been blocked out with pines to give serene, distant views of the San Gabriel Mountains to the east. The waterfall, spilling over tufa stone into the pool, and the bubbling fountain give soothing sounds. At night, ancient lanterns hung from the trees glow with candlelight. In the photograph, a waterfall of tufa stone spills into a fish pond, with day- and night-blooming water-lilies and cyperus. Twisted junipers and Alaska azaleas grow behind the tufa. Wisteria is on either side of the waterfall, with rabbit's-foot ferns at the base and saxifraga in crevices of the tufa. The planting plan below, suggested by the D. Hill Nursery Company, has been scaled down to fit a much smaller space, perhaps the corner of a suburban back yard. Japanese gardens traditionally have disappearing paths, no matter how small the area, and subtle contrasts in color and texture are sought instead of bold differences or brilliant flower colors. The reward of such a garden is that it is pleasing in all seasons and each plant plays an important role.

1. Juniper or pine tree pruned in bonsai style
2. Low-growing juniper
3. Japanese umbrella pine or Japanese maple
4. Waterfall with hardy ferns
5. Dwarf euonymus along edges of pool
6. Maney juniper with lantern
7. Water basin
8. Stepping stones

The Garden of Serenity

This seventeenth-century Japanese stroll garden grows today on a hilltop in North Salem, New York, meticulously designed and lovingly planted by Natalie Hays Hammond, who has always wondered what it felt like to live in other times and other places. Fifteen separate Oriental landscapes blend with subtlety into one place of solitude where time is suspended. Evergreen trees and shrubs set among lasting elements of rock, gravel and sand detail a flowing pattern symbolic of nature's never-ending rhythm. Only fleeting blooms and deciduous trees mark the passing seasons. The reflecting pool shown here mirrors weeping willow, pine, juniper and cypress trees above carpets of moss, thyme and sedum. Five water-lilies represent humanity, justice, courtesy, wisdom and fidelity. Although this tranquil scene is part of a complex of separate, yet inter-relating gardens, it might be re-created alone on a much smaller parcel of land.

1. Dwarf juniper
2. Water-lilies
3. Weeping willow
4. Maple
5. Pine
6. Cypress
7. Arborvitae
8. Japanese and spuria iris

New Dimensions for a Small Lot

The idea behind this plan, designed for Henry Field Seed and Nursery Company by Kathleen Bourke, is to make a narrow lot look wide, provide vegetables and fruit, plus flowers for making bouquets like the one shown of roses, lilacs and peonies. 1. Hedge of American arborvitae or Austrian pine. 2. Tulips and daffodils, followed by annual flowers. A planting of Emerald euonymus or Clavey's dwarf honeysuckle might also be used. 3. Spreading yew, interplanted each summer with impatiens, tuberous begonias and caladiums for color in the shade. 5. Flowering quince. 6. Flowering crab apple underplanted with English ivy. 7. Emerald euonymus or dwarf crape-myrtle. 8. Kazan pyracantha trained or espaliered on a six- to eight-foot trellis as a privacy screen. 9. Potentilla. 10. Same as 8; for less formal effect, use Persian lilac or highbush cranberry. 11. Redbud, flowering peach or dogwood. 12. Russian olive. 13. Spring bulbs overplanted with hybrid petunias in summer. 14. Dogwood. 15 and 16. Spirea, lilac, dwarf crape-myrtle, mock-orange and other flowering shrubs. 17. Hedge of blueberries. 18. Vegetable garden; train tomatoes on fence. 19. Apple tree. 20, 21, 22. Fruit trees or flowering crab apple. 23. Bush cherries. 24. Rose garden. 25. Perennial flower garden. 26. White birch clump un-

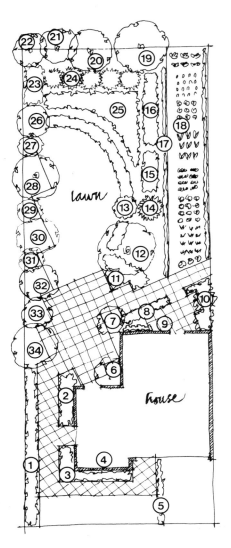

derplanted with spring bulbs and annual flowers. 27. Same as 15, 16. 28. Same as 26. 29. Same as 15, 16. 30. Same as 26. 31. Same as 15, 16. 32. Same as 26. 33. Same as 15, 16. 34. Sunburst locust.

Planting for Sun and Shade

A garden with a scattering of tall, high-branched deciduous trees like this one makes possible the cultivation of a tremendous variety of plants in terms of sun and shade requirements. One of the first things needed in designing such a garden is to live with it through one growing season in order to study the sun and shade patterns so that you have a realistic idea of where to plant the shade-lovers and where to position kinds that require direct sun. The garden shown has been designed as a series of curving beds, detailed by flagstones and small stones. As the property was approached originally, the larger trees were practically lost in a tangle of undergrowth. Once that was removed, the position of important trees could be indicated on a plot plan and effective design work could proceed. The paved terrace was of major importance since the owners wanted it to be as sunny as possible and located at some distance from the house in order to have a feeling of getting away from it all. Once the sun pocket was found for the terrace, the rest of the design fell into place naturally. The planting materials used were selected to give flowers in the spring but a variety of restful greens in other seasons. A similar design might accommodate plants selected mostly for summer bloom, or to give a scattering of flowers from the earliest crocus to the last chrysanthemum of autumn.

1. Red and white azaleas
2. Ajuga
3. Lawn
4. Pebble-surface concrete terrace
5. Flagstone paths
6. Dwarf evergreens and hardy ferns

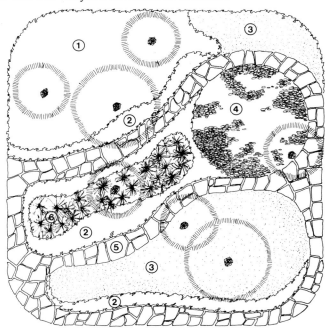

Low Upkeep for a One-story Ranch

This plan for a one-story ranch or provincial house features all curved edges for the lawn—to speed up maintenance time. The spacious entry court with a bricked surface from the drive to the front door, and also the bricked surfaces in the side yards—all reduce lawn upkeep. Designed by Kathleen Bourke for the Henry Field Seed and Nursery Company. 1. Clipped English ivy as a low hedge. Boston ivy on north-facing wall. 2. Andorra juniper. 3. Pyracantha espaliered on wall. 4. Spring bulbs followed by summer annuals interplanted with hardy chrysanthemums and dwarf asters for fall. 5. Savins juniper. 6. Fall-planted spring bulbs overplanted with Iceland poppies (color photograph), followed by summer annuals. 7. Pin oak. 8. Espalier tomatoes or grapevines on wall.

9. Vegetable garden
10. Lilliputian magnolia
11. Border of perennial flowers and shrubs
12. Apple or cherry tree
13. Same as 11, but keep tall plants away from front view of the espaliers against the fence
14. Dwarf apples or pears espaliered on fence
15. Dwarf bush cherries
16. Rose garden
17. Same as 4
18. Same as 4 with clematis on trellises attached to house
19. Sunburst locust, Russian olive or paper-white birch

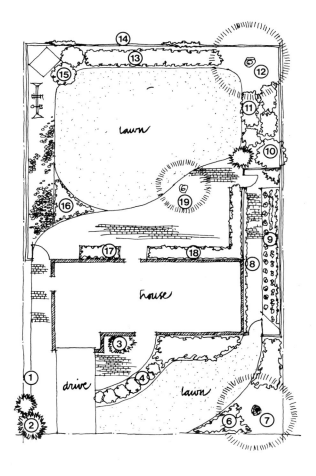

Tulips on the Module

One of the easiest ways to design a garden, especially one incorporating an area for outdoor living, is to use the modular approach whereby one standard-size unit is simply repeated, as in the plan shown here. The basic module for this garden is a three-foot square, so that if executed as sketched, it would require a space 18 by 24 feet. The planting areas 1 and 2, which could be at terrace level or raised beds as shown in the photograph, might be filled with any of hundreds of different annual, biennial or perennial flowers, bulbs or dwarf shrubs, limited only by the amount of sunlight available. If tulips are used for spring bloom, and uniformity of height and flowering time is important, it will be necessary to plant new bulbs every fall; otherwise the tulips can be left in the ground permanently and allowed to grow and bloom as they will in future years. Tulips or other spring bulbs might be followed by annuals for summer and fall. A garden designed by this approach and used as the surround for an outdoor living area makes a perfect place for the development of a color-scheme garden, perhaps monochromatic as shown, or using colors in subtle or sharp contrast. An all-pink spring garden might also give way to all-white in summer and perhaps all-yellow in autumn, simply by careful selection of seasonal-flowering plants.

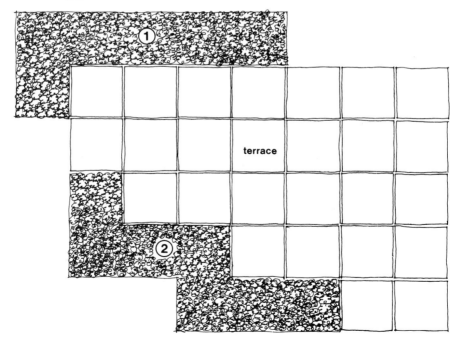

terrace

Green-and-white Viewing Garden

Boxwood frames azalea trees and ajuga ground cover, with St. Augustine-grass and flagstones, in this all green-and-white New Orleans garden. For a brief period in the spring the azaleas offer white flowers and the ajuga is covered with blue. Otherwise the garden is mostly a study of leaf greens with the grayish white accents of flagstones and the piece of statuary. The surrounding plantings include sweet-olive (*Osmanthus fragrans*), jasmine, yew and white-flowered camellias. A space approximately 24 by 24 feet would be needed to plant a garden similar to this one. Low hedges that might be used instead of the boxwood include *Ilex crenata* (Japanese holly), taxus (yew), *Iberis sempervirens* (evergreen candytuft, which has white flowers in spring), *Myrtus communis* (myrtle; not winter-hardy where temperatures drop below 20 degrees F.) and *Teucrium chamaedrys* (germander; hardy to about ten degrees F.). Other suitable ground covers include *Vinca minor* (periwinkle), *Ceratostigma plumbaginoides* and creeping thyme. Tree-form roses or lilac standards might be used instead of the azaleas. Although a garden like this one is always pleasant to walk through and to work in, it is especially beautiful viewed from above, perhaps a second-floor balcony or bedroom window. To keep up its manicure, a formal garden like this one requires a considerable commitment to upkeep almost year 'round, although the simplicity of design and limited number of different plants helps reduce the work. On the other hand, the upkeep of a garden like this is highly satisfying work and the space small enough to permit its grooming in a short enough period of time for the improvement in appearance to be quickly rewarding. This kind of gardening activity proves soothing to many people, a time-honored alternative to pills or alcohol for relieving everyday stresses and tensions.

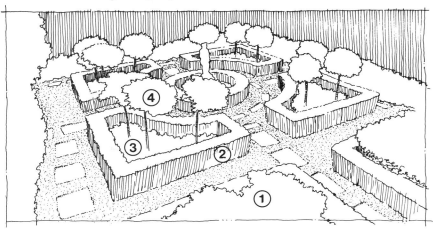

New Garden for an Old House

Some old houses are worth renovating, some are not. The same is true of gardens. This terrace is a good case in point since the house dated from the 19th century and was eminently restorable, but the small garden behind it had fallen into such ruin that the owners elected to start over. Weedy trees, shrubs and vines had long since choked out the finer species planted a hundred years earlier. In time the new magnolia trees will create welcome shade for the dining area, but the raised planting bed of tree roses will continue to receive a full quota of slightly more than a half day of direct sun. The fountain, a part of the brick wall at the back of the garden, provides the pleasant sound of splashing water and the pool is home for a school of goldfish. Ledges on the wall behind the pool hold seasonal flowering plants in clay pots. The plan for this garden is easily adaptable to almost any back yard where outdoor living space surrounded by a few beautiful plants is desired, but without the maintenance of a lawn or of extensive flower and shrubbery borders. The plants used in this New Orleans garden are easily replaced in colder climates by other kinds of similar appearance. The boxwood might be replaced by clipped yew or Japanese holly; the magnolia trees by American holly, one of the hardier, deciduous magnolias or dogwood. Tree roses might be cultivated in large containers sunk into the planting bed and wintered in a garage.

Spring Color Pool-side

This swimming pool in a narrow side yard is surrounded by six feet of space, half of which is taken by the brick walkway. The three-foot planting bed is filled with azaleas ranging from white to pale pink to near-red. These provide spring bloom, but the rest of the year this planting is a study in greens with the design interest of English ivy espaliered on the wall in a treillage pattern. One of the charms of this garden is this view through an archway—a near foolproof element in landscape design where the space and architecture permit. Obviously, a pool-side planting area like this one need not be limited to one plant that gives only a brief period of bloom in spring. Such a space might be filled with all kinds of hardy spring-flowering bulbs, to be followed by annual and perennial flowers selected to give an abundance of flowers every month until there is likelihood of ice on the pool. Of course, if you'd rather be mostly in the pool or on the tennis court, a simple planting all of azaleas—or geraniums, petunias or zinnias—will be more to your liking.

1. Boston ferns
2. Assorted azaleas, white, pale pink, rose-pink

A Mere Formality

A Victorian-style lath house for orchids inspired this formal garden in Florida, the plan for which is a classic, readily adapted to a variety of gardening interests in almost any climate. For best effect the ground should be level and of course it helps to have a focal point such as a greenhouse—or perhaps a lath house that in northern climates makes a perfect place in summer to cultivate fuchsias, tuberous-rooted begonias, impatiens, achimenes and gloxinias, not to mention orchids, which benefit from spending warm months outdoors. The four planting beds may be filled with plants at the pleasure of the owner. Here the two beds seen are filled on one side with the yellow and pink spires of snapdragons and on the other with red roses. The beds might be filled in spring with the flowers of fall-planted bulbs; in summer with annuals; in autumn with chrysanthemums and dwarf asters. If perfect symmetry of color and form is not a requisite, one bed might be given to roses, one to hybrid daylilies, one with geraniums like the red and pink Carefree hybrids shown and perhaps one to petunias. The pedestals and urns suggested in the plan to mark the four corners of the garden might be filled in early spring with primroses and forget-me-nots; in summer with ivyleaf geraniums or cascade petunias; or they might be planted in the Victorian manner with a fountain-form plant such as yucca in the center, surrounded by geraniums and variegated trailing vinca.

1. Sundial or birdbath
2. *Vinca minor*, or evergreen candytuft hedges
3. Brick edging
4. Clipped grass, dichondra or thyme
5. Paving stones
6. Boxwood, yew or privet
7. *Teucrium chamaedrys* or evergreen candytuft hedges
8. Urn on pedestal
9. Flower beds

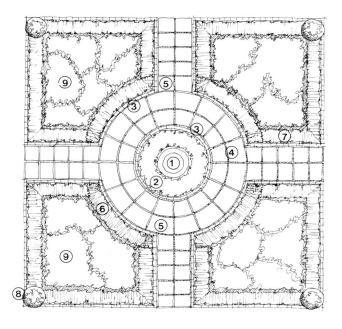

Dry-wall Rockery

A two-foot retaining wall of native stones set in place without mortar, called dry-wall construction, is the inspiration for the rock garden shown here, photographed through the pale pink of a dogwood in full springtime bloom. The planting plan represents a cutaway that might be repeated as a guide for planning a similar rockery of almost any length. Any of the low-growing hardy bulb flowers might be underplanted in the beds in autumn, or tucked into soil pockets of the wall, for example *Anemone blanda*, chionodoxa, crocus, winter aconite, galanthus, hyacinth, *Iris reticulata* and *I. danfordiae*, leucojum, muscari, species narcissus and tulips, and scilla. Depending on your interests, and whether or not you are at home in summer, the plantings in such a garden can be selected for flowers from late winter until fall freeze-up; or bloom can be concentrated in spring, summer or autumn. If the wall receives light shade, there are also suitable flowering and foliage plants (see the Plant Finder section of this book). 1. Silver Mound artemisia. 2. Arabis. 3. Aethionema. 4. Dwarf iris. 5. *Aquilegia canadensis* (columbine). 6. *Dianthus* species. 7. Dwarf platycodon. 8. *Aurinia saxatilis* (basket-of-gold alyssum). 9. *Campanula* species. 10. *Cerastium tomentosum*. 11. Heuchera (coral-bells). 12. *Iberis* species. 13. Mazus. 14. Aubrieta. 15. Armeria. 16. *Bellis perennis* (English daisy). 17. Hybrid English primroses. 18. *Achillea* species. 19. *Hypericum* species. 20. Dwarf iris.

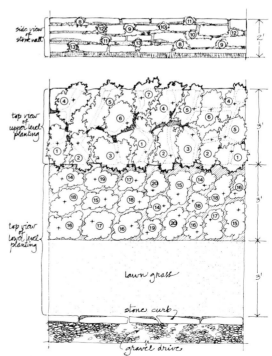

Flowers for a Shaded Entry

The number of flowering plants suitable for a sunny entry garden is practically unlimited, but where the area is mostly shaded there are considerably fewer possibilities. Two excellent choices are shown in color on the opposite page—a pink azalea and the green foliage of lily-of-the-valley, which is treasured for its exquisite, white, fragrant flowers in spring, but also as a hardy ground cover in shaded to partly sunny areas. The idea behind the planting plan below is to have some evergreen foliage for color even in winter (azaleas are suggested here since they also give spring bloom, but euonymus with plain or variegated leaves might be used or Japanese holly), plus a variety of flowering plants from early spring until the end of the growing season. For spring and early summer bloom there are azaleas, Lilliputian magnolia, lily-of-the-valley, Royal Robe violet, mertensia (Virginia bluebells) and fernleaf bleeding-heart (*Dicentra eximia*, which also gives some summer flowers). Spring-planted tuberous begonias and impatiens will provide bloom until frost, along with the colorful foliage of caladiums and the bold leaf contrast of giant elephant's-ear; excepting impatiens, all are tender bulbs that need to be dug and brought indoors just before fall frost. Cuttings from the impatiens can be made and rooted indoors in early fall and carried over for planting out the following spring, or new seedlings may be started or purchased each spring. Daffodils might be planted throughout this area in autumn to give earliest spring bloom, along with polyanthus primroses and pansies. Since the area will be mostly bare from fall freeze-up until spring, a mulch of bark chips is suggested to give it a tidy appearance. 1. Azalea. 2. Lilliputian magnolia. 3. Hardy ferns. 4. Giant elephant's ear. 5. Lily-of-the-valley. 6. Royal Robe violet. 7. Mertensia. 8. Tuberous begonias. 9. Caladiums. 10. Impatiens. 11. Fernleaf bleeding-heart.

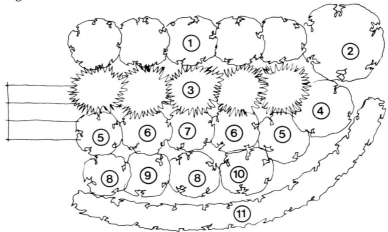

Sawed-off Barrel Garden

When Textile Designer Hans Koch looked for an apartment in New York, his main requirement was that it have a small, sunny terrace on which he could garden. His dreams came true, as shown by the photographs taken from the same angle in spring and in late summer. The sawed-off barrel which measures about 36 inches in diameter and 18 inches tall is filled with a mixture of equal parts all-purpose potting soil, sphagnum peat moss and vermiculite. In late fall it is planted with: 1. Grape-hyacinth. 2. Crocus. 3. Glory-of-the-snow. 4. Hyacinth. 5. Narcissus. 6. Red Emporor and Gudoshnik Darwin hybrid tulips. As soon as all these flowers fade, they are clipped off, leaving the foliage to mature naturally. Meanwhile started seedlings are planted in-between: 1. Portulaca or rose-moss. 2. Verbena. 3. Pink *Begonia semperflorens*. 4. *Phlox drummondi*. 5. White petunia. 6. Scarlet sage or salvia. To keep the annuals blooming, Koch removes spent flowers immediately, and also cuts freshly-opened ones for bouquets. In addition, he applies fertilizer diluted in water once every two weeks, alternating between a chemical all-purpose food and organic fish emulsion.

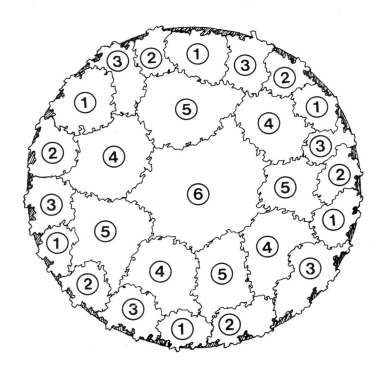

Hanging Gardens

Airborne flowering and foliage plants can help create a beautiful surround for an outdoor living area. Hanging containers can be suspended from eye screws installed in a roof overhang or tree limb, or from brackets mounted on walls or posts. Among the best for flowers in summer in part shade with up to two or three hours of direct sun are Catalina begonia *(opposite)*, cascade tuberous begonia, achimenes, browallia, fuchsia, impatiens, lobelia, nierembergia and torenia. For flowers in sun: ageratum, wax begonia, shrimp plant, African daisy, lantana, sweet-alyssum, ivyleaf and other geraniums, petunia, dwarf marigold, nasturtium, verbena and portulaca. The sketch below suggests various hanging containers and plantings, from left to right: Tuberous begonia in redwood box; maidenhair fern in tree-fern basket (for shade); echeverias in wire sphere stuffed with sphagnum moss (for sun); asparagus-fern in 25-inch pottery planter (for sun or shade); and Cascade petunias in clay pot with chain hanger. The main requirement for hanging gardens is that the soil never dry out.

All-Season Flower Border: Phase I

The plan shown here and on page 86 is designed to give a continuous display of flowers over as long a season as possible. The photographs by George De Gennaro, made in his own garden, include: 1. Potted spring bulbs. 2. Orange Kennedy tulip. 3. Sorbet tulip. 4. Lady Derby hyacinth. 5. Tulips and poet's narcissus. These and other bulbs listed below are planted in early to mid fall. Other plantings, which include a tree, shrubs and hardy perennial flowers, may be planted in early fall or spring in mild climates; elsewhere spring planting is recommended except for the hardy bulbs, which always require fall planting.

A. Spuria iris
B. Gypsophila
C. Heuchera
D. Dictamnus
E. Delphinium
F. Bergenia
G. Shasta daisy
H. Plume poppy
I. Japanese anemone
J. Monkshood
K. Hosta
L. Helleborus
M. Dogwood
N. Maidenhair fern
O. Inspiration rose
P. Jackmani clematis
Q. Bittersweet vine
R. Silverlace vine
S. Sparrieshoop rose

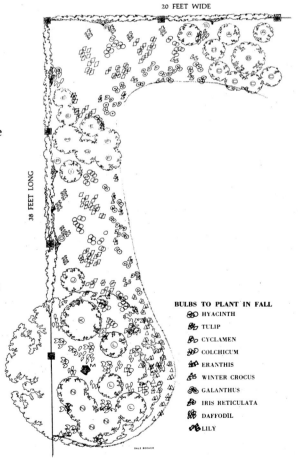

20 FEET WIDE

38 FEET LONG

BULBS TO PLANT IN FALL

HYACINTH
TULIP
CYCLAMEN
COLCHICUM
ERANTHIS
WINTER CROCUS
GALANTHUS
IRIS RETICULATA
DAFFODIL
LILY

All-Season Flower Border: Phase II

The plan shown here, like that on page 84, is designed to give flowers over as long a season as possible, with most of the planting work grouped in fall (bulbs listed on page 84) and spring (see list below). The photographs by George De Gennaro, made in his own garden, include: 1. Felicia. 2. Pink Glory lily. 3. Imperial Crimson lily. Unnumbered: Apricot-colored dahlia and Red Champion lily. The lilies are all hardy hybrids which may be planted in fall or early spring and might be scattered in clumps of three throughout the border; varieties are available for blooms from May until early September.

A. Spuria iris
B. Gypsophila
C. Heuchera
D. Dictamnus
E. Delphinium
F. Bergenia
G. Shasta daisy
H. Plume poppy
I. Japanese anemone
J. Monkshood
K. Hosta
L. Helleborus
M. Dogwood
N. Maidenhair fern
O. Inspiration rose
P. Jackmani clematis
Q. Bittersweet vine
R. Silverlace vine
S. Sparrieshoop rose

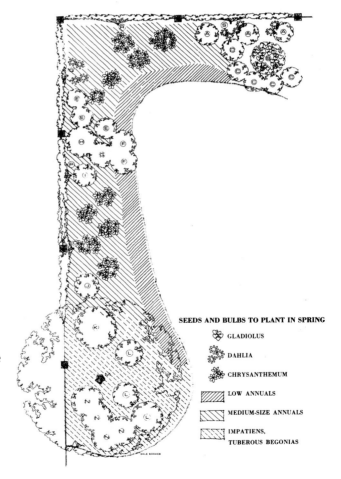

SEEDS AND BULBS TO PLANT IN SPRING

GLADIOLUS

DAHLIA

CHRYSANTHEMUM

LOW ANNUALS

MEDIUM-SIZE ANNUALS

IMPATIENS, TUBEROUS BEGONIAS

The Collector's Garden

If you have a passion for one kind of flower, for example the tall bearded irises shown here, it may be difficult to work all the varieties you want into the usual mixed perennial border. Gardeners who like to specialize often find the simple solution is to set aside one part of the landscape in which all of the space is devoted to the specialty plant, ideally with the walkways surfaced in such a way as to require no maintenance such as weeding or mowing of grass. Obviously, the plan shown might be used for any number of mixed gardens such as spring bulbs, annual or perennial flowers, or even vegetables and herbs, but the collector will find it adaptable to accommodate almost any number of cacti, geraniums, penstemons, iris, daffodils, gladiolus, roses, peonies, hostas, delphiniums, chrysanthemums, dahlias, daylilies (hemerocallis) or lilies. By isolating the collection, it is possible to cater to the soil, moisture and light needs of the specialty plants, and in off-seasons when they are not in bloom, or possibly not even in foliage, the appearance of the garden is of relatively little importance in the total landscape picture.

1. Brick walkways, three feet wide, except 18 inches between beds
2. Low hedge such as boxwood, privet or Japanese holly
3. Flower beds three feet wide
4. Wall 18 inches wide (pots of flowering plants may be set on top)

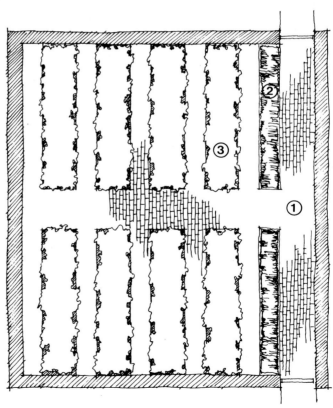

Raised Planting Beds

The rose garden shown opposite was designed for minimum upkeep with the maximum number of flowers. Bricking around the beds eliminates the tedious labor of maintaining, mowing and hand-edging grass and provides relatively dry footing even in extended periods of wet weather.

Raised planting beds offer a number of advantages: It is easier to isolate the soil in such a bed and improve it to meet the needs of a particular kind of plant—roses, lilies or strawberries, for example.

Raised planting beds assure better drainage of excess moisture, and in some gardens they are the only way it is possible to grow plants that require perfect drainage, such as tall bearded iris and lilies.

Various materials may be used for framing raised beds, for example rot-resistant redwood, bricks, stones or railroad ties. If a ledge is added at the top, as in the photographs, working the bed can be accomplished while sitting comfortably on the edge.

For convenience in maintaining a raised planting bed, a width of about three feet is right if it will be accessible from only one side, up to six feet if the bed is accessible from both sides. Handsomely constructed walls for raised planting beds help give the landscape architectural interest even in the bleakest months of the year when plants are dormant.

Border for Non-stop Bloom

The plan below suggests the plants for a perennial border that will bloom from early spring until autumn freeze-up. Although the color theme is white, lavender, purple and blue, it might also carry another color theme, perhaps as daring as that used in the flower arrangement opposite, harvested from a similar perennial border, using Tangerine carnations, pink-and-red rubrum lilies, red and orange anemones, a red rose and scented geranium foliage. 1. Phlox. 2. Dropmore Purple lythrum. 3. White King Oriental poppy. 4. *Clematis jackmani* and Ramona. 5. Peonies Festiva Maxima, Mons. Jules Elie and Kelway's Glorious. 6. Delphiniums. 7. Olympic lilies. 8. Phlox. 9. White King Oriental poppy. 10. Hardy asters. 11. Hemerocallis. 12. Rubrum lilies. 13. Platycodon. 14. Shasta daisies. 15. Phlox. 16. Platycodon. 17. Mertensia. 18. Hemerocallis. 19. Columbine. 20. Platycodon. 21. Poppy-flowered anemones. 22. White King Oriental poppy. 23. Hemerocallis. 24. Purple and white cushion chrysanthemums. 25. Mertensia. 26. Columbine. 27. Rose-scented geraniums. 28. Blue flax. 29. Maidenhair fern. 30. Purple cushion chrysanthemums. 31. Shasta daisies. 32. Hardy fern. 33. White painted daisy. 34. Chives. 35. White and purple cushion chrysanthemums. 36. Penstemon Henry hybrid mixture. 37. Blue flax. 38. Hardy fern. 39. Canterbury cushion aster. 40. Snowcap dwarf iris. 41. Dragon's Blood sedum. 42. Dwarf iris Ink Spot. 43. Dragon's Blood sedum. 44. Penstemon Henry hybrid mixture. 45. Silver Mound artemisia. 46. Purple cushion chrysanthemums. 47. Persian Rose cushion asters. 48. Blue Mound ruta. 49. Chives. 50. Purple cushion chrysanthemums. 51. Blue Moon cornflower aster. 52. Dwarf iris Tinker Bell. 53. Snow Maiden creeping phlox. 54. Dragon's Blood sedum. 55. Violets. 56. Blue creeping phlox. 57. Purple and white violets. 58. Blue creeping phlox. 59. Purple cushion chrysanthemums. 60. Sweet Memories carnation. Design by Kathleen Bourke for Henry Field Seed and Nursery Company.

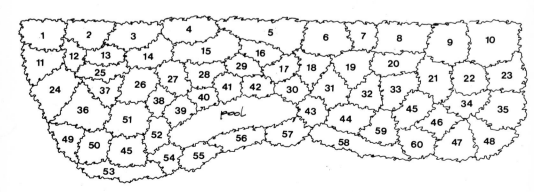

Biennial Border

This garden depends on biennials for a major part of the spring and early summer flower show. A biennial requires two growing seasons in order to complete its life cycle. Seeds are planted every year in late spring or summer; they produce only vegetative growth the first year, but the seedlings live over winter and blossom beautifully in the second spring or summer. The biennials used in this garden include bellis, pansy, myosotis and cheiranthus (wallflower). *Campanula medium* (Canterbury bells) is another favorite biennial, as are the fragrant sweet rocket *(Hesperis matronalis)* and sweet William *(Dianthus barbatus)*. Delphiniums and foxgloves are perennials sometimes treated as biennials. Other biennials are listed in the Plant Finder section of this book. The terra-cotta vase with its classic shape makes a striking focal point.

1. *Iberis sempervirens*
2. *Aurinia saxatilis* (basket-of-gold alyssum)
3. Myosotis forget-me-not
4. Pansies
5. Terra-cotta container of pansies
6. *Bellis perennis*
7. Tulips
8. *Cheiranthus cheiri* (wallflower)
9. Slate-topped brick wall
10. Pottery vase (might be filled with cut flowers or branches for special effects)
11. Boxwood hedge
12. Polyanthus primroses
13. Sandstone pebbles

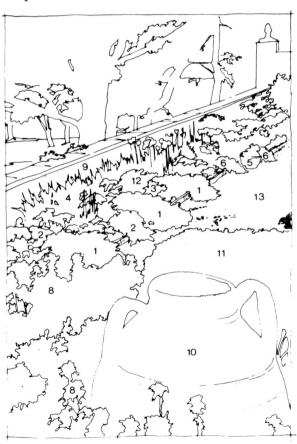

Spring Color, Summer Green

This plan shows half of a hedge-enclosed square back yard designed with a circular lawn and plant materials selected to bloom in the spring. The rest of the year the space is a study in pleasant greens. If you would like to copy the plan, but want flowers in a different season—or several—check the Plant Finder section of this book for other shrubs, perennials and bulbs.

1. White azalea*
2. Pink azalea*
3. Purple azalea*
4. Red azalea*
5. Hybrid lilac
6. Clipped boxwood hedge; Japanese holly or yew might also be used
7. *Phlox divaricata*
8. Brick edging
9. Lawn
10. Birdbath
    *Underplanted with tulip and narcissus bulbs in autumn for spring bloom

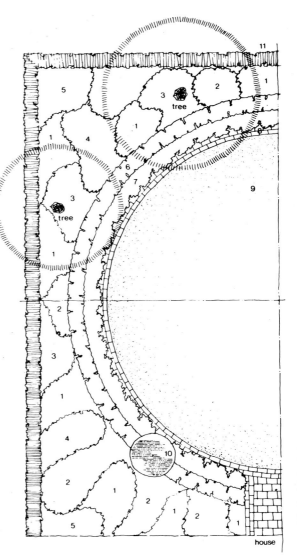

Monochromatic Gardens

The bed of Sensation cosmos and Rose Topper snapdragons (*opposite*) suggests the beauties of a garden planned around a single color. Whatever your favorite color, the Plant Finder section of this book is filled with many lists of different kinds of flowers, shrubs and trees grouped according to flower color as well as height and bloom time. The plan below suggests how plants for a color-scheme garden might be grouped in a border of annual, biennial or perennial flowers. The color you choose is of course a matter of personal taste, but in addition you will probably want it to be complementary to that of the house or other major architectural feature in the immediate surround of the garden. All-white gardens have a crisp, cool appearance in summer and are especially nice next to an outdoor living area. White flowers also mix well with those of various yellows or pinks. Light colors generally make an excellent choice for a shaded part of the garden. An extraordinary effect can also be achieved by using a range of related colors, for example, from palest pink through rose to red to lavender all the way to dark purple. By careful initial planning, plus some plant changes and transplanting as experience guides you, it is also possible to have the color theme of a garden change from season to season, although there is bound to be some overlapping. You might want only yellows and sky blues in spring followed by pinks-reds-purples in summer, ending the season with chrysanthemums in a range of fall colors from yellow through pumpkin to russet red. Plants suggested for the pink border plan below include: 1. Sensation cosmos. 2. Carefree Fickle Rose geranium. 3. Princess Sakura balsam. 4. Rosy Future zinnia. 5. Rose Topper snapdragon. 6. Pink Delight petunia. 7. Rosie O'Day sweet-alyssum. 8. Linda begonia (a hybrid of *B. semperflorens*). 9. Little Pinkie vinca. 10. Toreador celosia.

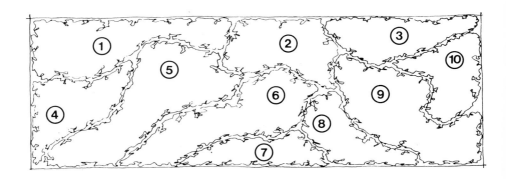

Constructed Shade for Plants—and People

Shade for the white azaleas in this raised planting bed is provided by pieces of redwood in an adaptation of typical lath-house construction. The azaleas themselves serve to screen this garden from that of the neighbors on the other side. The plantings have been designed for most flowering to occur in the springtime since the climate is too hot in summer for the owners to enjoy being outdoors except on a few cool evenings. English ivy is trained up each of the columns. Halfway between each, a large pot resting on the ground holds a white azalea and asparagus-fern. In young gardens where trees are still small, or in places where growing a tree is not practical, constructed shade can be the answer, either for plants or for people. Besides laths or treillage (trelliswork), canvas awnings can be used effectively as well as an open (egg-crate) roof framework on which a fast-growing vine is trained, for example wisteria, grape, silver-lace-vine, honeysuckle or trumpetcreeper.

1. English ivy
2. White wisteria
3. White azaleas
4. Asparagus-fern

A Garden of Old Roses

This plan for a round planting design within a square garden suggests a combination of old roses with modern. The rose is considered by many the supreme of garden plants and one bush at least is usually found in every garden. The rose has been linked with man's history for more than 5,000 years. Its romance, beauty and fragrance have been described in poetry, and roses have been collected by the greats of history and grown by the humblest. There are approximately 100 species of roses, many of them obscure botanical varieties, but some of the roses from history, often referred to as the old-fashioned roses, are readily obtainable from several mail-order nurseries. Collecting some of these can be a highly rewarding pursuit. Many of them are shrub roses that are not constantly in flower like the everblooming hybrids (also suggested for this garden), but as shrubs they are more rugged and durable and often disease- and pest-resistant. The bouquet shown here is made of three lovely old-fashioned roses: Leda (small and white), General Jacqueminot (crimson) and Mrs. John Laine (pink). The space chosen for a rose garden needs to have well-drained soil (or raised planting beds can be used), at least a half day of direct sun and good air circulation to reduce problems of disease. Suggested varieties: 1. New Dawn. 2. *Rosa gallica versicolor*. 3. *Rosa rugosa* hybrid.

4. *Rosa spinosissima*
5. Flowering crab apple
6. Prosperity rose
7. Blue Boy rose
8. Eddie's Crimson
9. Dorothy Perkins rose
10. Harison's Yellow rose
11. Miniature roses
12. Tree roses
13. Hybrid roses

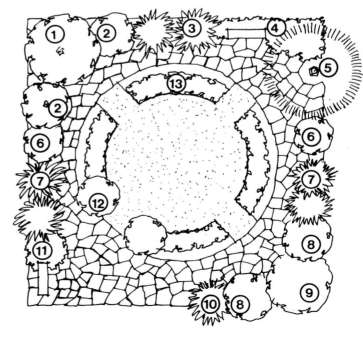

Container Rose Garden

Changing nursery practices have recently brought the rose into much wider use as an outdoor container plant, especially where fragrant blooms can be enjoyed up close by a dining or relaxing area, on a high-rise terrace, a rooftop garden or spacious country patio. Roses growing in containers, such as the tree, floribunda and miniatures shown sketched below in classic Italian terra-cotta tubs 12 to 24 inches in diameter, need at least a half day of direct sun, the same as other roses. These rose types plus the large-flowered hybrid teas and grandifloras shown in the bouquet *(opposite)* are available from local nurseries in spring and summer, growing in containers. This practice of selling the roses in pots or cans, usually already in bloom, makes it possible to select by the color, form—and fragrance—of a bloom produced by the actual bush you choose. At home, transfer to a permanent container at least four inches larger in diameter. First add a layer of drainage, then a mixture of two parts each all-purpose potting soil, sphagnum peat moss and vermiculite to one-half dried blood meal or well-rotted cow manure. Pack firmly about the rootball. Water heavily. Never allow the soil of a

container-grown rose to dry out. Granules of an all-purpose systemic rose pesticide may be applied to the soil to control insects and diseases. Apply rose fertilizer according to directions on the label. In severely cold climates, winter over container roses in a protected place such as an un-heated garage, or treat them as annuals and replant each spring. When cutting for bouquets, remove the rose above a five-leaflet leaf which has a growth bud pointing to the outside of the bush; remove spent blooms at the same point.

Container Water Garden

Fascinating and beautiful aquatics may be cultivated in large fiberglass or ceramic cylinders like those sketched below which hold, *left to right*, horsetail equisetum, dwarf water-lily (a form of *Nymphaea* like that shown in color on the facing page) and blue water-hyacinth. The roots of the equisetum and water-lily are contained by sizable wood boxes or clay flowerpots filled with rich potting soil, the surface then thickly mulched with pebbles. The water-hyacinth simply floats on the water with the roots suspended in it. A container garden like this one is especially convenient where it is not possible to be at home every day in the summer to moisten soil; although water evaporates from these containers and may need replenishing, they can go for a week without any attention. Catalogs of specialists in aquatic plants and goldfish list many other species that might be enjoyed in a container water garden, both for interesting foliage and colorful flowers. Small goldfish might also be placed in one or more of the containers. Where freezing temperatures occur, move inside if possible; otherwise, replant as necessary in spring.

The Fragrant Year

This entry courtyard garden with a paved surface in which pockets have been left open for plants might be adapted to a variety of situations and the possibilities for plant selection are unlimited. Here the plan has been devoted entirely to plants selected for their fragrant blossoms, which appear from earliest spring when the fruit trees and lily-of-the-valley bloom to the last roses in autumn. In order to include as many different fragrant flowers as possible with bloom spread over a wide season, the relatively large-growing lilacs have not been included; however, a hybrid lilac might be used in any of the planting pockets instead of other plants, possibly with sweet violets or lily-of-the-valley planted as a ground cover around it. The arrangement of rose petals, sweet violets and lilacs *(opposite)* in a tall glass cylinder suggests one use indoors for fragrant flowers; fresh, dew-covered petals placed in an arrangement like this in early evening will last several hours before wilting. They may also be dried to be used in the making of sweet potpourri.

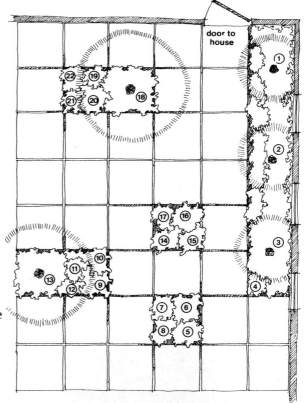

1. Apricot tree
2. Cherry tree
3. Peach tree
4. Lily-of-the-valley
5. Lavender
6. Daphne
7. Dwarf honeysuckle
8. *Rosa spinosissima*
9. Dwarf viburnum
10. Hybrid lilies
11. *Monarda didyma*
12. Summer phlox
13. Plum tree
14. Chrysler Imperial rose
15. Pink Peace rose
16. Sterling Silver rose
17. Lowell Thomas rose
18. Apple tree
19. *Hosta plantaginea*
20. *Centranthus ruber*
21. Hemerocallis
22. Peony

The Cutting Garden

Whether you are a serious flower arranger or a casual bouquet-maker, a cutting garden can be tremendously rewarding. The idea is to grow flowers in an out-of-the-way part of the garden where you won't mind cutting all of the blooms to take indoors, and to plant them in simple, easily cultivated rows, vegetable-garden style. The site you choose will need direct sun for at least half a day and moist, well-drained soil; if drainage is poor, raised planting beds offer a simple solution. The garden can be limited to annual flowers, or it might include rows of annuals, biennials, perennials and bulbs. Favorites for cutting are listed below. The color photograph shows white Queen Anne's lace, red zinnias, blue delphinium, yellow black-eyed Susan, red-and-mahogany Gloriosa daisy and red-and-yellow gloriosa-lily, all arranged in individual vials.

ANNUALS

ACROCLINIUM
ANTIRRHINUM
CALENDULA
CALLIOPSIS
CALLISTEPHUS
CELOSIA
CENTAUREA
CHRYSANTHEMUM
CLARKIA
COREOPSIS
COSMOS
DAHLIA
DELPHINIUM
DIANTHUS
ESCHSCHOLTZIA
GAILLARDIA
GODETIA
GYPSOPHILA
HELICHRYSUM
HELIPTERUM
LATHYRUS
LEPTOSYNE
LINARIA
LUPINUS
LYCHNIS
MATRICARIA
MATHIOLA
NIEREMBERGIA
NIGELLA
PENSTEMON
RESEDA
RHODANTHE
RUDBECKIA
SALPIGLOSSIS
SCABIOSA
STATICE
TAGETES
TROPAEOLUM
VERBENA
ZINNIA

BIENNIALS

ALTHAEA
CAMPANULA
CHEIRANTHUS
DAUCUS
DIANTHUS
DIGITALIS
HESPERIS
MYOSOTIS
VERBASCUM
VIOLA

PERENNIALS

ACHILLEA
ANEMONE
AQUILEGIA
ASTER
CAMPANULA
CATANANCHE
CHRYSANTHEMUM
COREOPSIS
DELPHINIUM
DIANTHUS
DORONICUM
ECHINOPS
DIANTHUS
DORONICUM
ECHINOPS
ERIGERON
ERYNGIUM
GYPSOPHILA
HELENIUM
HELIANTHUS
HEUCHERA
IRIS
KNIPHOFIA
LYTHRUM
MONARDA
PAEONIA
PHLOX
PHYSALIS
PLATYCODON
POLYGONUM
PYRETHRUM
SOLIDAGO
THALICTRUM
TROLLIUS

BULBS

ACIDANTHERA
ALLIUM
DAHLIA
GALTONIA
GLADIOLUS
HYACINTHUS
HYMENOCALLIS
IRIS
LILIUM
LYCORIS
MONTBRETIA
MUSCARI
NARCISSUS
POLIANTHES
RANUNCULUS
TULIPA

Forever Flowers

The bouquet shown here consists entirely of garden flowers dried in silica gel to preserve their natural beauty for several months if not a year or more. High humidity and excessive heat are the enemies of dried flowers like these, otherwise they will last almost indefinitely. The plan below suggests four-foot-square raised planting beds divided in half and separated by paths two feet wide. As sketched this garden would require a space approximately 16 by 22 feet. The plants suggested for it include annuals (1 through 15) and perennials (16 through 28), and mostly kinds whose flowers or seedpods may be cut, tied loosely in small bunches and hung upside down to dry in the air of a well-ventilated room. Air-dried flowers and seedpods generally do not have the brilliant colors of kinds dried in silica gel, but their soft pastels make up into beautiful, long-lasting arrangements, wreaths and Christmas-tree decorations.

1. Ammobium
2. Celosia
3. Emilia
4. Gomphrena
5. Gypsophila
6. Helianthus
7. Helichrysum
8. Helipterum
9. Hordium
10. Limonium
11. Lonas
12. Lunaria
13. Molucella
14. Nigella
15. Polygonum
16. Achillea
17. Allium
18. Anaphalis
19. Artemisia
20. Atriplex
21. Catananche
22. Antennaria
23. Echinops
24. Eryngium
25. Lavandula
26. Liatris
27. Solidago
28. Stachys

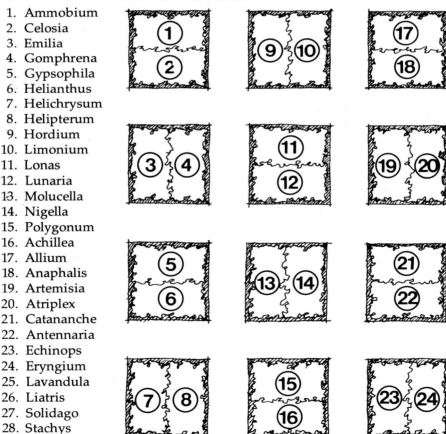

Sand and Sea Gardening

Gardens by the sea, whether cultivated or wild, have a special kind of beauty born of endless struggle with the elements. The relentless wind that sculptures a fantasy tree can also flatten a tender flower and shift the very anchor of its roots to another part of the beach. A friendly sun that chases away the morning mist and reveals flower colors of unmatched brilliance can change by noon to a blazing torch that sears every young leaf and bud. The bracing, salty air that sharpens the spicy fragrance of pine and rosemary may affect other plants as if it were a killing spray. Gardening in this atmosphere can be frustrating and impossible, but it can also be a breathtaking success, supercharged with the excitement of life where ocean meets continent.

The easiest way to have a thriving garden by the sea is to cultivate the plants that grow naturally in the area. On a single dune you may find as many as a dozen or more different kinds, and some will be on the seaward slopes, some on the crest and others on the more protected land side. The native denizens of our coastlines, such as beachgrass, bayberry, beach plum, dusty miller, beach pea and seaside aster are commonly joined today by Japanese black pines and rugosa roses from the Orient, and by such European favorites as the sea buckthorn, Russian olive, Austrian pine, heather and sea lavender. This kind of international exchange between seaside gardens continues as we look to New Zealand and Australia for new varieties; at the same time our California coastal wildings are taking up residence along the French Riviera.

As you study plant life by or near the sea, you will discover a pattern for where various kinds grow. In the parlance of seaside gardening, there are Belt I (fully exposed, with salt in the soil); Belt II (somewhat protected, often by plants in Belt I); and Belt III (well back and protected). These divisions intermingle in subtle ways, but they do provide a basis on which to select plant materials. When planting in the dunes, first make pockets in the sand and fill with rich garden soil. This technique encourages the plants to send out roots quickly in the new location. One way to grow flowers, herbs or vegetables in the midst of sand is to sink clay flue tiles into the ground, replacing all the sand with rich garden soil (*sketch below*). Container plantings next to a protective wall of the house (*opposite*) also are likely to prosper. For lists of flowers, shrubs, trees and vines suited to seaside gardens, see the Plant Finder section of this book.

Water-fall Shade Garden

A steep bank may present a difficult problem in landscaping, but it also offers an opportunity for creating a beautiful garden like that shown here. While the initial labor may be substantial, the rewards make it worthwhile. In the garden shown, boulder-size rocks were left in place and the other elements planned around them. A minimum of copper pipe and a re-circulating pump made possible the waterfall which gives both visual and aural pleasure. On this particular property, the native soil was excellent and many wild flowers, shrubs and young trees already inhabited the site. Only the area shown in the foreground was cleared, partly to accommodate construction of the waterfall, using native stones, but also to allow the planting of selected cultivated flowers that, once established, grow nearly wild in perfect harmony with the surroundings. If a hillside planting like this one receives a half day or more of sun in summer, seeds of Iceland poppies, sweet rocket, dianthus, godetia, clarkia, arctotis, and anchusa broadcast over it in early spring will provide unexpected patches of flower color all season; most will self-sow for future years of bloom. 1. Epimedium. 2. Asarum. 3. Mazus. 4. *Phlox divaricata*. 5. Mertensia. 6. *Begonia evansiana*. 7. *Nepeta hederacea*. 8. Daffodils. 9. *Aquilegia canadensis*. 10. *Anemone japonica*. 11. *Aconitum uncinatum*. 12. *Thymus vulgaris*.

Drought-tolerant Plantings

In semi-arid climates, or where the water supply for irrigation is limited, or you don't want to always be watering, rely mostly on drought-tolerant plantings like the red, orange and yellow daylilies, Mugho pines and white-flowered yucca shown in this garden *(opposite)*. The landscape design shown here, by Kathleen Bourke for the Henry Field Seed and Nursery Company, uses mostly plant materials that will do exceptionally well in a dry year. Although the plan might be adapted to a flat property, it was planned for a hilly site with soil that rapidly drains off excess moisture. Lists of plants recommended for dry locations included in the Plant Finder section of this book are: annuals (page 155), bulbs (page 165), ferns (page 166), ground covers that tolerate poor soil (page 170), hedge plants for poor growing conditions (page 172), perennials (page 195), shrubs (page 233), trees (page 244) and wild flowers (page 251).

1. Ginkgo
2. Redbud
3. Savins juniper
4. Red barberry
5. Tamarix
6. Redmond linden
7. Hybrid lilacs
8. Honeysuckle
9. Barberry
10. Sedums
11. Golden elder
12. Potentilla
13. Hybrid daylilies
14. *Vinca minor*
15. Golden-rain tree
16. Crape-myrtle
17. Mugho pines
18. Ginkgo
19. Viburnum
20. Russian olive
21. Weigela
22. Amur cork tree
23. Crown-vetch
24. Locust tree
25. Pyracantha
26. Russian olive
27. White birch
28. Yucca

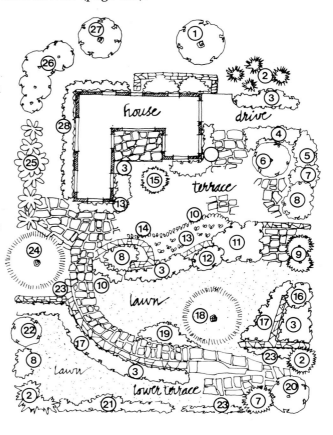

Nearly Wild Garden

If you have a sunny meadow, you can turn it into acres of carefree flowers simply by sowing seeds of cultivated types broadcast-fashion over the area. There are several ways to do this. One that works particularly well for the hardy annuals such as Iceland poppies (opposite), larkspur, sweet-alyssum, baby's-breath, nemophila, viola, snapdragon, calendula, clarkia, godetia, gaillardia, bachelor's-button, nigella, coreopsis and rudbeckia is to broadcast the seeds over the meadow on a sunny winter day when it is covered by snow. Eventually, as the snow melts, it will carry the seeds into the surface soil, allowing them to find a lodging place where they will sprout and begin to grow in the first warm days of spring. Another way is to scatter the seeds over the meadow following an April shower; first flowers should appear in June and continue until frost. The third way is to plow and harrow the section to be planted in any sunny field, then to broadcast pounds of hardy annual seeds sold for this purpose by mail-order seed houses. The whole idea, based somewhat on survival of the fittest, is that the flowers will spring up among the grasses and other meadow plants, and without any coddling—no weeding, feeding or watering—they will grow, bloom, set seeds which they drop to the ground, or which animals and the wind will scatter, and these will increase and perpetuate themselves year after year. This plan can also be put into practice along any country road where municipal maintenance does not include mowing along the roadsides. Not everything you plant will grow, and some that sprout and flower beautifully the first year may not return, depending on the coldness of your winter climate and the hardiness of the seeds themselves. Tender annuals such as nicotiana (flowering tobacco) may scatter millions of seeds, but if the winter is too severe, few if any may survive.

ANNUALS FOR NEARLY WILD GARDENS

ADONIS	COLLOMIA	GODETIA	MALOPE
ALYSSUM	CONVOLVULUS	GYPSOPHILA	MATHIOLA
ANCHUSA	CYNOGLOSSUM	HELIANTHUS	NEMOPHILA
ARCTOTIS	DELPHINIUM	IBERIS	NICOTIANA
BORAGO	DIMORPHOTHECA	IPOMOEA	NIGELLA
CALENDULA	DOWNINGIA	LATHYRUS	PAPAVER
CALLIOPSIS	ECHIUM	LAVATERA	PHACELIA
CAMPANULA	EMILIA	LEPTOSYNE	RESEDA
CENTAUREA	ERYSIMUM	LIMNANTHES	RUDBECKIA
CHRYSANTHEMUM	ESCHSCHOLTZIA	LINARIA	TAGETES
CLARKIA	EUPHORBIA	LINUM	TROPAEOLUM
CLEOME	GILIA	LUPINUS	VISCARIA
COLLINSIA	GLAUCIUM	MALCOMIA	ZINNIA

Landscaping with Edibles

This design by Kathleen Bourke for Henry Field Seed and Nursery Company accommodates a vegetable garden, fruit and nut trees, bramble fruits and strawberries, all treated also as ornamentals in the landscape. Although this plan is for a narrow lot, the idea can be adapted to almost any sunny site. 1. Onions, beets, carrots, beans. 2. Corn, squash, cabbage. 3. Peas, radishes, peppers, spinach and green onions. 4. Grape arbor. 5. Blueberry bushes with Nanking cherries as a hedge. 6. Pachysandra. 7. Sunburst locust. 8. Lilac or azalea.

9. Evergreen windbreak
10. Perennial border flowers
11. Nut trees
12. Pin oak
13. Annuals over spring bulbs
14. Fruit trees
15. Clematis
16. Tree hydrangea
17. Climbing rose
18. Hybrid roses
19. Ajuga
20. Miniature roses
21. Russian olive
22. Gravel or tanbark
23. Climbing rose
24. Herbs
25. Fig trees
26. Strawberries
27. Yews
28. Raspberry and blackberry bushes trained on fence
29. Potted tuberous begonias under lath shade

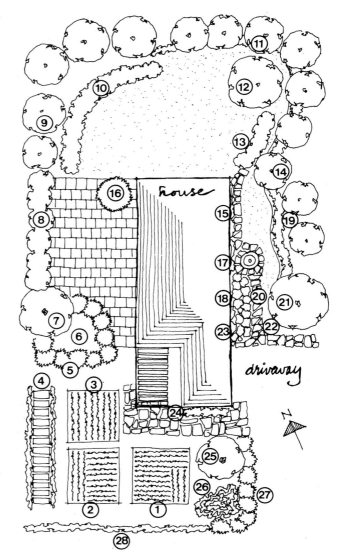

Big Crop from A Small Plot

Depending on your available space and interests, you can copy or adapt this little kitchen garden that measures all of eight by ten feet. The designers, Grant and Holly Gilmore, have used new varieties of midget vegetables in a mini-nursery system combined with succession planting, interplanting, high fertility and one inch of water a week. The Gilmores' garden in summer and fall takes advantage of mini-nursery techniques. For example, parsley, tomatoes, peppers, kale and Chinese cabbage can be brought to planting-out size in flats kept elsewhere (either in the garden or purchased at a nursery). This keeps actual garden space working hard. When you remove one crop and replace it with another, you are practicing suckession planting. When you plant vegetables of different maturity times in the same row, you are interplanting. Study the plans to see how the two practices increase productivity.

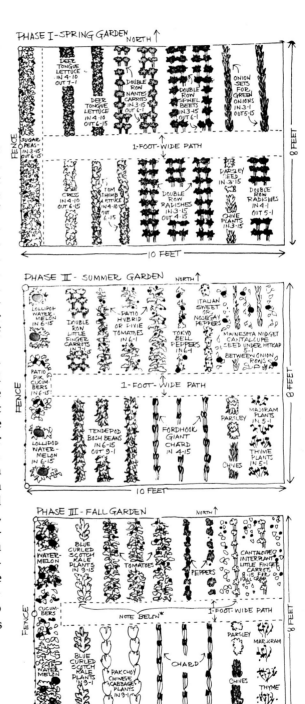

Vegetables on a Rooftop

The owners of this rooftop garden in Manhattan, Mr. and Mrs. William B. Crane, Jr., elected to turn it into a vegetable truck patch instead of a flower border. Raised planting beds on three sides, 12 inches deep and three feet wide, were filled with a mixture of rich garden loam, peat moss, perlite and vermiculite, plus some well-rotted compost (dried cow manure might also be used). The fourth side, a brick wall facing east, provides an ideal place to espalier hybrid beefsteak tomatoes, an ideal way to increase the harvest, at the same time reducing the amount of space required by the plants. Before planting on a rooftop, be sure that it is waterproof and strong enough to carry the weight of soil and plantings. Where weight may be a problem, lightweight soil-less planting mediums may be used, combined with a feeding-with-every-watering program.

1. Tomatoes espaliered on wall
2. Vegetables and herbs
3. Impatiens
4. Geraniums
5. Rhubarb
6. Asparagus
7. Potting shed
8. Shelf added as a bar
9. Lawn
10. Ten-inch wide ledge on raised planting beds

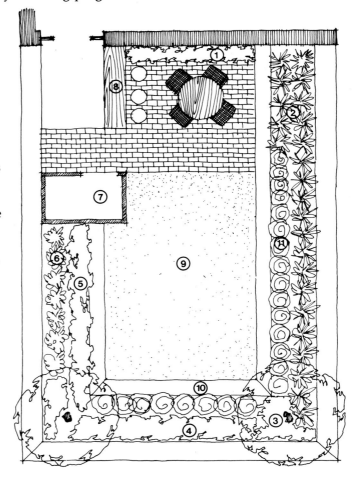

Container Vegetable Garden

If you have no ground space for growing vegetables and herbs, try them in containers. There are two requisites that stand above all others in importance: a site that receives a half day or more of direct sun and a growing medium that is *never* allowed to dry out. Otherwise, the needs of container edibles are fairly easily met. Herbs will grow nicely in six- to eight-inch pots; vegetables are likely to do better in pots ten inches or larger in diameter, or in wooden tubs, plastic-lined fruit baskets, plastic garbage pails, or in planter boxes like those in the patio, rooftop or high-rise terrace garden below, designed by Ron Hildebrand for Ortho. Planter boxes can be made of rot-resistant redwood or cypress if budget permits; otherwise, you can build them of shipping-crate lumber, easily salvaged from city streets on heavy-pickup day, or from a municipal dump. For best results, minimum depth should be eight inches. Prepare a growing medium by mixing two parts each of garden loam or all-purpose potting soil, well-rotted compost, peat moss and vermiculite to one-half part blood meal or dried cow manure. After vegetables have been in active growth for about a month, regular feedings of fish emulsion fertilizer will prove beneficial throughout the balance of the season. Dwarf, midget or mini-varieties of vegetables are excellent for container gardening; also standard varieties of rhubarb and Swiss chard, eggplant, leaf lettuce, peppers, New Zealand spinach (a great warm-weather substitute for regular spinach), zucchini and okra. Strawberries may be cultivated in hanging baskets (one everbearing plant to each ten-inch hanging pot), or the runnerless *fraises des bois* varieties such as Baron Solemacher or Alexandria may be planted in pots or boxes. Dwarf fruit trees of all types, including Bonanza peach and fig, will do well in individual tubs 18 to 24 inches in diameter, as will blueberries, raspberries and grapes (for which a fence, trellis or arbor will be needed).

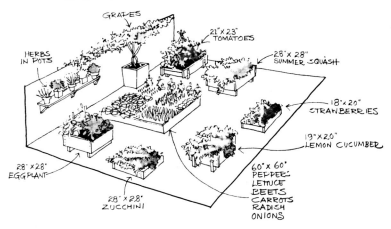

Victorian Knot Garden of Herbs

An herb garden can be located anywhere—from a small window box perched above a busy street to a secluded, quiet half-acre, neatly hedged and green-ribboned. Most herbs need only two things: a soil that is not overly rich and sunshine. To plant the Victorian knot garden sketched below you will need a sunny site at least 12 feet square. Favorite herbs best started by purchasing growing plants from a nursery include chives, tarragon, lovage, lemon balm, mint, pot-marjoram, rosemary, sage, burnet, winter savory and thyme. Herbs fairly easy to start from seeds—though your local garden center will likely have them in small flats at planting time in spring—include dill, chervil, caraway, coriander, fennel, sweet marjoram, basil, parsley and summer savory. The photograph *(opposite)* shows fresh harvest from an herb garden, including curly and plain parsley, sweet bay, thyme and basil with sweet peppers. Of the 14 herbs suggested below, only dill, fennel, basil and parsley require annual planting in spring; the others are perennials that should live over winter and grow larger year after year. (In severely cold climates, rosemary may need to be carried over winter indoors in a cool, sunny window or greenhouse.) To grow herbs indoors, provide a sunny sill or grow under fluorescent lights (a unit with two 20- or 40-watt tubes is suggested, one Gro-Lux and one Gro-Lux Wide Spectrum) burned 14 to 18 hours daily. Herbs need fresh, moist air and moist soil.

 1. Dill
 2. Tarragon
 3. Sage
 4. Fennel
 5. Chives
 6. Basil
 7. Parsley
 8. Mint
 9. Lavender
10. Culinary thyme
11. Green santolina
12. Gray santolina
13. Germander
14. Rosemary

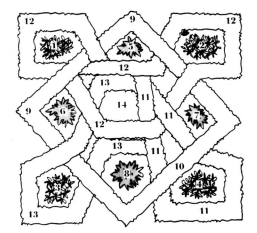

Dining Terrace on the Module

To design a modular garden, a simple shape of a specific size is selected, usually a square or a rectangle, and this shape is repeated, using two or more materials in various combinations, to form the surface pattern of the garden. The modular method almost invariably produces an attractive garden even when it is used by an inexperienced gardener with no particular training in design. The first step in designing a modular garden is to choose the shape and size of the modular unit. If a square is chosen, and it is the easiest to use, the size should be between two and five feet square; in most gardens three or four feet will be the most desirable. The garden design below, by Landscape Architect Betty Ajay, uses a modular unit three by three feet for a total area 30 by 39 feet; all of the gardens that follow, on pages 134, 136, 138, 140 and 142, show variations on this same theme. When the shape and size of the module have been decided, the next step is to determine the materials to be used in the modular units. In most gardens a place to sit and a place to walk will be required, and, therefore, a permanent surfacing material such as flagstone, brick, poured concrete or crushed stone should be one of the materials selected. The other materials can be water, trees, shrubs, flowers, ground covers, tan bark, sand or any other material the gardener finds particularly appealing. However, while the choice is wide, the selection should be limited. If a few materials are used, it is much easier to produce a unified design than if a wide assortment of different materials is used. The specific choices should depend on the personal preferences of the gardener, not only in the limited sense of which surfacing materials and plants are preferred, but in the larger sense of what kind of garden is wanted. If a cool, restful, low-maintenance garden is desired, stone, water, trees and a ground cover would be logical choices. If a profusion of color and texture is wanted, brick, flowers and herbs might be selected. The simple plan below is designed for minimum upkeep.

This modular garden is enclosed by a rock wall with flagstone surface, and a medium-size tree in each corner with ground cover. The dining terrace *(opposite)* uses tile and brick surface; potted tropical plants give accent.

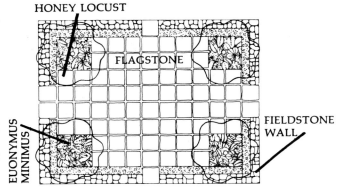

HONEY LOCUST

FLAGSTONE

EUONYMUS MINIMUS

FIELDSTONE WALL

Blue-and-Gold Modular Garden

This garden, like those on pages 132, 136, 138, 140 and 142, was designed by Landscape Architect Betty Ajay, and uses a basic modular unit three by three feet for a total space 30 by 39 feet. Color is provided by blue ageratum and dwarf French marigolds, shown closeup (*opposite*) with an inset of the high-rise terrace garden of Mr. and Mrs. William B. Crane, Jr., where pots of marigolds are used for movable living bouquets. After the materials have been chosen for a modular garden, the basic pattern into which the modular units will be fitted should be designed. The pattern will be determined by the available space, the materials which have been selected and the ingenuity and skill of the gardener. The only requirement to be met is that the allotted space must be level, with just enough pitch for adequate drainage. The modular concept does not work on sloping land, since a discernible pitch distorts proportions. If the land is not level, it must be leveled by cutting or filling or both, and the necessary retaining walls must be built before a pattern is laid out. This modular approach to landscaping remedies the most common fault in amateur gardens; namely, the absence of a coherent design of any kind. This unfortunate and widespread lack is responsible for the disappointing appearance of thousands of well-tended gardens filled with beautiful plants. The modular method is the simplest way to introduce a unified pattern into the garden. Far from being the straitjacket that some gardeners fear it to be, use of the module brings clarity and crispness to the garden and, within its firm structure, allows the complexity of plant material to show to full advantage. In the garden sketched below, blue- and yellow-flowered hardy spring bulbs (see the Plant Finder section of this book) might precede the blue ageratum and yellow marigolds. In another season, an entirely different color scheme might be used—perhaps white petunias with pink snapdragons, or purple petunias with red dwarf zinnias for a vivid, daring combination.

A clipped taxus (yew) hedge frames this garden with surface of gray crushed stone. Favorite herbs are used in the corner planting modules with flowers in the middle. Lawn furniture might be used in the open center space.

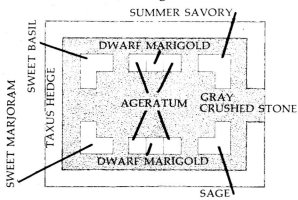

SUMMER SAVORY

SWEET BASIL

SWEET MARJORAM

TAXUS HEDGE

DWARF MARIGOLD

AGERATUM

GRAY CRUSHED STONE

DWARF MARIGOLD

SAGE

Grandeur on a Small Scale

The modular approach to landscaping, shown here and on pages 132, 134, 138, 140 and 142, in designs by Landscape Architect Betty Ajay, is an excellent way to capture the grandeur of an estate garden like that shown in color (*opposite*) in a small space. All of the major features of the grand garden, which include wisteria trained on an arbor, a reflecting pool, an abundance of tulips and a bench to sit and contemplate the beauty might be adapted to the 30- by 39-foot terrace garden sketched below. Wisteria could be trained on the fence; a reflecting pool is part of the design; instead of myrtle as a ground cover beneath the white birch trees, tulips or other spring bulbs might be planted in autumn, to be followed after bloom the next year by favorite annual flowers, geraniums, wax begonias—or impatiens if the trees cast considerable shade. Instead of white birch, any number of other small trees might be used, such as flowering dogwood, redbud, flowering crab apple, peach or cherry. The open spaces of the terrace allow for the placement of a small dining table and chairs, or simply of comfortable outdoor furniture for reading and relaxing. Usually the last step in designing a modular garden is to enclose it. If the garden is directly adjacent to the house, the enclosure should surround three sides; but, if the garden is not adjacent, it should be enclosed on all four sides, with appropriate openings for entrance and exit. The enclosure can be a wall, a fence or a hedge; it can be high or low, formal or informal. It can be one material throughout or a mixture of several materials, but it should never be omitted. Without it the garden will be incomplete, for a sense of containment, desirable in all gardens, is vital to a modular garden. If the enclosing wall is six to eight feet tall, it can provide an excellent place to espalier some dwarf fruit trees, pyracantha, cotoneaster, viburnum or yew, or it can be used as the support for training wisteria or clematis flowering vines.

A fence surrounds this modular garden with flagstone surface. A taxus (yew) hedge frames the reflecting pool; other plants are white birch trees underplanted with myrtle. Spring bulbs such as tulips might be used instead of myrtle, to be followed by annual flowers.

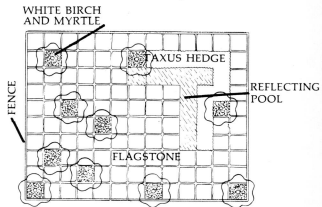

WHITE BIRCH AND MYRTLE

TAXUS HEDGE

REFLECTING POOL

FENCE

FLAGSTONE

Spring Flowers, All-season Greens for a Modular Terrace

This modular garden, like those sketched on pages 132, 134, 136, 140 and 142, is based on a module three feet square, repeated for a total area of 30 by 39 feet. The plant materials suggested by Landscape Architect Betty Ajay have been selected to bring a spring season of glorious bloom from dogwood and broadleaf evergreens including rhododendron, azalea and mountain-laurel. In all other months of the year this landscape would be a pleasant surround of various greens, the only deciduous plantings being the dogwood and pin oak trees. While dogwood limbs are bare in winter, the bud-tipped branches silhouette beautifully. The oak leaves, which turn russet in autumn, tend to cling to the branches through winter, finally falling as new growth begins in spring. Although mountain-laurels all tend to bloom at the same time, the rhododendrons and azaleas might be selected to bloom simultaneously or chosen in early, midseason and late varieties in order to spread flowers over the longest period possible. Hybrids like the rhododendron shown on the opposite page in color are available with relatively compact, dwarf growth habit that packs the most bloom possible into the least amount of space, almost always a desirable trait to keep in mind when selecting planting materials for a small-space garden. Although pebble-surface concrete with wood dividers is the paving material suggested, bricks might be used instead, or white crushed gravel, flagstones or gray crushed stone, depending on the architecture and color of the house or other materials used in the surrounding landscape. In a dry, windy climate, an entirely different selection of plant materials would be desirable; choose from lists of trees and shrubs recommended for dry soil in the Plant Finder section of this book; for a terrace by the ocean, check the lists of plants recommended for Belts I, II and III under Seaside plants.

A hemlock hedge frames this modular garden with dogwood and pin oak trees shading plantings of rhododendron, azaleas and mountain-laurel, underplanted with pachysandra ground cover. The paving is pebble-surface concrete with redwood dividers.

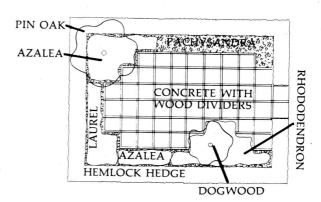

Outdoor Living Room Designed on the Module

The terrace design below, like those on pages 132, 134, 136, 138 and 142, by Landscape Architect Betty Ajay, is based on a modular unit three by three feet square, repeated for a total space of 30 by 39 feet. In the photographs (*opposite*) this same concept has simply been adapted to fit the available space behind a townhouse. Gray flagstone surrounds a bricked area used for dining and other outdoor living furniture. Purple wisteria grows on an arbor attached to the house, as well as on the walls of the garden. Depending on your own preferences, the dogwood trees suggested in the planting plan might be replaced by almost any flowering tree listed in the Plant Finder section of this book. The English ivy ground cover might be any of the many ground covers listed (also in the Plant Finder), or the space could be used for fall-planted spring bulb flowers, followed by annual flowers that tolerate some shade, or a permanent border of hardy perennials. If summer-flowering trees are selected instead of the dogwoods, the red maples might be replaced by spring-flowering trees (also listed in the Plant Finder), and if the upkeep of mowing grass is not appealing, it might be replaced by a low-upkeep ground cover, or the area simply used for a garden of low-growing bulbs, annuals, biennials and perennials, selected to give patches of bloom from the first warm days of spring to the last frost-free weather of autumn. One of the advantages of a modular landscape design like this one, and the others shown on these pages, is that the planting spaces left open for shrubs, ground covers and flowers can be changed completely every few years, thus creating the effect of a new garden without the expense and labor of a major overhaul.

A brick wall surrounds this modular garden. Dogwood trees underplanted with English ivy edge the bricked surface, which frames a 12- by 21-foot lawn in which two red maples are planted. Containers of flowers might be added for color.

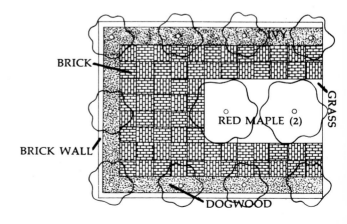

Contemporary Terrace Designed on the Module

This terrace, like those sketched on pages 132, 134, 136, 138 and 140, has been designed by Landscape Architect Betty Ajay, using a basic module three by three feet, repeated for a total area of 30 by 39 feet. The modular concept of landscaping is surprisingly adaptable to almost any level-ground space, and may be used with relative ease to achieve a delightful effect that may be traditional or contemporary. The design below, like the five preceding, creates a garden that is as pleasant to walk through or sit in as it is when viewed from above, perhaps a second-story window or balcony. This garden with its frame of clipped Tatarian honeysuckle hedge gives a contemporary appearance, and would be especially appropriate next to a house of contemporary design. Pink petunias, like the Pink Cascade variety shown in color (opposite) may be purchased in full bloom at a local garden center or nursery in spring. Since they offer the only long-term color from flowers, almost any other variety might be chosen for a different color scheme. Fall-planted spring bulbs might also precede the petunias or other annual flowers. Or, a no-maintenance hardy perennial such as hybrid daylilies might be used in the planting pockets; four different daylilies could be planted in each pocket, the varieties selected for early, midseason and late bloom, all in one color or mixed; for example, all yellows, all oranges or all pinks and reds. If only annual flowers such as petunias are used in a garden like this one, the planting pockets need not be planted in a season when you plan to be away from home; for example, if one year you plan to take a long trip in summer, the spaces can be left empty until your return, at which time you could easily fill the pockets with seasonal chrysanthemums for an almost-instant effect.

A Tatarian honeysuckle hedge frames this modular garden with a surface of white crushed stone. Three flowering crab apple trees are underplanted with English ivy. Pockets of pink petunias provide bloom all summer.

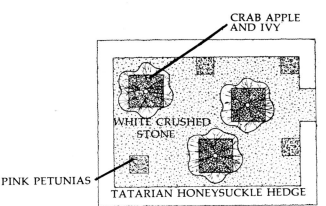

CRAB APPLE AND IVY

WHITE CRUSHED STONE

PINK PETUNIAS

TATARIAN HONEYSUCKLE HEDGE

How To Use the Plant Finder

You can spend a lifetime gathering the information needed to plan a garden that blooms all season long. Or a landscape with plantings that achieve specific purposes—shade, or scent, screening, or your favorite color. With the Plant Finder you can do it in minutes. Main categories are indexed in the Contents, below.

If you are looking for an annual, for instance, that is fragrant, grows in shade and tolerates damp ground, a quick cross-check of the Plant Finder will tell you whether or not there is such an annual. If you want several species of fern for a rock garden in the sun, the Plant Finder will tell you which to plant. You can use the Plant Finder to select plants of all sorts for gardens by the seashore, or trees with brilliant autumn coloring or decorative bark; shrubs that provide fruit for the birds or grow no taller than three feet or flower in winter.

Having the Plant Finder for reference at the time you are planning a garden is almost like having your own horticultural computer. While it might be nice to have a machine race through all the variables and possibilities for a request such as blue flowers in spring on a plant less than 12 inches tall that grows in damp ground in the shade, and then spew out the answer (*Ajuga reptans*), finding the answer yourself in the Plant Finder is like a fascinating game, the playing of which is guaranteed to help you better understand plants, how they grow and how to use them effectively.

Plant Finder Contents

Annuals

Annuals
BY HEIGHT: DWARF, UNDER 1 FOOT

Ageratum houstonianum
Anagallis arvensis—Pimpernel
 A. linifolia
Antirrhinum majus—Snapdragon
Begonia semperflorens—Wax begonia
Calandrinia umbellata—Rock-purslane
Campanula drabifolia—Bellflower
Coreopsis tinctoria nana—Plains coreopsis
Dorotheanthus gramineus
Eschscholtzia caespitosa
Felicia bergeriana—Kingfisher daisy
Gamolepis tagetes
Gazania longiscapa
Gilia dianthoides
 G. lutea
Ionopsidium acaule—Diamond-flower
Lathyrus odoratus, dwarf varieties—
 Sweet-pea
Limnanthes douglasii—Meadow-foam
Limonium spicatum—Sea-lavender
Linaria alpina—Alpine toadflax
 L. bipartita—Cloven-lip toadflax
 L. broussonnetia
Lobelia erinus—Edging lobelia
Lobularia maritima—Sweet-alyssum
Mimulus moschatus—Musk-flower
Myosotis welwitschii—Forget-me-not
Nemophila maculata—Five-spot
 N. menziesii—Baby blue-eyes
Nierembergia hippomanica caerulea—
 Cup-flower
 N. repens rivularis—White cup-
 flower
NOLANA—Chilean-bellflower
Omphalodes linifolia—Navelwort
Papaver pavoninum—Peacock poppy
Petunia x hybrida, dwarf varieties
Phacelia campanularia
Platystemon californicus—Cream-cups
Portulaca grandiflora—Rose-moss
Reseda odorata—Mignonette
Sanvitalia procumbens—Creeping-zinnia
Saponaria calabrica—Soapwort
Schizopetalon walkeri
Sedum caeruleum—Stone crop

Tagetes erecta, dwarf varieties—African
 marigold
 T. patula—French marigold
Thymophylla tenuiloba—Dahlberg daisy
Torenia fournieri—Wishbone flower
Tropaeolum minus—Nasturtium
Ursina anthemoides
 U. pulchra
 U. pygmaea
Viola tricolor var. hortensis—Pansy
Zinnia elegans varieties—Garden zinnia
 Z. linearis

Annuals
BY HEIGHT: LOW, 1 TO 1½ FEET

Adonis aestivalis—Summer adonis
Alonsoa species—Mask-flower
Anchusa capensis—Alkanet. Bugloss
Antirrhinum majus varieties—Snap-
 dragon
Asperula orientalis—Woodruff
Brachycome iberidifolia—Swan River
 daisy
Browallia americana
Calandrinia ciliata—Rock-purslane
Calendula officinalis—Pot-marigold
Callistephus chinensis—China-aster
Centaurea cyanus dwarf varieties—
 Cornflower. Bachelor's-button
 C. moschata—Sweet sultan
Collinsia heterophylla
 C. verna—Blue-eyed Mary
Collomia linearis
Convolvulus tricolor—Dwarf glorybind
Coreopsis drummondii—Golden wave
Cuphea ignea—Cigarflower
Dianthus chinensis var. heddewigii—
 China pink
Diascia barberae—Twinspur
Dimorphotheca annua—Cape-marigold
Echium creticum—Viper's bugloss
 E. plantagineum varieties
Eschscholtzia californica—California-
 poppy
Euphorbia marginata—Snow-on-the-
 mountain
Felicia adfinis
Gaillardia amblyodon—Maroon gaillardia
 G. pulchella—Painted gaillardia
Gilia liniflora

G. tricolor—Bird's-eyes
Glaucium corniculatum—Sea-poppy
Godetia grandiflora—Satin flower
Gomphrena globosa—Globe-amaranth
Gypsophila elegans—Baby's-breath
    G. muralis
Helipterum manglesii—Swan River ever-
    lasting
Hunnemannia fumariaefolia—Mexican
    golden-cup
Iberis affinis—Candytuft
    I. amara—Rocket candytuft
    I. umbellata
Impatiens walleriana—Busy Lizzie
Lathyrus odoratus—Sweet-pea
Layia elegans—Tidy-tips
    L. glandulosa—White daisy
Limonium suworowii—Rattail statice
Linaria maroccana—Toadflax
    L. reticulata—Purplenet toadflax
Linum grandiflorum—Flowering flax
Lobelia gracilis
Lonas inodora—African daisy
Lupinus densiflorus—Lupine
    L. nanus
    L. subcarnosus—Bluebonnet
Lychnis species—Campion. Catchfly
Mimulus brevipes—Monkey-flower
Nemesia floribunda
Nigella sativa—Black cumin
Papaver californicum—Mission poppy
Petunia x hybrida varieties
Phacelia viscida
    P. whitlavia—California-bluebell
Phlox drummondii—Annual phlox
Salvia patens—Gentian sage. Blue sage
Satureja hortensis—Summer savory
Schizanthus retusus—Fringe flower
Tagetes erecta varieties—African marigold
Tropaeolum species—Nasturtium
Verbena x hybrida—Garden verbena
Zinnia elegans varieties—Garden zinnia

Annuals
BY HEIGHT: MEDIUM, 1½ TO 3 FEET

Adonis annua—Autumn adonis. Red-
    chamomile
Alonsoa warscewiczii—Mask flower
Amaranthus tricolor—Joseph's-coat
Ammobium alatum—Winged-everlasting
Antirrhinum species—Snapdragon
Arctotis stoechadifolia—African daisy
Argemone grandiflora—Prickly-poppy
Borago officinalis—Borage
Browallia speciosa
Calandrinia grandiflora—Rock-purslane
Calceolaria chelidonioides—Slipperwort
Callistephus chinensis—China-aster
Campanula medium varieties—Canter-
    bury-bells
Celosia argentea var. cristata—Cocks-
    comb
Centaurea cyanus—Cornflower
Cerinthe retorta—Honeywort
Chrysanthemum carinatum—Tricolor
    chrysanthemum
Clarkia concinna—Red-ribbons
    C. elegans
Collomia cavanillesii
    C. grandiflora
Coreopsis atkinsonia—Tickseed
    C. tinctoria—Plains coreopsis
Crepis rubra—Hawkweed
Cynoglossum amabile—Chinese-forget-
    me-not
Delphinium ajacis—Rocket larkspur
Echium creticum—Viper's bugloss
    E. plantagineum
Emilia sagittata—Tassel-flower
Euphorbia heterophylla—Mexican fire-
    plant. Painted spurge
Eustoma russellianum—Russell prairie-
    gentian
Gaillardia amblyodon—Maroon gaillardia
    G. aristata—Blanket-flower
Gilia abrotanifolia
    G. achilleaefolia
Godetia amoena—Farewell-to-spring
Helichrysum bracteatum—Strawflower
Heliotropium arborescens—Heliotrope
Helipterum roseum—Everlasting
Hibiscus trionum—Flower-of-an-hour

Impatiens balsamina—Garden balsam
Limonium bonduellii—Sea-lavender
Lupinus hirsutus—Blue lupine
Malope trifida
Mathiola incana—Stock. Gilliflower
Matricaria chamomila—German-chamomile
   M. inodora—Scentless false chamomile
Mentzelia decapetala
   M. laevicaulis—Blazing-star
Mimulus guttatus—Yellow monkey-flower
   M. lewisii—Pink monkey-flower
Mirabilis jalapa—Four-o'clock
   M. longiflora—Marvel-of-Peru
Molucella laevis—Bells-of-Ireland
Nemesia strumosa
Nicotiana sanderae—Tobacco plant
Nierembergia scoparia frutescens—Cupflower
Nigella damascena—Love-in-a-mist
Papaver glaucum—Tulip poppy
Penstemon x *gloxinioides*—Border penstemon. Garden penstemon
Petunia x *hybrida*
Phacelia minor—Canterbury-bells
Rudbeckia bicolor—Thimbleflower
   R. hirta—Gloriosa daisy
Salpiglossis sinuata—Painted-tongue
Salvia splendens—Scarlet sage
Scabiosa atropurpurea—Sweet scabious
Schizanthus pinnatus—Butterfly-flower
Senecio elegans—Purple ragwort
Silene armeria—Sweet William-catchfly
Tagetes erecta—African marigold
Trachymene caerulea—Blue laceflower
Tropaeolum majus—Nasturtium
Venidium species
Vinca rosea—Madagascar periwinkle
Xanthisma texanum—Star-of-Texas
Xeranthemum annuum—Immortelle
Zinnia elegans varieties—Garden zinnia

Annuals
BY HEIGHT: TALL, OVER 3 FEET

Althaea rosea—Hollyhock
Amaranthus caudatus—Love-lies-bleeding
   A. x *hybridus* var. Prince's-feather
Antirrhinum majus varieties—Snapdragon

Argemone platyceras—Crested-poppy
Calonyction aculeatum—Moonflower
Centaurea americana—Basket flower
Cleome spinosa—Spider flower
Cosmos species
Cuphea lanceolata—Lanceleaf cigarflower
Datura metel—Hindu datura
   D. meteloides
Dolichos lablab—Hyacinth-bean
Felicia amelloides—Blue daisy
Hebenstretia comosa
Helianthus annuus—Sunflower
   H. argyrophyllus—Silver-leaf sunflower
   H. debilis—Cucumber-leaf sunflower
Hibiscus manihot—Queen-of-the-border
   H. sabdariffa—Roselle
Ipomoea hederacea—Ivy-leaved morning-glory
   I. nil
   I. purpurea—Morning-glory
Kochia scoparia—Summer-cypress
Lathyrus odoratus—Sweet-pea
Lavatera trimestris—Tree-mallow
Lupinus caucasicum—Lupine
   L. macrostomum
Malva crispa—Curled mallow
Mentzelia lindleyi
Molucella spinosa
Nicotiana alata—Flowering tobacco
Phacelia tenacetifolia
Polygonum orientale—Prince's-feather
Ricinus communis—Castor-bean
Schizanthus grahamii—Poor-man's-orchid
Tithonia rotundifolia—Mexican-sunflower
Tropaeolum peltophorum—Shield nasturtium
   T. peregrinum—Canary nasturtium
Verbena bonariensis—Vervain
Zinnia elegans varieties—Garden zinnia

Annuals
BY COLOR: BLUE

Ageratum houstonianum
Anagallis linifolia—Pimpernel
Anchusa capensis—Alkanet. Bugloss
Arctotis stoechadifolia—African daisy

Asperula orientalis—Woodruff
Borago officinalis—Borage
Brachycome iberidifolia—Swan River
    daisy
Browallia americana
Callistephus chinensis—China-aster
Campanula drabifolia—Bellflower
Centaurea cyanus—Cornflower
Collinsia verna—Blue-eyed Mary
Convolvulus tricolor—Dwarf glorybind
Cynoglossum amabile—Chinese-forget-
    me-not
Delphinium ajacis—Larkspur
Echium plantagineum—Viper's bugloss
Felicia adfinis
    F. bergeriana—Kingfisher daisy
Gilia capitata
Ipomoea purpurea—Morning-glory
Lathyrus odoratus—Sweet-pea
Linum usitatissimum—Common flax
Lobelia erinus—Edging lobelia
Lupinus hirsutus—Blue lupine
    L. subcarnosus—Blue-bonnet
Myosotis sylvatica—Forget-me-not
Nemophila menziesii—Baby blue-eyes
Nierembergia hippomanica caerulea—
    Cupflower
Nigella damascena—Love-in-a-mist
NOLANA—Chilean-bellflower
Petunia x hybrida
PHACELIA
Salpiglossis sinuata—Painted-tongue
Salvia patens—Blue sage
Scabiosa atropurpurea—Sweet scabious
Sedum caeruleum—Stonecrop
Torenia fournieri—Wishbone flower
Trachymene caerulea—Blue laceflower
Verbena x hybrida—Garden verbena
Viola tricolor var. hortensis—Pansy

Annuals
BY COLOR: ORANGE

Antirrhinum majus—Snapdragon
Arctotis breviscapa—African daisy
Argemone mexicana—Prickly-poppy
Calendula officinalis—Pot-marigold
Collomia cavanillesii
Cosmos sulphureus hybrids—Yellow
    cosmos
Diascia barberae—Twinspur

Dimorphotheca annua—Cape-marigold
    D. aurantiaca
Eccremocarpus scaber—Glory-flower
Emilia sagittata—Tassel-flower
Eschscholtzia californica varieties—
    California-poppy
Gaillardia pulchella varieties—Painted
    gaillardia
Gamolepis tagetes
Helichrysum bracteatum—Strawflower
Linaria maroccana varieties—Toadflax
Nemesia strumosa var. suttonii
Papaver rhoeas—Shirley poppy. Corn
    poppy
Penstemon x gloxinioides—Border pen-
    stemon. Garden penstemon
Tagetes erecta—African marigold
    T. patula—French marigold
Tropaeolum majus—Garden nasturtium
    T. peltophorum—Shield nasturtium
Ursinia pulchra
Venidium fastuosum
Zinnia elegans varieties—Garden zinnia

Annuals
BY COLOR: PINK

Abronia umbellata—Prostate sand-ver-
    bena
Amaranthus caudatus—Love-lies-bleeding
Antirrhinum majus varieties—Snapdragon
Begonia semperflorens—Wax begonia
Brachycome iberidifolia—Swan River
    daisy
Calandrinia grandiflora—Rock-purslane
Callistephus chinensis—China-aster
Campanula medium varieties—Canter-
    bury-bells
Celosia argentea varieties
    C. a. var. cristata—Cockscomb
Centaurea cyanus—Cornflower. Bache-
    lor's-button
Clarkia concinna—Red-ribbons
    C. elegans
Cleome spinosa—Spider-flower
Collinsia heterophylla
Collomia linearis
Cosmos bipinnatus
Crepis rubra—Hawkweed
Delphinium ajacis—Rocket larkspur
Echium plantagineum—Viper's bugloss

Gilia achilleaefolia
  G. androsacea
  G. liniflora
Godetia species and varieties—Farewell-
  to-spring. Satin flower
Gomphrena globosa—Globe-amaranth
Gypsophila elegans—Baby's-breath
  G. muralis
Helichrysum bracteatum—Strawflower
Helipterum manglesii—Swan River ever-
  lasting
  H. roseum
Iberis umbellata—Candytuft
Impatiens balsamina—Garden balsam
  I. walleriana—Busy Lizzie
Ipomoea nil—Morning-glory
  I. purpurea
Lathyrus odoratus—Sweet-pea
Lavatera trimestris—Tree-mallow
Limonium spicatum—Sea-lavender
Linum grandiflorum—Flowering flax
Lupinus densiflorus—Lupine
  L. hirsutus varieties
Lychnis coeli-rosa—Rose-of-heaven
Malcomia maritima—Virginia-stock
Malope trifida
Malva sylvestris—Mallow
Mathiola incana var. annua—Stock
Mirabilis jalapa—Four-o'clock
Molucella laevis—Bells-of-Ireland. Shell-
  flower
Myosotis sylvatica var. fischeri—Forget-
  me-not
Nemesia chamaedrifolia
Nicotiana alata—Flowering tobacco
  N. sanderae
Papaver rhoeas—Shirley poppy
Penstemon x gloxinioides—Border pen-
  stemon. Garden penstemon
Petunia x hybrida varieties
Phlox drummondii—Annual phlox
Portulaca grandiflora—Rose-moss
Saponaria calabrica—Soapwort
Satureja hortensis—Summer savory
Scabiosa atropurpurea—Sweet scabious
Schizanthus grahamii—Poor-man's-
  orchid
  S. pinnatus—Butterfly-flower
Silene armeria—Sweet William-catchfly
Verbena x hybrida—Garden verbena
Vinca rosea—Madagascar periwinkle

Xeranthemum annuum—Immortelle. Everlasting
Zinnia elegans varieties—Garden zinnia

Annuals
BY COLOR: PURPLE

Arctotis stoechadifolia—African daisy
Browallia speciosa
Calandrinia ciliata—Rock-purslane
  C. grandiflora
Callistephus chinensis—China-aster
Celosia argentea varieties
  C. a. var. cristata—Cockscomb
Centaurea cyanus—Cornflower
Clarkia concinna—Red-ribbons
  C. elegans
Cleome spinosa varieties—Spider-flower
Cobaea scandens—Cup-and-saucer vine
Collinsia bartsiaefolia—Seaside collinsia
  C. heterophylla
Cosmos bipinnatus
Datura meteloides
Dolichos lablab—Hyacinth-bean
Eustoma russellianum—Russell prairie-
  gentian
Gilia achilleaefolia
  G. androsacea
  G. californica—Prickly-phlox
  G. dianthoides
Godetia grandiflora—Satin flower
Heliotropium arborescens—Heliotrope
Iberis umbellata—Candytuft
Impatiens balsamina—Garden balsam
  I. walleriana—Busy Lizzie
Ipomoea purpurea—Morning-glory
Lathyrus odoratus—Sweet-pea
Limonium puberulum—Sea-lavender
Linaria bipartita var. splendida—Cloven-
  lip toadflax
Lobelia erinus—Edging lobelia
  L. siphilitica—Blue lobelia
Lobularia maritima varieties—Sweet-
  alyssum
Malcomia maritima—Virginia-stock
Malope trifida
Mathiola incana var. annua—Stock
Mirabilis multiflora
Nemophila maculata var. purpurea—
  Five-spot
  N. menziesii varieties—Baby blue-eyes

Penstemon x *gloxinioides*—Border penstemon. Garden penstemon
Petunia x *hybrida*
    P. violacea
Phacelia minor—Canterbury-bells
    P. whitlavia—California-bluebell
Phlox drummondii—Annual phlox
Salpiglossis sinuata—Painted-tongue
Salvia splendens varieties—Sage
Scabiosa atropurpurea—Sweet scabious
Schizanthus grahamii—Poor-man's-orchid
Senecio elegans—Purple ragwort
Verbena bonariensis—Vervain
    V. x *hybrida*—Garden verbena
Viola tricolor var. *hortensis*—Pansy
Xeranthemum annuum—Immortelle. Everlasting

Annuals
BY COLOR: RED

Adonis annua—Autumn adonis. Redchamomile
Amaranthus caudatus—Love-lies-bleeding
    A. x *hybridus* var. *hypochondriacus*
Anagallis arvensis—Pimpernel
Antirrhinum majus varieties—Snapdragon
Begonia semperflorens
Calandrinia ciliata var. *menziesii*—Rock-purslane
    C. umbellata
Callistephus chinensis—China-aster
Celosia argentea
    C. a. var. *cristata*—Cockscomb
Centaurea cyanus—Cornflower. Bachelor's-button
Collomia cavanillesii
Cosmos bipinnatus
CUPHEA—Cigar-flower
Dianthus chinensis var. *heddewigii*—China pink
Eccremocarpus scaber—Glory-flower
Echium creticum—Viper's bugloss
Emilia sagittata—Tassel-flower
Euphorbia heterophylla—Mexican fireplant. Painted spurge
Gaillardia amblyodon—Maroon gaillardia
    G. pulchella varieties
Glaucium corniculatum—Sea-poppy

Godetia species and vareties—Farewell-to-spring. Satin flower
Helichrysum bracteatum—Strawflower
Helipterum manglesii—Swan River everlasting
Iberis umbellata—Candytuft
Impatiens walleriana—Busy Lizzie
Lathyrus odoratus—Sweet-pea
Lavatera trimestris—Tree-mallow
Linaria maroccana varieties—Toadflax
Linum grandiflorum varieties—Flowering flax
Lunaria annua—Money plant
Lychnis coeli-rosa—Rose-of-heaven
Malcomia maritima—Virginia-stock
Mirabilis jalapa—Four-o'clock. Marvel-of-Peru
Nemesia strumosa varieties
Nicotiana alata—Flowering tobacco
Papaver californicum—Mission poppy
    P. caucasicum—Annual poppy
    P. glaucum—Tulip poppy
Penstemon x *gloxinioides*—Border penstemon. Garden penstemon
Petunia x *hybrida* varieties
Phaseolus coccineus—Scarlet runner bean
Phlox drummondii—Annual phlox
Portulaca grandiflora—Rose-moss
QUAMOCLIT—Star-glory
Salpiglossis sinuata—Painted-tongue
Salvia splendens—Scarlet sage
Scabiosa atropurpurea—Sweet scabious
Tithonia rotundifolia—Tithonia
Tropaeolum majus varieties—Nasturtium
Verbena x *hybrida*—Garden verbena
    V. peruviana—Vervain
Zinnia elegans varieties—Garden zinnia

Annuals
BY COLOR: WHITE

Ageratum houstonianum
Ammobium alatum—Winged-everlasting
Antirrhinum coulterianum—Chaparral snapdragon
    A. majus—Snapdragon
Arctotis stoechadifolia—African daisy
Argemone grandiflora—Prickly-poppy
Begonia semperflorens
Brachycome iberidifolia—Swan River daisy

Browallia americana var. *alba*
Callistephus chinensis—China-aster
Calonyction aculeatum—Moonflower
Centaurea cyanus—Cornflower
   C. imperialis—Royal centaurea
   C. moschata—Sweet sultan
Chrysanthemum segetum—Corn-marigold
Clarkia elegans
Cleome spinosa varieties—Spider-flower
Cobaea scandens varieties—Cup-and-saucer vine
Collinsia bartsiaefolia—Seaside collinsia
Cosmos bipinnatus
Datura metel—Hindu datura
Delphinium ajacis—Rocket larkspur
Dianthus chinensis—China pink
Dimorphotheca annua—Cape-marigold
Dolichos lablab—Hyacinth-bean
Echium plantagineum—Viper's bugloss
Euphorbia marginata—Snow-on-the-mountain
Gilia species
Godetia amoena—Farewell-to-spring
   G. grandiflora—Satin flower
Gomphrena globosa—Globe-amaranth
Gypsophila elegans—Baby's-breath
Hebenstretia comosa
Helichrysum bracteatum varieties—Strawflower
Heliotropium arborescens—Heliotrope
Helipterum manglesii—Everlasting
Iberis affinis—Candytuft
   I. amara—Rocket candytuft
   I. umbellata
Impatiens balsamina—Garden balsam
   I. walleriana—Busy Lizzie
Ionopsidium acaule—Diamond-flower
Ipomoea purpurea—Morning-glory
Lathyrus odoratus—Sweet-pea
Lavatera trimestris var. *alba*—Tree-mallow
Layia glandulosa—White daisy
Limonium spicatum—Sea-lavender
Linum usitatissimum—Common flax
Lobularia maritima—Sweet-alyssum
Lunaria annua—Money plant
Lupinus hartwegii—Lupine
Malcomia maritima—Virginia-stock
Malva crispa—Curled mallow
Mathiola incana var. *annua*—Stock

Matricaria inodora—Scentless false chamomile
Mentzelia decapetala
Mirabilis jalapa—Four-o'clock. Marvel-of-Peru
   M. longiflora
Molucella laevis—Bells-of-Ireland. Shell-flower
Myosotis sylvatica var. *alba*—Forget-me-not
Nemesia floribunda
Nemophila maculata—Five-spot
Nicotiana alata var. *grandiflora*—Flowering tobacco
Penstemon x *gloxinioides*—Border penstemon. Garden penstemon
Petunia x *hybrida* varieties
Phacelia campanularia var. *alba*
Phlox drummondii—Annual phlox
Portulaca grandiflora—Rose-moss
Salvia splendens varieties—Scarlet sage
Saponaria calabrica var. *alba*—Soapwort
Scabiosa atropurpurea—Sweet scabious
Schizanthus grahamii—Poor-man's-orchid
   S. retusus varieties
Schizopetalon walkeri
Silene armeria—Sweet William-catchfly
Thunbergia alata—Clock-vine
Torenia fournieri—Wishbone flower
Verbena x *hybrida* varieties—Garden verbena
Viola tricolor var. *hortensis*—Pansy
Xeranthemum x *annuum*—Common immortelle
Zinnia elegans varieties—Garden zinnia

Annuals
BY COLOR: YELLOW

Althaea ficifolia—Fig-leaved hollyhock
Antirrhinum majus—Snapdragon
Arctotis laevis—African daisy
Argemone grandiflora—Prickly-poppy
   A. platyceras—Crested-poppy
Calendula officinalis—Pot-marigold
Celiosa argentea var. *cristata*—Cockscomb
Centaurea moschata—Sweet sultan
Cerinthe retorta—Honeywort

Chrysanthemum coronarium—Crown
daisy
Coreopsis calliopsidea—Tickseed
C. tinctoria—Plains coreopsis
Cosmos sulphureus—Yellow cosmos
Dimorphotheca annua—Cape-marigold
Emilia sagittata var. lutea—Tassel-flower
Eschscholtzia californica—California-
poppy
Gaillardia pulchella—Painted gaillardia
Gamolepis tagetes
Gazania longiscapa
Hebenstretia comosa
Helianthus annuus—Sunflower
H. argophyllus—Silver-leaf sunflower
H. debilis—Cucumber-leaf sunflower
Helichrysum bracteatum—Strawflower
Helipterum humboldtianum—Everlasting.
Immortelle
Hibiscus trionum—Flower-of-an-hour
Hunnemannia fumariaefolia—Mexican
golden-cup. Mexican tulip-poppy
Layia elegans—Tidy-tips
Limonium bonduellii—Sea-lavender
L. sinense
Linaria broussonnetia—Toadflax
Lonas inodora—African daisy
Lupinus densiflorus—Lupine
L. luteus—Yellow lupine
Mathiola incana var. annua—Stock
Matricaria chamomila—German-chamo-
mile
Mentzelia laevicaulis—Blazing-star
Mimulus brevipes—Monkey-flower
M. guttatus—Yellow monkey-flower
Mirabilis jalapa—Four-o'clock. Marvel-
of-Peru
Nemesia strumosa
Papaver rhoeas—Shirley poppy. Corn
poppy
Platystemon californicus—Cream-cups
Portulaca grandiflora—Rose-moss
P. oleracea—Purslane
Quamoclit lobata—Star-glory
Reseda odorata—Mignonette
Rudbeckia bicolor—Thimbleflower
R. hirta—Gloriosa daisy
Salpiglossis sinuata—Painted-tongue
Sanvitalia procumbens—Creeping-zinnia
Tagetes species and varieties—Marigold

Thunbergia alata—Black-eyed Susan vine
Tithonia rotundifolia—Mexican-sun-
flower
Tropaeolum majus—Garden nasturtium
T. pergrinum—Canary nasturtium
Ursinia anthemoides
Viola tricolor var. hortensis—Pansy
Xanthisma texanum—Star-of-Texas
Zinnia elegans varieties—Garden zinnia

Annuals
FOR DRIED ARRANGEMENTS

Amaranthus caudatus—Love-lies-bleeding
Ammobium alatum—Winged-everlasting
Celosia argentea
C. a. var. cristata—Cockscomb
Emilia sagittata—Tassel-flower
Gomphrena globosa—Globe-amaranth
Gypsophila elegans var. grandiflora—
Baby's-breath
G. muralis
Helianthus argophyllus—Silver-leaf sun-
flower
Helichrysum bracteatum—Strawflower
HELIPTERUM—Everlasting. Immortelle
Hordium jubatum—Squirrel-tailgrass
Limonium bonduellii—Sea-lavender
L. suworowii—Rattail statice. Russian
statice
Lonas inodora—African daisy
Lunaria annua—Money plant
Molucella laevis—Bells-of-Ireland. Shell-
flower
Nigella damascena (pods)—Love-in-a-mist
Polygonum orientale—Prince's-feather

Annuals
WITH SCENTED FLOWERS

Abronia umbellata—Prostrate sand-ver-
bena
Asperula orientalis—Oriental woodruff
Calonyction aculeatum—Moonflower
Centaurea imperialis—Royal centaurea
C. moschata—Sweet sultan
Cleome spinosa—Spider-flower
Datura meteloides
Hebenstretia comosa

Heliotropium arborescens—Heliotrope
Iberis affinis—Candytuft
  I. amara—Rocket candytuft
Lathyrus odoratus—Sweet-pea
Limnanthes douglasii—Meadow-foam
Lobularia maritima—Sweet-alyssum
Lunaria annua—Money plant
Mathiola incana var. annua—Stock
  M. longipetala—Night-scented stock
Mentzelia lindleyi
Mimulus moschatus—Musk-flower
Molucella laevis—Bells-of-Ireland.
  Shellflower
Monopsis campanulata
Myosotis sylvatica—Forget-me-not
Nemophila species
Nicotiana alata var. grandiflora—
  Flowering tobacco
  N. sanderae—Tobacco plant
  N. suaveolens macrantha
Petunia x hybrida
Reseda odorata—Mignonette
Schizopetalon walkeri
Tagetes lucida—Marigold
Torenia fourneri—Wishbone flower
Tropaeolum majus—Nasturtium
Verbena x hybrida—Garden verbena
Viola cornuta—Horned violet. Tufted
  pansy
  V. x hybrida
  V. tricolor—Johnny-jump-up. Pansy
Zaluzianskya capensis—Night-stock

Annuals
THAT FLOWER IN LIGHT SHADE

Ageratum houstonianum
Antirrhinum majus—Snapdragon
Asperula orientalis—Woodruff
Begonia semperflorens—Wax begonia
Bellis perennis—English daisy
Calendula officinalis—Pot-marigold
Callistephus chinensis—China-aster
Clarkia concinna—Red-ribbons
  C. elegans
Cobaea scandens—Cup-and-saucer vine
Coleus blumei—Foliage plant
COLLINSIA
Cynoglossum amabile—Chinese forget-
  me-not
Eschscholtzia californica—California-

poppy
Godetia amoena—Farewell-to-spring
  G. grandiflora—Satin flower
Impatiens balsamina—Garden balsam
  I. walleriana—Busy Lizzie
Ionopsidium acaule—Diamond-flower
Ipomoea purpurea—Morning-glory
Lobelia erinus—Edging lobelia
Malva crispa—Curled mallow
Matricaria inodora—Bridal-rose
Mimulus moschatus—Musk-flower
Molucella laevis—Bells-of-Ireland. Shell-
  flower
Myosotis species and varieties—Forget-
  me-not
Nemophila maculata—Five-spot
  N. menziesii—Baby blue-eyes
Nicotiana alata—Flowering tobacco
Phlox drummondii—Annual phlox
Reseda odorata—Mignonette
Salpiglossis sinuata—Painted-tongue
Salvia splendens—Flowering sage
Schizanthus grahamii—Poor-man's-
  orchid
Torenia fourneri—Wishbone flower
Verbena x hybrida—Garden verbena
Vinca rosea—Madagascar periwinkle
Viola tricolor var. hortensis—Pansy

Annuals
THAT TOLERATE DAMP GROUND

Asperula orientalis—Woodruff
Browallia americana
Calendula officinalis—Pot-marigold
Datura metel—Hindu datura
  D. meteloides
Iberis affinis—Candytuft
  I. umbellata
Impatiens balsamina—Garden balsam
  I. walleriana—Busy Lizzie
Ionopsidium acaule—Diamond-flower
Lathyrus odoratus—Sweet-pea
Limnanthes douglasii—Meadow-foam
Linaria reticulata—Purplenet toadflax
Mimulus guttatus—Yellow monkey-flower
  M. lewisii—Pink monkey-flower
  M. moschatus—Musk-flower
Myosotis azorica—Forget-me-not
  M. sylvatica
Nemophila maculata—Five-spot

N. menziesii—Baby blue-eyes
Nicotiana alata—Flowering tobacco
Reseda odorata—Mignonette
Ricinus communis—Castor-bean
Torenia fournieri—Wishbone flower
Vinca rosea—Madagascar periwinkle
Viola tricolor var. *hortensis*—Pansy

Annuals
THAT TOLERATE HEAT AND DROUGHT

Abronia umbellata—Prostrate sand-verbena
Amaranthus caudatus—Love-lies-bleeding
ARGEMONE—Prickly-poppy
Calandrinia ciliata var. *menziesii*—Rock-purslane
Centaurea americana—Basket flower
  C. cyanus—Cornflower. Bachelor's-button
Cleome spinosa—Spider-flower
Convolvulus mauritanicus—Ground morning-glory
Coreopsis tinctoria—Plains coreopsis
Cosmos bipinnatus
Crepis rubra—Hawkweed
Cynoglossum amabile—Chinese forget-me-not
Dimorphotheca annua—Cape-marigold
Echium plantagineum—Viper's bugloss
Emilia sagittata—Tassel-flower
Eschscholtzia californica—California-poppy
Euphorbia heterophylla—Mexican fire-plant
  E. marginata—Snow-on-the-mountain
Gaillardia amblyodon—Maroon gaillardia
  G. pulchella—Painted gaillardia
Gazania longiscapa
Glaucium corniculatum—Sea-poppy
Gypsophila elegans var. *grandiflora*—Baby's-breath
  G. muralis
Helianthus annuus—Sunflower
Helipterum manglesii—Swan River everlasting
Kochia scoparia var. *trichophila*—Summer-cypress
Lupinus hartwegii—Lupine
Mirabilis jalapa—Four-o'clock.

Papaver rhoeas—Shirley poppy. Corn poppy
Pelargonium hortorum—Geranium
Perilla frutescens—Beefsteak plant
Phacelia campanularia
Phlox drummondii—Annual phlox
Portulaca grandiflora—Rose-moss
Rudbeckia bicolor—Thimbleflower
Sanvitalia procumbens—Creeping-zinnia
Tagetes erecta—African marigold
Tropaeolum majus—Nasturtium
  T. minus
Ursinia pulchra
Xanthisma texanum—Star-of-Texas
Zinnia angustifolia—Mexican zinnia

Biennials

Biennials
BY HEIGHT: LOW, UNDER 1 FOOT

Anchusa capensis—Alkanet. Bugloss
Bellis perennis—English daisy
Cheiranthus cheiri—Wallflower
Viola tricolor var. *hortensis*—Pansy

Biennials
BY HEIGHT: MEDIUM, 1 TO 3 FEET

Argemone grandiflora—Prickly-poppy
Campanula medium—Canterbury-bells
Cynoglossum amabile—Chinese forget-me-not
Dianthus barbatus—Sweet William
Digitalis species—Foxglove
Gentiana crinita—Fringed gentian
Gilia aggregata
Glaucium flavum—Horned-poppy
Hesperis species—Sweet rocket
Limonium bonduellii—Sea-lavender
Lunaria annua—Money plant
Lychnis alba—Evening campion
Machaeranthera tanacetifolia—Tahoka daisy
Mathiola incana—Gilliflower
Mentzelia decapetala
  M. laevicaulis—Blazing-star
Myosotis sylvatica—Forget-me-not
Verbascum species—Mullein

Biennials
BY HEIGHT: TALL, OVER 3 FEET

Adlumia fungosa—Allegheny vine
Althaea ficifolia—Fig-leaved hollyhock
  A. rosea—Hollyhock
Digitalis purpurea—Common foxglove
Meconopsis integrifolia—Yellow Chinese-
  poppy
Salvia argentea—Silver sage. Silver clary
  S. sclarea—Clary
Verbascum chaixii—Nettle-leaved mullein
  V. olympicum—Olympian mullein

Biennials
BY COLOR: BLUE

Anchusa capensis—Alkanet. Bugloss
Campanula medium—Canterbury-bells
Cynoglossum amabile—Chinese-forget-
  me-not
Gentiana crinita—Fringed gentian
Myosotis sylvatica —Forget-me-not
Salvia sclarea—Clary
Viola tricolor var. *hortensis*—Pansy

Biennials
BY COLOR: ORANGE

Althaea ficifolia—Fig-leaved hollyhock
Cheiranthus cheiri—Wallflower

Biennials
BY COLOR: PINK

Althaea rosea—Garden hollyhock
Bellis perennis—English daisy
Campanula medium—Canterbury-bells
Dianthus barbatus—Sweet William
Digitalis purpurea—Common foxglove
Mathiola incana—Gilliflower
Myosotis sylvatica varieties—Forget-me-
  not
Salvia argentea—Silver sage. Silver clary

Biennials
BY COLOR: PURPLE

Adlumia fungosa—Allegheny vine
Digitalis purpurea—Common foxglove
Hesperis species—Sweet rocket

Lunaria annua—Money plant
Machaeranthera tanacetifolia—Tahoka
  daisy
Mathiola incana—Gilliflower
Salvia argentea—Silver sage. Silver clary
Viola tricolor var. *hortensis*—Pansy

Biennials
BY COLOR: RED

Althaea rosea—Garden hollyhock
Cheiranthus cheiri—Wallflower
Dianthus barbatus—Sweet William
Gilia aggregata

Biennials
BY COLOR: WHITE

Adlumia fungosa—Allegheny vine
Althaea rosea—Garden hollyhock
Argemone grandiflora—Prickly-poppy
Bellis perennis—English daisy
Campanula medium—Canterbury-bells
Dianthus barbatus—Sweet William
Digitalis purpurea—Foxglove
Hesperis matronalis—Sweet rocket
  H. tristis—Rocket
Lunaria annua—Money plant
Lychnis alba—Evening campion
Mathiola incana—Gilliflower
Mentzelia decapetala
Myosotis sylvatica varieties—Forget-me-
  not
Verbascum chaixii var. *album*—Nettle-
  leaved mullein
Viola tricolor var. *hortensis*—Pansy

Biennials
BY COLOR: YELLOW

Althaea ficifolia—Fig-leaved hollyhock
Argemone grandiflora—Prickly-poppy
Cheiranthus cheiri—Wallflower
Digitalis purpurea—Common foxglove
Glaucium flavum—Horned-poppy
Limonium bonduellii—Sea-lavender
Mathiola incana—Gilliflower
Meconopsis integrifolia—Yellow Chinese-
  poppy
Mentzelia laevicaulis—Blazing-star

Verbascum chaixii—Nettle-leaved mullein
V. olympicum—Olympian mullein
Viola tricolor var. hortensis—Pansy

Biennials
WITH FRAGRANT FLOWERS

Cheiranthus cheiri—Wallflower
Hesperis matronalis—Sweet rocket
Lychnis alba—Evening campion
Mathiola incana—Gilliflower
Mentzelia decapetala

Biennials
THAT SELF-SOW

Adlumia fungosa—Allegheny vine
Althaea rosea—Garden hollyhock
Anchusa capensis—Alkanet. Bugloss
ARGEMONE—Prickly-poppy
Digitalis purpurea—Common foxglove
Lunaria annua—Money plant
Salvia argentea—Silver sage. Silver clary
S. sclarea—Clary
Verbascum chaixii—Nettle-leaved mullein

Biennials
THAT FLOWER IN LIGHT SHADE

Adlumia fungosa—Allegheny vine
Anchusa capensis—Alkanet. Bugloss
Digitalis purpurea—Common foxglove
Gentiana crinita—Fringed gentian
Myosotis sylvatica—Forget-me-not
Viola tricolor var. hortensis—Pansy

Bulbs

Bulbs
BY HEIGHT: LOW, UNDER 1 FOOT

Allium cyaneum—Ornamental onion
A. karataviense—Turkestan onion
Anemone species and hybrids—Wind-flower
Arum maculatum—Cuckoo-pint. Lords-and-ladies
A. palestinum—Black-calla
Babiana stricta
Brodiaea bridgesii
B. crocea

B. uniflora—Spring star-flower
Bulbocodium vernum—Spring meadow-saffron
Caladium humboldtii—Miniature caladium
Calochortus caeruleus—Cat's-ears
C. kennedyi—Mariposa-lily
C. maweanus
C. venustus—White mariposa-lily
Chionodoxa luciliae—Glory-of-the-snow
C. sardensis
Chlidanthus fragrans
CLAYTONIA—Spring-beauty
COLCHICUM—Autumn-crocus.
Meadow-saffron
Convallaria majalis—Lily-of-the-valley
Cooperia drummondii—Rain-lily
CROCUS
CYCLAMEN
CYRTANTHUS
Eranthis hyemalis—Winter aconite
Erythronium species and hybrids—Dog-tooth-violet
Eucharis fosterii
Fritillaria pluriflora—Pink fritillary.
Adobe-lily
F. pudica—Yellow fritillary
Galanthus elwesii—Giant snowdrop
G. nivalis—Snowdrop
Habranthus species
Haemanthus coccineus—Blood-lily
H. katherinae
Hyacinthus amethystinus—Hyacinth
H. azureus
Iris species and hybrids
Ixia maculata—Corn-lily
LACHENALIA—Cape-cowslip
Lapeirousia cruenta
Leucocrinum montanum—Star-lily
LEUCOJUM—Snowflake
LIRIOPE—Lily-turf
MUSCARI—Grape-hyacinth
Narcissus species and hybrids
OPHIOPOGON—Lily-turf
Ornithogalum biflorum
Oxalis species and hybrids
Puschkinia scilloides
Ranunculus amplexicaulis—Buttercup
Scilla species and hybrids—Squill
Sternbergia lutea—Lily-of-the-field
Trillium nivale—Dwarf trillium

Tulipa species and hybrids—Tulip
Watsonia coccinea—Bugle-lily
Zantedeschia elliottiana—Golden calla
   Z. rehmannii—Pink calla-lily
ZEPHYRANTHES—Rain-lily

Bulbs
BY HEIGHT: MEDIUM, 1 TO 2 FEET

Achimenes species and hybrids—Magic
   flower
Acidanthera murieliae
Agapanthus campanulatus—Lily-of-the-
   Nile
Albuca minor
Allium flavum—Yellow onion
   A. neapolitanum—Naples onion
Amaryllis belladonna—Belladonna-lily
Anemone species and hybrids—Wind-
   flower
Arisaema triphyllum—Jack-in-the-pulpit
Arum italicum—Italian arum
Begonia tuberhybrida cultivars and
   hybrids—Tuberous begonia
   B. evansiana—Hardy begonia
Brodiaea capitata—Blue-dicks
   B. ixioides—Pretty face
   B. lactea—Wild-hyacinth
   B. laxa
Caladium bicolor
Calochortus albus—Mariposa-lily
   C. gunnisonii
   C. macrocarpus
Camassia species and hybrids—Camass
Clivia x *cyrtanthiflora*—Kaffir-lily
Cooperia pedunculata—Rain-lily
Crocosmia aurea—Copper-tip
Dahlia, dwarf varieties
Erythronium oregonum—Oregon fawn-lily
Eucharis grandiflora—Amazon-lily
Eucomis comosa—Pineapple-lily
Freesia refracta hybrids and varieties
Fritillaria species and hybrids—Fritillary
Gladiolus species and hybrids
HIPPEASTRUM—Amaryllis
Hyacinthus orientalis var. *albulus* and
   hybrids—Common hyacinth
Hymenocallis amancaes—Spider-lily
   H. calathina—Basket-flower. Peruvian-
   daffodil

H. occidentalis—Inland spider-lily
Iris species and hybrids
Ixia viridifolia—Corn-lily
Leucocoryne ixioides—Glory-of-the-sun
Lilium species and hybrids—Lily
MORAEA
Narcissus species and hybrids
Nerine curvifolia
   N. sarniensis—Guernsey-lily
Ornithogalum species and hybrids
Ranunculus aconitifolius—Buttercup
   R. asiaticus—Persian buttercup
Smithiantha cinnabarina—Temple bells
   S. zebrina
Sparaxis tricolor—Wand flower
Sprekelia formosissima—Jacobean-lily.
   St. James-lily
Tigridia pavonia—Tiger-flower
Trillium grandiflorum
Tritonia crocata—Saffron tritonia
Tulbaghia cepacea
   T. fragrans—Pink-agapanthus
Tulipa species and hybrids—Tulip
Veltheimia glauca
   V. viridifolia
Zantedeschia aethiopica—Calla-lily
   Z. albo-maculata—Spotted calla-lily

Bulbs
BY HEIGHT: TALL, 2 TO 4 FEET

Acidanthera bicolor—Fragrant-gladiolus
Agapanthus africanus—African-lily
   A. orientalis—Lily-of-the-Nile
Albuca major
Allium caeruleum—Ornamental onion
ALSTROEMERIA
Amaryllis belladonna—Belladonna-lily
Anemone species and hybrids—Wind-
   flower
Anthericum liliago—St. Bernard's-lily
Arisaema dracontium—Green dragon
Begonia, tuberous species and hybrids
Belamcanda chinensis—Blackberry-lily
Bessera elegans
Calochortus clavatus—Mariposa-lily
Camassia quamash—Camass
Canna x *generalis*, Pfitzer hybrids, Opera
   Series—Indian shot
x *Crinodonna corsii*

x C. howardii
CRINUM
Crocosmia x crocosmaeflora—Copper-tip
  C. pottsii
Dahlia species and hybrids
Fritillaria imperialis—Crown imperial
Galtonia candicans—Summer-hyacinth
Gladiolus species and hybrids
Hymenocallis littoralis—Spider-lily
Iris species and hybrids
Lilium species and hybrids—Lily
Lycoris aurea—Golden spider-lily
  L. squamigera—Naked ladies
Polianthes tuberosa—Tuberose
Polygonatum multiflorum—Solomon's seal
Smilacina racemosa—False Solomon's-seal
Tulbaghia violacea—Society-garlic
Tulipa species and hybrids—Tulip
Vallota speciosa—Scarborough-lily
Watsonia iridifolia—Bugle-lily
  W. meriana

Bulbs
BY HEIGHT: VERY TALL, OVER 4 FEET

Allium giganteum—Giant onion
Anemone tomentosa—Windflower
Brodiaea volubilis—Snake-lily
Canna edulis—Indian shot
  C. x generalis hybrids
Cardiocrinum giganteum—Giant-lily
Colocasia antiquorum—Elephant's-ear
  C. esculenta—Taro
Dahlia pinnata varieties and hybrids
EREMURUS—Desert candle. Foxtail-lily
GLORIOSA—Glory-lily
Polygonatum commutatum—Great Solomon's seal
Watsonia longifolia—Bugle-lily

Bulbs
BY COLOR: BLUE

Achimenes species and varieties—Magic flower
Agapanthus species and varieties—Lily-of-the-Nile
Allium caeruleum
  A. cyaneum
  A. giganteum—Giant onion

Anemone apennina—Italian windflower
  A. blanda—Greek anemone
  A. coronaria—Poppy-flowered anemone
  A. glaucifolia—Windflower
  A. patens—Spreading pasque-flower
  A. pulsatilla—European pasque-flower
Babiana stricta varieties
Brodiaea capitata—Blue-dicks
Calochortus caeruleus—Cat's-ears
  C. gunnisonii—Fairy lantern. Globe-tulip. Mariposa-lily
Camassia cusickii—Camass
  C. howellii
  C. leichtlinii
  C. quamash
  C. scilloides—Wild-hyacinth
Chionodoxa luciliae—Glory-of-the-snow
  C. sardensis
Crocus species and varieties
Endymion hispanica—Spanish bluebell. Spanish hyacinth. Spanish squill
  E. nonscripta—Blue squill. English bluebell. Harebell
Griffinia hyacinthina—Blue-amaryllis
  G. ornata
Hyacinthus amethystinus—Spanish hyacinth
  H. azureus
  H. orientalis varieties—Common hyacinth
Iris species and varieties
Ixia varieties—Corn-lily
IXIOLIRION
Lapeirousia species and varieties
Leucocoryne ixioides—Glory-of-the-sun
Liriope muscari var. variegata—Blue lily-turf
Muscari species and varieties—Grape-hyacinth
PUSCHKINIA
Scilla species—Squill

Bulbs
BY COLOR: ORANGE

Alstroemeria aurantiaca var. major—Yellow alstroemeria
  A. a. var. 'Doves Orange'
  A. litgu hybrids
Begonia (tuberous) varieties and hybrids
Belamcanda chinensis—Blackberry-lily

Clivia miniata—Kaffir-lily
Crocosmia aurea—Copper-tip
  C. x crocosmaeflora
Crocus species and varieties
Dahlia species and varieties
Eremurus x shelfordii—Desert-candle
Freesia refracta
Fritillaria imperialis variety—Fritillary.
  Crown imperial
  F. pudica—Yellow fritillary
Gladiolus species and varieties
Hyacinthus orientalis varieties—Common
  hyacinth
Iris species and varieties
Ixia varieties—Corn-lily
Lilium species, varieties and hybrids—Lily
Oxalis (tuberous) species
Ranunculus asiaticus—Persian buttercup
Tigridia pavonia variety—Tiger-flower
Tulipa biflora var. turkestanica—Tulip

Bulbs
BY COLOR: PINK

Achimenes species and varieties—Magic
  flower
Allium ostrowskianum—Ostrowsky onion
Alstroemeria chilensis—Chilean alstro-
  emeria
  A. litgu and hybrids
AMARYLLIS—Naked ladies. Naked lads
Anemone apennina varieties—Italian
  windflower
  A. blanda varieties—Greek anemone
  A. coronaria—Poppy-flowered anemone
  A. hortensis—Garden anemone
  A. hupehensis and varieties—Dwarf
    Japanese anemone
  A. narcissiflora—Narcissus windflower
  A. tomentosa
  A. vitifolia varieties—Grape-leaved
    windflower
Begonia (tuberous) varieties and hybrids
Brodiaea ixioides—Pretty face
  B. volubilis—Snake-lily
Chionodoxa luciliae variety—Glory-of-
  the-snow
Claytonia caroliniana—Spring-beauty
  C. megarrhiza

C. nivalis
C. rosea
Colchicum speciosum—Autumn-crocus
Convallaria majalis var. rosea—Lily-of-
  the-valley
x CRINODONNA
Crinum amabile varieties
  C. longifolium
  C. moorei variety and hybrids
Crocus species and varieties
Cyclamen species and varieties
Dahlia species and varieties
Endymion hispanica and variety—Span-
  ish bluebell. Spanish hyacinth. Span-
  ish squill
  E. nonscripta varieties—Blue squill.
  English bluebell. Harebell
Eremurus elwesii—Elwes desert-candle
  E. robustus—Giant desert-candle
  E. x shelfordii—Shelford desert-candle
Erythronium species and varieties—
  Dogtooth-violet
Freesia refracta
Fritillaria pluriflora—Pink fritillary
Gladiolus species and varieties
Hyacinthus orientalis and varieties—
  Common hyacinth
Iris species and varieties
Ixia varieties—Corn-lily
Lilium species, varieties and hybrids—
  Lily
Lycoris incarnata
  L. sprengeri
Muscari botryoides variety—Grape-
  hyacinth
Narcissus named varieties—Daffodil. Jon-
  quil. Narcissus
Nerine bowdenii
  N. sarniensis varieties
Oxalis (tuberous) species
Scilla bifolia variety—Squill
Sparaxis tricolor—Wand flower
Tigridia pavonia varieties—Tiger-flower
Tulbaghia fragrans—Pink-agapanthus
Tulipa biflora—Tulip
  T. pulchella
Watsonia iridifolia—Bugle-lily
  W. longifolia
  W. meriana
Zephyranthes grandiflora—Zephyr-lily

Bulbs
BY COLOR: PURPLE

Achimenes species and varieties—Magic
flower
Allium albopilosum
    A. schoenoprasum—Chives
Alstroemeria litgu
    A. pelegrina—Inca-lily alstroemeria
Anemone caroliniana—Carolina wind-
flower
    A. coronaria—Poppy-flowered anemone
    A. halleri—Haller's anemone
    A. hortensis—Garden anemone
    A. patens—Spreading pasque-flower
    A. pulsatilla—European pasque-flower
    A. tuberosa
Babiana stricta varieties
Brodiaea bridgesii
    B. laxa
BULBOCODIUM—Spring meadow-
saffron
Calochortus macrocarpus—Green-banded
mariposa-lily
Camassia leichtlinii—Camass
Chionodoxa luciliae—Glory-of-the-snow
Colchicum agrippinum—Autumn-crocus
    C. alpinum
    C. autumnale
    C. bornmuelleri
    C. byzantinum
    C. speciosum

Crocus species and varieties
Cyclamen species and varieties
Dahlia species and varieties
Erythronium species and varieties—
Dogtooth-violet
Fritillaria lanceolata—Riceroot fritillary
    F. persica—Fritillary
Gladiolus species and varieties
Hyacinthus orientalis varieties—Common
hyacinth
Iris species and varieties
Ixia varieties—Corn-lily
IXIOLIRION
Lilium species, varieties and hybrids—Lily
Liriope muscari—Blue lily-turf
    L. spicata—Creeping lily-turf
Moraea pavonia variety

Muscari moschatum—Musk grape-
hyacinth
Ophiopogon japonicus—Lily-turf
Oxalis (tuberous) species
Sparaxis tricolor—Wand flower
Tigridia pavonia variety—Tiger-flower
Tricyrtis macropoda—Toad-lily
    T. stolonifera
Trillium erectum—Birthroot. Purple
trillium. Wake robin
Tulbaghia cepacea
    T. violacea—Society-garlic
Tulipa saxatilis—Tulip

Bulbs
BY COLOR: RED

Achimenes species and varieties—Magic
flower
Alstroemeria chilensis
    A. litgu hybrids
    A. pulchella—Parrot alstroemeria
Anemone coronaria—Poppy-flowered
anemone
    A. fulgens—Scarlet windflower
    A. hortensis—Garden anemone
    A. hupehensis—Dwarf Japanese
anemone
    A. h. var. *japonica*—Japanese anemone
    A. pulsatilla—European pasque-flower
Babiana stricta varieties
Begonia (tuberous) varieties and hybrids
Bessera elegans
Calochortus kennedyi—Fairy lantern
Clivia x *cyrtanthiflora*—Kaffir-lily
Crinum amabile and varety
    C. moorei
Cyclamen species and varieties
Dahlia species and varieties
Freesia refracta
Fritillaria imperialis and variety—Fritil-
lary. Crown imperial
Gladiolus species and varieties
Gloriosa rothschildiana—Glory-lily.
Rothschild gloriosa-lily
Habranthus robustus
HAEMANTHUS—Blood-lily

Hippeastrum x *ackermannii*—Amaryllis
    H. x *johnsonii*

H. reginae
Hyacinthus orientalis varieties—Common
  hyacinth
Iris sibirica variety
Ixia varieties—Corn-lily
Lapeirousia cruenta varieties
Lilium species, varieties and hybrids—Lily
Lycoris radiata—Spider-lily
Moraea pavonia
Nerine curvifolia
  N. filifolia
  N. sarniensis—Guernsey-lily
Oxalis (tuberous) species
Scilla bifolia variety—Squill
Smithiantha cinnabarina—Temple bells
  S. zebrina
Sprekelia formosissima—Jacobean-lily. St.
  James-lily
Tigridia pavonia—Tiger-flower
Trillium chloropetalum
  T. sessile—Toad trillium
  T. vaseyi—Sweet trillium
Tritonia crocata—Saffron tritonia
Tulipa species—Tulip
Vallota speciosa—Scarborough-lily
Veltheimia viridifolia
Watsonia coccinea—Bugle-lily
  W. rosea
Zephyranthes rosea—Zephyr-lily

Bulbs
BY COLOR: WHITE

Achimenes species and varieties—Magic
  flower
Acidanthera bicolor—Dark-eye gladixia.
  Fragrant-gladiolus
  A. murieliae
Agapanthus orientalis—Lily-of-the-Nile
  A. o. var. *albus*
  A. o. var. *maximus albus*
  A. o. var. 'Rancho'
Albuca varieties
Allium karataviense—Turkestan onion
  A. neapolitanum—Naples onion
  A. triquetrum
  A. tuberosum—Chinese chives
Alstroemeria litgu
Anemone species and varieties—Wind-
  flower

Anthericum liliago—St. Bernard's-lily
  A. ramosum
Babiana stricta varieties
Begonia (tuberous) hybrids
Brodiaea lactea—Wild-hyacinth
  B. uniflora—Spring star-flower
Calochortus albus—Fairy lantern. Globe-
  tulip. Mariposa-lily
  C. apiculatus—Giant star globe-tulip
  C. gunnisonii
  C. maweanus
Camassia leichtlinii—Camass
  C. scilloides—Wild-hyacinth
Cardiocrinum giganteum—Giant-lily
Chionodoxa luciliae variety
Claytonia megarrhiza—Spring-beauty
  C. virginica
Colchicum autumnale—Autumn-crocus
  C. bornmuelleri
  C. speciosum var. *album*
Convallaria majalis—Lily-of-the-valley
COOPERIA—Rain-lily
Crinum americanum
  C. asiaticum
  C. kirkii
  C. longifolium
  C. moorei variety and hybrid
  C. sanderianum—Milk-and-wine lily

Crocus species and varieties
Cyclamen species and varieties
Dahlia species and varieties
Endymion hispanica variety—Spanish
  bluebell. Spanish hyacinth. Spanish
  squill
  E. nonscripta variety—Blue squill. Eng-
  lish bluebell. Harebell
Eremurus elwesii var. *albus*—Elwes
  desert-candle
  E. himalaicus—Himalayan desert-candle
  E. x shelfordii—Shelford desert-candle
Erythronium species and varieties—
  Dogtooth-violet
EUCHARIS
EUCOMIS—Pineapple-lily
Freesia refracta
GALANTHUS—Snowdrop
Galtonia candicans—Summer-hyacinth
Gladiolus species and varieties
Griffinia blumenavia
Haemanthus varieties—Blood-lily

Hippeastrum hybrids—Amaryllis
Hyacinthus orientalis varieties—Common
hyacinth
HYMENOCALLIS—Spider-lily
Iris species and varieties
Ixia varieties—Corn-lily
LEUCOCRINUM—Sand-lily. Star-lily
LEUCOJUM—Snowflake
Lilium species, varieties and hybrids—Lily
Liriope spicata—Creeping lily-turf
Lycoris radiata var. *alba*—Spider-lily
MILLA—Mexican star
Moraea glaucopsis—Peacock-iris
M. *pavonia* variety
Muscari species and varieties—Grape-
hyacinth
Narcissus species—Daffodil. Narcissus
Ophiopogon jaburan—Jaburan
ORNITHOGALUM
PARADISEA—St. Bruno-lily
POLIANTHES—Tuberose
Ranunculus aconitifolius—Buttercup.
Crowfoot
R. *amplexicaulis*
R. *lyallii*
Scilla bifolia variety—Squill
SMILACINA—False Solomon's-seal
Sparaxis tricolor—Wand flower
Tigridia pavonia variety—Tiger-flower
Tricyrtis affina—Toad-lily
T. *hirta*
Trillium cernuum—Nodding trillium
T. *chloropetalum*
T. *erectum* var. *album*—Birthroot.
Purple trillium. Wake robin
T. *grandiflorum*
T. *nivale*—Dwarf trillium
T. *ovatum*
T. *undulatum*—Painted trillium
Tulipa species—Tulip
Vallota speciosa var. *alba*—Scarborough-
lily
Veltheimia glauca
Watsonia iridifolia var. *obrienii*—Bugle-
lily
W. *longifolia*
Zantedeschia aethiopica—Common calla
Z. *albo-maculata*—Spotted calla-lily
Z. *rehmannii*—Pink calla-lily
Zephyranthes atamasco—Zephyr-lily
Z. *candida*

Bulbs
BY COLOR: YELLOW

Achimenes species and varieties—Magic
flower
Albuca major
A. *minor*
Allium flavum—Yellow onion
A. *moly*—Golden garlic
Alstroemeria aurantiaca—Yellow alstro-
emeria
A. *a.* var. *lutea*
A. *litgu* hybrids
Anemone alpina var. *sulphurea*—Moun-
tain anemone
A. *narcissiflora*—Narcissus windflower
A. *ranunculoides*—Yellow wood
anemone
Begonia (tuberous) varieties and hybrids
Belamcanda flabellata
Brodiaea crocea
B. *ixioides* varieties—Pretty face
Calochortus amabilis—Golden globe-tulip
C. *apiculatus*—Giant star globe-tulip
C. *clavatus*—Fairy lantern. Globe-tulip.
Mariposa-lily
Chlidanthus fragrans
Clivia miniata var. *flava*—Kaffir-lily
Colchicum luteum—Autumn-crocus.
Meadow-saffron
Crocosmia pottsii—Copper-tip
Crocus species and varieties
Dahlia species and varieties
Eranthis hyemalis—Winter-aconite
Eremurus bungei—Desert-candle. Foxtail-
lily
E. x *shelfordii*—Shelford desert-candle
Erythronium species and varieties—
Dogtooth-violet
Freesia refracta
Fritillaria imperialis variety—Fritillary.
Crown imperial
F. *pudica*—Yellow fritillary
Gladiolus species and varieties
Gloriosa simplex—Glory-lily
G. *superba*
Habranthus andersonii
Hyacinthus orientalis varieties—Common
hyacinth
Iris species and varieties
Ixia species and varieties—Corn-lily

Lachenalia aloides var. *aurea*—Cape-
  cowslip
Lilium species, varieties and hybrids—Lily
Lycoris aurea—Golden spider-lily
Moraea bicolor—Yellow moraea
  M. pavonia variety
Muscari moschatum var. *flavum*—Musk
  grape-hyacinth
Narcissus species—Daffodil. Jonquil
Oxalis (tuberous) species
Ranunculus species and varieties—Butter-
  cup. Crowfoot
Sparaxis tricolor—Wand flower
Sternbergia lutea—Lily-of-the-field
Tigridia pavonia variety—Tiger-flower
Tricyrtis flava—Toad-lily
Trillium chloropetalum
  T. luteum
  T. sessile—Toad trillium
Tritonia crocata—Saffron tritonia
Tulipa species—Tulip
Veltheimia viridifolia
Zantedeschia elliottiana—Golden calla
  Z. melanoleuca—Calla-lily
Zephyranthes x *ajax*—Zephyr-lily
  Z. citrina
  Z. longifolia

Bulbs
WITH FRAGRANT FLOWERS

Acidanthera bicolor—Fragrant-gladiolus
  A. murieliae
Amaryllis belladonna—Belladonna-lily
Brodiaea lactea—Wild-hyacinth
Cardiocrinum giganteum—Giant-lily
Chlidanthus fragrans
Convallaria majalis—Lily-of-the-valley
Cooperia drummondii—Rain-lily
  C. pedunculata
x *Crinodonna corsii*
  x *C. howardii*
Crinum amabile
  C. americanum—Florida swamp-lily
Cyclamen europaeum
Endymion nonscripta—Harebell. English
  bluebell
Eucharis grandiflora—Amazon-lily
Freesia refracta
HYACINTHUS—Hyacinth

Hymenocallis calathina—Basket-flower.
  Peruvian-daffodil
Iris species and hybrids
Leucocoryne ixioides—Glory-of-the-sun
Leucocrinum montanum—Star-lily. Sand-
  lily
Lilium species and hybrids—Lily
Lycoris squamigera—Naked ladies
Milla biflora—Mexican star
Narcissus species and hybrids
Ornithogalum arabicum
Polianthes tuberosa—Tuberose
Trillium vaseyi—Sweet trillium
Tulbaghia fragrans—Pink-agapanthus
Tulipa patens—Persian tulip
  T. suaveolens—Duc Van Thol tulip
  T. sylvestris—Florentine tulip
Zephyranthes citrina—Zephyr-lily. Rain-
  lily

Bulbs
THAT TOLERATE SUMMER SHADE

ACHIMENES—Magic flower
ALLIUM—Ornamental onion
ALSTROEMERIA
Amaryllis belladonna—Belladonna-lily
ANEMONE—Windflower
Arisaema dracontium—Green dragon
  A. triphyllum—Jack-in-the-pulpit
Begonia, tuberous species and hybrids
Bletilla striata
CALADIUM—Fancy-leaved caladium
CALOCHORTUS—Mariposa-lily. Globe-
  tulip
CAMASSIA—Camass
CLAYTONIA—Spring-beauty
CLIVIA—Kaffir-lily
Colocasia antiquorum—Elephant's-ear
Convallaria majalis—Lily-of-the-valley
x *Crinodonna corsii*
CRINUM
ERANTHIS—Winter aconite
ERYTHRONIUM—Dogtooth-violet
EUCHARIS
FRITILLARIA—Fritillary
GALANTHUS—Snowdrop
HIPPEASTRUM—Amaryllis
LEUCOJUM—Snowflake
Lilium species and varieties—Lily

LYCORIS
MUSCARI—Grape-hyacinth
POLYGONATUM—Solomon's seal
Scilla, most species and varieties—Squill
SMILACINA—False Solomon's-seal
TRILLIUM
ZANTEDESCHIA—Calla-lily
ZEPHYRANTHES—Zephyr-lily. Rain-lily

Bulbs
THAT TOLERATE HOT, DRY LOCATIONS

BRODIAEA
CALOCHORTUS—Mariposa-lily. Globe-tulip
COOPERIA—Rain-lily
CROCOSMIA—Copper-tip
GLADIOLUS
Iris, bearded varieties
IXIA—Corn-lily
Leucocrinum montanum—Star-lily. Sand-lily
Schizobasopsis volubilis—Climbing-onion
TIGRIDIA—Tiger-flower
TRITONIA
TULIPA—Tulip
VALLOTA—Scarborough-lily
WATSONIA—Bugle-lily

Bulbs
THAT TOLERATE DAMP GROUND

AGAPANTHUS—Lily-of-the-Nile
ALSTROEMERIA
Arisaema dracontium—Green dragon
   A. triphyllum—Jack-in-the-pulpit
ARUM
Begonia, tuberous species and hybrids
CALADIUM—Fancy-leaved caladium
CAMASSIA—Camass
CANNA—Indian shot
CLAYTONIA—Spring-beauty
CLIVIA—Kaffir-lily
Colocasia antiquorum—Elephant's-ear
Convallaria majalis—Lily-of-the-valley
ERYTHRONIUM—Dogtooth-violet
EUCHARIS
GALANTHUS—Snowdrop
Iris, beardless species and hybrids, especially Japanese varieties

LEUCOJUM—Snowflake
Lilium canadense—Canada lily. Meadow lily
ORNITHOGALUM
POLYGONATUM—Solomon's seal
SMILACINA—False Solomon's-seal
TRILLIUM
ZANTEDESCHIA—Calla-lily
ZEPHYRANTHES—Zephyr-lily. Rain-lily

Ferns

Ferns
COMMONLY GROWN OUTDOORS: IN SHADY LOCATIONS

Adiantum capillus-veneris—Southern maidenhair fern
   A. pedatum—American maidenhair fern
Asplenium platyneuron—Ebony spleenwort
   A. trichomanes—Maidenhair spleenwort
Athyrium species and hybrids
Blechnum gibbum
BOTRYCHIUM—Grape fern
Camptosorus rhizophyllus—Walking fern
CRYPTOGRAMMA—Rock-brake
CYSTOPTERIS—Bladder fern
Dennstaedtia punctilobula—Hay-scented fern
Lygodium palmatum—Hartford fern
Onoclea sensibilis—Sensitive fern
Ophioglossum vulgatum—Adder's-tongue fern
Osmunda claytoniana—Interrupted fern
POLYSTICHUM
Pteridium aquilinum—Bracken. Brake

Ferns
COMMONLY GROWN OUTDOORS: IN PARTIAL SHADE

Adiantum pedatum—American maidenhair fern
Asplenium platyneuron—Ebony spleenwort
Athyrium filix-femina—Lady fern
BOTRYCHIUM—Grape fern
CERATOPTERIS—Water fern. Floating fern

CHEILANTHES—Lip fern
Cibotium schiedei—Mexican tree fern
Cyrtomium falcatum—Japanese holly
   fern
CYSTOPTERIS—Bladder fern
DAVALLIA—Hare's-foot fern
Dennstaedtia punctilobula—Hay-scented
   fern
DRYOPTERIS—Wood fern
Matteuccia struthiopteris var. *pensylvan-
   ica*—Ostrich fern
Onoclea sensibilis—Sensitive fern
Ophioglossum vulgatum—Adder's-
   tongue fern
Osmunda regalis—Royal fern
PELLAEA—Cliff-brake
Phyllitis scolopendrium—Hart's-tongue
   fern
PITYROGRAMMA
Polypodium polypodioides—Resurrection
   fern
   P. vulgare—Common polypody
Pteridium aquilinum—Bracken. Brake
PTERIS—Brake. Table fern
WOODSIA
WOODWARDIA—Chain fern

Ferns
COMMONLY GROWN OUTDOORS: POSSIBLY IN FULL SUN

Dennstaedtia punctilobula—Hay-scented
   fern
Onoclea sensibilis—Sensitive fern
Osmunda cinnamomea—Cinnamon fern
PELLAEA—Cliff-brake
Pteridium aquilinum—Bracken. Brake
WOODSIA
Woodwardia virginica—Common chain
   fern

Ferns
THAT TOLERATE DRY GROUND

ATHYRIUM
Camptosorus rhizophyllus—Walking fern
CHEILANTHES—Lip fern
Osmunda claytoniana—Interrupted fern
PELLAEA—Cliff-brake

Phyllitis scolopendrium—Hart's-tongue
   fern
Pteridium aquilinum—Bracken. Brake
WOODSIA

Ferns
THAT TOLERATE DAMP GROUND

ADIANTUM—Maidenhair fern
ASPLENIUM—Spleenwort
BOTRYCHIUM—Grape fern
CERATOPTERIS—Water fern. Floating
   fern
Cibotium schiedei—Mexican tree fern
CRYPTOGRAMMA—Rock-brake
CYRTOMIUM
CYSTOPTERIS—Bladder fern
Dennstaedtia punctilobula—Hay-scented
   fern
DRYOPTERIS—Wood fern. Shield fern
LYGODIUM—Climbing fern
Matteuccia struthiopteris var. *pensylvan-
   ica*—Ostrich fern
Onoclea sensibilis—Sensitive fern
Ophioglossum vulgatum—Adder's-tongue
   fern
OSMUNDA
PITYROGRAMMA
Polypodium polypodioides—Resurrection
   fern
   P. vulgare—Common polypody
POLYSTICHUM
Pteridium aquilinum—Bracken. Brake
WOODWARDIA—Chain fern

Ferns
FOR THE ROCK GARDEN

Adiantum pedatum—American maiden-
   hair fern
Asplenium platyneuron—Ebony spleen-
   wort
   A. trichomanes—Maidenhair spleen-
     wort
Athyrium thelypteroides
Camptosorus rhizophyllus—Walking fern
CHEILANTHES—Lip fern
CRYPTOGRAMMA—Rock brake
CYSTOPTERIS—Bladder fern
Dennstaedtia punctilobula—Hay-scented

fern
Dryopteris filix-mas—Male fern
Matteuccia struthiopteris var. *pensylvan-*
ica—Ostrich fern
Osmunda regalis—Royal fern
Pellaea atropurpurea—Purple-stemmed
cliff-brake
P. densa
Pityrogramma x *hybrida*
Polypodium vulgare—Common polypody
POLYSTICHUM
Pteridium aquilinum—Bracken. Brake
Woodsia obtusa—Common woodsia
W. scopulina—Rocky Mountain woodsia

Ground-cover Plants

Ground Covers
WITH DECORATIVE FLOWERS:
SPRING-BLOOMING

AJUGA—Bugleweed
ARABIS—Rock-cress
Arenaria caroliniana—Sandwort
Armeria maritima—Sea-pink
Asperula odorata—Sweet woodruff
Cerastium alpinum—Alpine chickweed
Chiogenes hispidula—Creeping snowberry
Convallaria majalis—Lily-of-the-valley
Cornus canadensis—Bunchberry dog-
wood
Cytisus x *kewensis*—Kew broom
Dianthus alpinus—Alpine pink
EPIMEDIUM—Barrenwort
Erica carnea—Spring heath
E. ciliaris—Fringed heath
Fragaria chiloensis—Chiloe strawberry
Genista pilosa—Silky-leaf woadwaxen
Helianthemum nummularium—Sun-rose
Heuchera glabra—Alum-root
Hypericum olympicum—St. John's-wort
Iberis saxatilis—Rock candytuft
I. sempervirens—Evergreen candytuft
Iris species and varieties
Lonicera species and varieties—Honey-
suckle
Mahonia repens
Mazus species and varieties
Myosotis alpestris—Forget-me-not

PACHYSANDRA—Spurge
Phlox subulata—Ground-pink. Moss
phlox
Primula species and varieties—Primrose
Ranunculus repens—Creeping buttercup
Saponaria calabrica—Soapwort
S. ocymoides
Vinca minor—Myrtle. Periwinkle
Viola blanda—Sweet white violet
Waldsteinia fragarioides—Barren-straw-
berry

Ground Covers
WITH DECORATIVE FLOWERS:
SUMMER-BLOOMING

Achillea clavennae—Silver yarrow
Arenaria caroliniana—Sandwort
A. verna
Calluna vulgaris varieties—Heather
Campanula portenschlagiana—Dalmatian
bellflower
C. rotundifolia—Common harebell.
Bluebells-of-Scotland
Cerastium alpinum—Alpine chickweed
Ceratostigma plumbaginoides—Leadwort
Convolvulus mauritanicus—Ground
morning-glory
Coronilla varia—Crown-vetch
Cytisus albus—Portuguese broom
Daboecia cantabrica—Irish-heath
Dianthus gratianopolitanus—Cheddar
pink
Galax aphylla
Geranium robertianum—Herb Robert.
Red robin
GLOBULARIA
Gypsophila cerastioides
G. repens
Hosta species and varieties—Plantain-lily
Hypericum calycinum—Aaron's-beard
Indigofera kirilowii—Indigo
Iris species and varieties
Lantana sellowiana—Weeping lantana
LIRIOPE—Lily-turf
Lobularia maritima—Sweet-alyssum
Lonicera species and varieties—Honey-
suckle
Lycium chinense—Box-thorn. Matrimony
vine

Lysimachia nummularia—Moneywort.
  Creeping Jenny
Matricaria tchihatchewii—Turfing daisy
Mazus reptans
Myosotis scorpioides var. *semper-*
  florens—Forget-me-not
Nepeta hederacea—Ground-ivy. Gill-
  over-the-ground. Field-balm
OPHIOPOGON—Lily-turf
Phlox species and varieties
Polygonum capitatum—Knotweed
Primula species and varieties—Primrose
Rosa species and varieties—Rose
Satureja calamintha—Calamint
Stachys olympica—Lamb's-ears
Viola rotundifolia—Roundleaf violet
Wedelia trilobata

Ground Covers
WITH DECORATIVE FLOWERS: AUTUMN-BLOOMING

Achillea clavennae—Silver yarrow
Camellia sasanqua var. 'White Doves'
Ceratostigma plumbaginoides—Leadwort
Coronilla varia—Crown-vetch
HOSTA—Plantain-lily
Polygonum reynoutria—Knotweed

Ground Covers
WITH EVERGREEN FOLIAGE

ACAENA
Achillea tomentosa—Woolly yarrow
Arctostaphylos uva-ursi—Bearberry
Armeria maritima—Sea-pink
Bruckenthalia spiculifolia—Spikeheath
Calluna vulgaris varieties—Heather
Chiogenes hispidula—Creeping snow-
  berry
Cornus canadensis—Bunchberry dogwood
Cotoneaster dammeri
Erica carnea varieties—Heath
Euonymus fortunei—Wintercreeper
Galax aphylla
Gaultheria species and varieties
Gaylussacia brachycera—Box huckleberry
Grevillea obtusifolia
Hedera helix—Common ivy. English ivy

Helianthemum nummularium—Sun-rose
Iberis gibraltarica—Gibraltar candytuft
  I. saxatilis—Rock candytuft
Juniperus species and varieties—Prostrate
  juniper
Leiophyllum species and varieties—Sand-
  myrtle
Linnaea borealis—Twin flower
Mahonia repens
Mitchella repens—Partridge-berry
OPHIOPOGON—Lily-turf
Pachistima canbyi
Pachysandra terminalis—Spurge
Sedum species and varieties—Stonecrop
SHORTIA
Thymus vulgaris—Common thyme
Trachelospermum jasminoides—Star-
  jasmine. Confederate-jasmine
Vaccinium angustifolium—Low-bush
  blueberry
Veronica repens—Speedwell
Vinca minor—Myrtle. Periwinkle

Ground Covers
FOR BANKS AND SLOPES

Akebia trifoliata
Anthemis species and varieties—
  Chamomile
Arabis alpina—Mountain rock-cress
Arctostaphylos uva-ursi—Bearberry
Calluna vulgaris varieties—Heather
Ceanothus prostratus—Squaw-carpet
Comptonia peregrina—Sweet-fern
Convolvulus mauritanicus—Bindweed
Coronilla varia—Crown-vetch
Cotoneaster dammeri
Cytisus x *kewensis*—Kew broom
Daboecia cantabrica—Irish-heath
Diervilla lonicera—Dwarf bush-honey-
  suckle
  D. sessilifolia—Southern bush-honey-
  suckle
Euonymus fortunei varieties—Winter-
  creeper
Forsythia suspensa—Golden bells
Fragaria chiloensis—Chiloe strawberry
Grevillea obtusifolia
Hedera helix varieties—Common ivy.
  English ivy

Hydrangea petiolaris—Climbing hydrangea
Hypericum calycinum—Aaron's-beard
Juniperus procumbens var. nana—Dwarf Japanese garden juniper
Lonicera species and varieties—Honeysuckle
Lycium chinense—Box-thorn. Matrimony vine
Menispermum canadense—Moonseed
Nepeta hederacea—Ground-ivy. Gill-over-the-ground. Field-balm
OPHIOPOGON—Lily-turf
Pachistima canbyi
Parthenocissus quinquefolia—Woodbine. Virginia creeper
Polygonum reynoutria—Knotweed
Pueraria lobata—Kudzu vine
Rhus aromatica—Fragrant sumac
Robinia hispida—Rose-acacia
Rosa wichuraiana—Memorial rose
Rubus hispidus—Swamp dewberry
Symphoricarpos orbiculatus—Indian-currant. Coralberry
Vaccinium angustifolium—Low-bush blueberry
Vinca species and varieties—Periwinkle
Waldsteinia species and varieties
Xanthorhiza simplicissima—Yellow-root

Ground Covers
THAT GROW WELL IN SHADE

AJUGA—Bugleweed
Arctostaphylos uva-ursi—Bearberry
Asarum caudatum—Wild-ginger
    A. virginicum
Asperula odorata—Sweet woodruff
Ceratostigma plumbaginoides—Leadwort
Chiogenes hispidula—Creeping snowberry
Convallaria majalis—Lily-of-the-valley
Epimedium species—Barrenwort
Galax aphylla
Gaultheria species and varieties
Hedera helix—Common ivy. English ivy
Helxine soleirolii—Baby's-tears
Hosta species and varieties—Plantain-lily
Linnaea borealis—Twin-flower
Liriope species and varieties—Lily-turf
Mahonia repens
Maianthemum canadense

Myosotis alpestris—Forget-me-not
Nepeta hederacea—Ground-ivy. Gill-over-the-ground. Field-balm
Ophiopogon species—Lily-turf
Pachysandra terminalis—Spurge
Sarcococca hookeriana
    S. ruscifolia
Thymus vulgaris—Thyme
Vaccinium angustifolium—Low-bush blueberry
Veronica repens—Speedwell
Vinca minor—Myrtle. Periwinkle
Waldsteinia species and varieties
Xanthorhiza simplicissima—Yellow-root

Ground Covers
THAT SPREAD RAPIDLY

Aegopodium podagraria—Bishop's-weed
AJUGA—Bugleweed
Akebia trifoliata
Arenaria caroliniana—Sandwort
Cerastium alpinus—Alpine chickweed
Ceratostigma plumbaginoides—Leadwort
Convallaria majalis—Lily-of-the-valley
Coronilla varia—Crown-vetch
Dichondra carolinensis—Lawn leaf
Euonymus fortunei varieties—Winter-creeper
Fragaria chiloensis—Chiloe strawberry
Galium verum—Yellow bedstraw
Hedera helix—Common ivy. English ivy
Helxine soleirolii—Baby's-tears
Hypericum calycinum—Aaron's-beard
Lonicera species and varieties—Honeysuckle
Lycium chinense—Box-thorn. Matrimony vine
Matricaria tchihatchewii—Turfing daisy
Mazus species and varieties
Menispermum canadense—Moonseed
Nepeta hederacea—Ground-ivy. Gill-over-the-ground. Field-balm
Ophiopogon species—Lily-turf
Parthenocissus quinquefolia—Woodbine. Virginia creeper
Polygonum reynoutria—Knotweed
PRUNELLA
Pueraria lobata—Kudzu vine
Rosa wichuraiana—Memorial rose

Rubus hispidus—Swamp dewberry
Sedum species and varieties—Stonecrop
Symphoricarpos orbiculatus—Indian-currant. Coralberry
Thymus species and varieties—Thyme
Vinca minor—Myrtle

Ground Covers
THAT TOLERATE POOR SOIL

Abronia latifolia—Yellow sand-verbena
Achillea tomentosa—Woolly yarrow
AJUGA—Bugleweed
Anthemis species and varieties—Chamomile
Arabis alpina—Mountain rock-cress
Arenaria caroliniana—Sandwort
Cerastium alpinum—Alpine chickweed
Coreopsis auriculata—Tickseed
Cytisus albus—Portuguese broom
Dianthus alpinus—Alpine pink
Gypsophila repens
Leiophyllum species and varieties—Sand-myrtle
Lippia canescens
Lycium chinense—Box-thorn. Matrimony vine
Nepeta hederacea—Ground-ivy. Gill-over-the-ground. Field-balm
Salix repens—Creeping willow
Sedum species and varieties—Stonecrop
Thymus species and varieties—Thyme

Ground Covers
FOR USE BETWEEN PAVING STONES

Arabis alpina—Mountain rock-cress
Arenaria balearica—Corsican sandwort
Armeria maritima—Sea-pink
Dichondra carolinensis—Lawn leaf
Lysimachia nummularia—Moneywort. Creeping Jenny
Matricaria tchihatchewii—Turfing daisy
Mazus species and varieties
Nepeta hederacea—Ground-ivy. Gill-over-the-ground. Field-balm
Portulaca species and varieties
Sedum species and varieties—Stonecrop
Thymus species and varieties—Thyme
Viola blanda—Sweet white violet

Hedge Plants

Hedge Plants
WITH DECIDUOUS FOLIAGE

ABELIA
Acanthopanax sieboldianus—Fiveleaf aralia
Acer campestre—Hedge maple
Berberis species and varieties—Barberry
Caragana frutex—Pea-tree
Carpinus betulus—European hornbeam
Chaenomeles speciosa—Japanese-quince
Cornus racemosa—Gray dogwood
Cotoneaster species and varieties
Crataegus crus-gallii—Cockspur thorn
C. monogyna—Single seed hawthorn
Deutzia gracilis—Slender deutzia
Elaeagnus angustifolia—Russian-olive
Euonymus alatus—Corkbush. Winged euonymus
Fagus grandifolia—American beech
F. sylvatica—European beech
Forsythia species and varieties
Hibiscus syriacus—Shrub althea. Rose-of-Sharon
Ligustrum species and varieties—Privet
Lonicera species and varieties—Honeysuckle
Philadelphus species and varieties—Mock-orange
Physocarpus opulifolius—Ninebark
Poncirus trifoliata—Hardy-orange
Populus alba var. *bolleana*—Poplar
PRINSEPIA
Rosa species and varieties—Rose
Salix purpurea—Purple osier
S. repens—Creeping willow
SPIRAEA—Spirea
Stephanandra species and varieties

SYRINGA—Lilac
Teucrium chamaedrys—Germander
    T. fruticans
Viburnum opulus—European cranberry
    bush
    V. trilobum—American cranberry bush

Hedge Plants
WITH EVERGREEN FOLIAGE

Berberis species and varieties—Barberry
BUXUS—Box. Boxwood
Chamaecyparis pisifera—Sawara-cypress
Elaeagnus pungens—Thorny elaeagnus
Euonymus japonicus—Evergreen
    euonymus
Iberis species and varieties—Candytuft
Ilex crenata—Japanese holly
Juniperus communis—Common juniper
Laurus nobilis—Bay. Bay tree
Ligustrum species and varieties—Privet

Hedge Plants
WITH DECORATIVE FRUIT

BERBERIS—Barberry
Cornus racemosa—Gray dogwood
Cotoneaster species and varieties
Crataegus species and varieties—Haw-
    thorn
Euonymus species and varieties—Spindle-
    tree
Ilex crenata—Japanese holly
Juniperus communis—Common juniper
LIGUSTRUM—Privet
Lonicera species and varieties—Honey-
    suckle
Myrtus communis—Myrtle
PERNETTYA
Physocarpus monogynus—Ninebark
    P. opulifolius
Poncirus trifoliata—Hardy-orange
PRINSEPIA
PYRACANTHA—Firethorn
Rosa species and varieties—Rose
SARCOCOCCA
TAXUS—Yew
Viburnum opulus—European cranberry
    bush
    V. trilobum—American cranberry bush

Hedge Plants
THAT TOLERATE HEAVY CLIPPING

Acanthopanax sieboldianus—Fiveleaf
    aralia
Acer campestre—Hedge maple
Berberis species and varieties—Barberry
BUXUS—Box. Boxwood
Carpinus betulus—European hornbeam
Chamaecyparis pisifera—Sawara-cypress
Fagus grandifolia—American beech
    F. sylvatica—European beech
Ilex crenata var. convexa—Japanese holly
Juniperus communis—Common juniper
Laurus nobilis—Bay. Bay tree
LIGUSTRUM—Privet
Myrtus communis—Myrtle
Picea glauca—White spruce
Pinus strobus—White pine
Pittosporum species and varieties
Poncirus trifoliata—Hardy-orange
PRINSEPIA
PYRACANTHA—Firethorn
Rosa species and varieties—Rose
SARCOCOCCA
Stephanandra species and varieties
TAXUS—Yew
Thuja occidentalis var. fastigiata—
    American arborvitae
TSUGA—Hemlock

Hedge Plants
LOW, UNDER 3 FEET

Berberis verruculosa—Barberry
Buxus microphylla—Japanese box
    B. sempervirens var. suffruticosa—
    Dwarf boxwood
Chaenomeles japonica—Japanese-quince
Chamaecyparis obtusa varieties—Hinoki-
    cypress
Cotoneaster species and varieties
Iberis sempervirens—Evergreen candy-
    tuft
Ilex crenata varieties—Japanese holly
Juniperus communis var. compressa—
    Common juniper
Ligustrum vicaryi—Privet
PERNETTYA
Physocarpus opulifolius var. nana—Nine-
    bark

Rosa species and varieties—Rose
Salix purpurea var. nana—Purple osier
Sarcococca species and varieties
Spiraea x bumalda—Spirea
Stephanandra incisa var. crispa
Taxus species and varieties—Yew
Teucrium chamaedrys—Germander
Viburnum opulus var. nanum—European
   cranberry bush

Hedge Plants
MEDIUM, 3 TO 6 FEET

Berberis species and varieties—Barberry
Buxus species and varieties—Box. Box-
   wood
Chaenomeles speciosa—Japanese-quince
Chamaecyparis obtusa varieties—Hinoki-
   cypress
Cotoneaster species and varieties
Euonymus species and varieties—Spindle-
   tree
Ilex crenata—Japanese holly
Juniperus communis var. depressa—
   Common juniper
Lonicera species and varieties—Honey
   suckle
Rosa species and varieties—Rose
Sarcococca species and varieties
Spiraea species and varieties—Spirea
Taxus species and varieties—Yew
Thuja occidentalis varieties—American
   arborvitae
Teucrium fruticans—Germander
Viburnum species and varieties

Hedge Plants
WITH THORNS OR PRICKLES

Acanthopanax sieboldianus—Fiveleaf
   aralia
BERBERIS—Barberry
Chaenomeles japonica—Japanese-quince
Crataegus crus-gallii—Cockspur thorn
   C. monogyna—Single seed hawthorn
Elaeagnus angustifolia—Russian-olive
   E. pungens—Thorny elaeagnus

Ilex crenata—Japanese holly
Poncirus trifoliata—Hardy-orange
PRINSEPIA
PYRACANTHA—Firethorn
Rosa species and varieties—Rose

Hedge Plants
THAT TOLERATE CONSIDERABLE SHADE

Acanthopanax sieboldianus—Fiveleaf
   aralia
Euonymus alatus—Corkbush. Winged
   euonymus
LIGUSTRUM—Privet
SARCOCOCCA
Stephanandra incisa
TAXUS—Yew
TSUGA—Hemlock

Hedge Plants
FOR POOR GROWING CONDITIONS

Acanthopanax sieboldianus—Fiveleaf
   aralia
Berberis species and varieties—Barberry
Caragana arborescens—Siberian pea-tree
Elaeagnus species and varieties
LIGUSTRUM—Privet
Philadelphus species and varieties—
   Mock-orange
Physocarpus monogynus—Ninebark
   P. opulifolius

Hedge Plants
FOR INFORMAL USE

Abelia species and varieties
Abies species and varieties—Fir
Acanthopanax sieboldianus—Fiveleaf
   aralia
Berberis species and varieties—Barberry
Buxus species and varieties—Box. Box-
   wood
Caragana arborescens—Siberian pea-tree
Carpinus species and varieties—Horn-
   beam
Chaenomeles species and varieties—
   Flowering-quince

Chamaecyparis species and varieties—
False cypress
Cornus racemosa—Gray dogwood
Cotoneaster species and varieties
Crataegus crus-gallii—Cockspur thorn
C. *monogyna*—Single seed hawthorn
Deutzia gracilis—Slender deutzia
Euonymus alatus—Corkbush. Winged
euonymus
Forsythia species and varieties
Hibiscus syriacus—Shrub althea. Rose-
of-Sharon
Iberis species and varieties—Candytuft
Ilex crenata—Japanese holly
Juniperus communis—Common juniper
Ligustrum obtusifolium—Border privet
Lonicera species and varieties—Honey-
suckle
Myrtus communis—Myrtle
PERNETTYA
Philadelphus species and varieties—
Mock-orange
Physocarpus monogynus—Ninebark
P. *opulifolius*
Pinus strobus—White pine
Pittosporum species and varieties
Poncirus trifoliata—Hardy-orange
PRINSEPIA
PYRACANTHA—Firethorn
Rosa species and varieties—Rose
SPIRAEA—Spirea
Stephanandra species and varieties
SYRINGA—Lilac
TAXUS—Yew
Teucrium chamaedrys—Germander
T. *fruticans*
TSUGA—Hemlock
Viburnum opulus—European cranberry
bush
V. *trilobum*—American cranberry bush

Hedge Plants
FOR FORMAL USE

Acanthopanax sieboldianus—Fiveleaf
aralia
Acer campestre—Hedge maple
Berberis species and varieties—Barberry
Buxus species and varieties—Box. Box-
wood
Carpinus betulus—European hornbeam

Chamaecyparis pisifera—Sawara-cypress
Fagus grandifolia—American beech
F. *sylvatica*—European beech
Ilex crenata var. *convexa*—Japanese holly
Juniperus communis—Common juniper
Laurus nobilis—Bay. Bay tree
LIGUSTRUM—Privet
SARCOCOCCA
Stephanandra species and varieties
Thuja occidentalis var. *fastigiata*—Amer-
ican arborvitae
TSUGA—Hemlock

Hedge Plants
FOR SCREENS OR WINDBREAKS

Abies species and varieties—Fir
Acer campestre—Hedge maple
Berberis species and varieties—Barberry
Caragana arborescens—Siberian pea-tree
Carpinus betulus—European hornbeam
Crataegus species and varieties—Haw-
thorn
Elaeagnus species and varieties
Forsythia species and varieties
Hibiscus syriacus—Shrub althea. Rose-
of-Sharon
Juniperus communis—Common juniper
Laurus nobilis—Bay. Bay tree
Ligustrum amurense—Amur privet
L. *vulgare*—Common privet
Lonicera species and varieties—Honey-
suckle
Philadelphus species and varieties—
Mock-orange
Physocarpus species and varieties—Nine-
bark
Picea species and varieties—Spruce
Pinus species and varieties—Pine
Poncirus trifoliata—Hardy-orange
Populus alba var. *bolleana*—Poplar
PRINSEPIA
Rosa species and varieties—Rose
Salix purpurea—Purple osier
TAXUS—Yew
Thuja occidentalis var. *fastigiata*—Amer-
ican arborvitae
TSUGA—Hemlock
Viburnum species and varieties

Perennials

Perennials
BY HEIGHT: DWARF, UNDER 1 FOOT

Acaena buchananii—Buchanan sheepbur
Achillea clavennae—Silver yarrow
Adonis chrysocyathus—Pheasant-eye
  A. pyrenaica—Pyrenees adonis
Aegopodium podagraria var. *variega-*
  tum—Bishop's-weed
Aethionema cordifolium—Lebanon stone-
  cress
Ajuga genevensis—Geneva bugleweed.
  Alpine bugleweed
  A. reptans—Bugleweed. Carpet bugle
Alchemilla vulgaris—Lady's-mantle
Alyssum murale—Yellow-tuft alyssum
Anaphalis nubegina—Pearly everlasting
Anemone species—Windflower
Antennaria aprica—Pussy-toes
  A. dioica—Common pussy-toes
  A. plantaginifolia—Plantainleaf pussy-
  toes
Aquilegia alpina—Alpine columbine
Arabis caucasica—Caucasian rock-cress
Arenaria laricifolia—Larchleaf sandwort
Armeria maritima—Sea-pink
Artemisia schimidtiana var. *nana*—Silver-
  mound artemisia
Asarum caudatum—Wild-ginger
Asperula odorata—Woodruff
Aster alpinus—Rock aster
Aubrieta deltoidea—Purple rock-cress
Aurinia saxatilis—Basket-of-gold.
  Golden tuft
Bellis perennis—English daisy
Bergenia ligulata
Campanula carpatica—Carpathian bell-
  flower
Cerastium tomentosum—Snow-in-summer
Ceratostigma plumbaginoides—Leadwort.
  Plumbago
Chrysanthemum arcticum—Arctic chry-
  santhemum
Chrysogonum virginianum—Golden-star
Chrysopsis bakeri—Golden-aster
Claytonia virginica—Spring-beauty
Convallaria majalis—Lily-of-the-valley
Coreopsis auriculata var. *nana*—Dwarf-
eared coreopsis
Corydalis bulbosa—Fumaria
Cyclamen coum
  C. neapolitanum
Dianthus deltoides—Maiden pink
  D. alpinus—Alpine pink
Dicentra cucullaria—Dutchman's-breeches
Draba sibirica—Siberian draba
EPIMEDIUM—Mitrewort. Bishop's-hat
Euphorbia epithymoides—Common
  euphorbia
  E. myrsinites—Myrtle euphorbia
Galax aphylla
Gentiana septemfida—Gentian
Geum reptans—Avens
Gypsophila cerastioides—Baby's-breath
  G. repens
Helleborus niger—Christmas-rose
  H. orientalis—Lenten-rose
HEPATICA—Liverleaf
Houstonia caerulea—Bluets
Hypericum calycinum—Aaron's-beard
Hypoxis hirsuta—Star-grass
Iberis saxatilis—Rock candytuft
  I. sempervirens—Evergreen candytuft
Incarvillea grandiflora—Bigflower incar-
  villea
Iris bracteata—Bracted iris
  I. cristata—Crested dwarf iris
  I. pumila—Dwarf iris
Jeffersonia diphylla—Twinleaf
LEWISIA
Limonium tataricum—Tatarian sea-
  lavender
Linaria alpina—Alpine toadflax
Linum alpinum—Alpine flax
Liriope muscari—Blue lily-turf
Lupinus subcarnosus—Bluebonnet
Lychnis alpina—Arctic campion
Matricaria tchihatchewii—Turfing daisy
Mertensia lanceolata—Prairie bluebells
  M. longiflora—Small bluebells
Myosotis alpestris—Alpine forget-me-not
Oenothera caespitosa—Tufted evening-
  primrose
  O. missouriensis—Ozark sundrop
  Missouri-primrose
Papaver alpinum—Alpine poppy
Penstemon cardwellii
  P. pinifolius—Beard-tongue
Phlox subulata—Ground-pink. Moss

phlox
Polemonium reptans—Creeping pole-
monium
Potentilla alba—White cinquefoil
Primula clusiana—Primrose
P. *elatior*—Oxlip
P. *farinosa*—Bird's-eye primrose
P. x *polyantha*—Polyantha primrose
Pulmonaria angustifolia—Cowslip lung-
wort
P. *officinalis*—Common lungwort
Pyrola elliptica—Shinleaf
Ranunculus amplexicaulis—Yellow-eye
buttercup
R. *repens*—Creeping buttercup
Roscoea cautleoides
R. *purpurea*
Sagina glabra var. *aurea*—Golden pearl-
wort
Sanguinaria canadensis—Bloodroot
Saponaria ocymoides—Soapwort
Saxifraga caespitosa—Saxifrage
S. *umbrosa*—London pride saxifrage
Sedum sieboldii—Stonecrop
SEMPERVIVUM—Hen and chickens
Senecio aureus—Golden ragwort
Shortia galacifolia—Oconee-bells
Silene maritima—Sea campion
Thymus serpyllum—Creeping thyme
Tiarella cordifolia—Foamflower
Tunica saxifraga—Tunic-flower
Vinca minor—Periwinkle. Myrtle
Viola cornuta—Horned violet. Tufted
pansy
V. *odorata*—Sweet violet

Perennials
BY HEIGHT: LOW, 1 TO 2 FEET

Achillea millefolium—Pink yarrow
A. *tomentosa*—Woolly yarrow
Actaea pachypoda—White baneberry
A. *rubra*—Red baneberry
Adonis amurensis—Amur adonis
Anchusa barrelieri—Alkanet. Bugloss
Anemone alpina—Alpine anemone
A. *hupehensis*—Dwarf Japanese
anemone
Antennaria rosea—Rose pussy-toes
Aquilegia vulgaris—European columbine
Armeria pseud-armeria—Thrift

Artemisia pontica—Roman wormwood
A. *stelleriana*—Beach wormwood
Aster amellus—Italian aster
Bergenia cordifolia
Brunnera macrophylla—Heartleaf brun-
nera
Callirhoe digitata—Poppy-mallow
Caltha palustris—Marsh-marigold
Campanula carpatica—Carpathian bell-
flower
Catananche caerulea—Blue cupidone
Centaurea gymnocarpa—Dusty miller
C. *montana*—Mountain bluet
Ceratostigma plumbaginoides—Leadwort.
Plumbago
Cheiranthus cheiri—Wallflower
Chrysanthemum segetum—Corn-marigold
Coreopsis grandiflora—Bigflower
coreopsis
C. *lanceolata*—Lance coreopsis
Corydalis flavula—Yellow fumewort
Cosmos diversifolius—Black cosmos
Delphinium nudicaule—Red larkspur
Dianthus latifolius—Button pink
D. *plumarius*—Grass pink
Dicentra eximia—Fringed bleeding-heart
D. *formosa*—Pacific bleeding-heart
D. *spectabilis*—Common bleeding-heart
Dodecatheon meadia—Shooting-star
Doronicum caucasicum—Caucasian
leopard's-bane
Erigeron speciosus—Oregon fleabane
Eryngium maritimum—Eryngo. Sea-holly
Erysimum asperum—Siberian wallflower
Eupatorium coelestinum—Mistflower
eupatorium
Geranium ibericum—Iberian cranesbill
G. *sanguineum*—Blood-red geranium
Geum chiloense—Chile avens
Heuchera sanguinea—Coral-bells
Hosta decorata—Blunt-leaved plantain
H. *fortunei*—Plantain-lily. Funkia
H. *lancifolia*
H. *plantaginea*—Fragrant plantain
Hypericum x *moserianum*—Goldflower
Incarvillea delavayi—Hardy-gloxinia
Iris kaempferi—Japanese iris
I. *sibirica*—Siberian iris
Limonium sinuatum—Florists' statice
Linum flavum—Golden flax
L. *grandiflorum*—Flowering flax

L. perenne—Garden flax
Liriope muscari—Blue lily-turf
Lupinus perennis—Wild lupine
Lychnis flos-cuculi—Cookoo-flower.
   Ragged Robin
   L. flos-jovis—Flower-of-Jove
   L. viscaria—German catchfly
Meconopsis cambrica—Welsh-poppy
Mertensia virginica—Virginia bluebells
Myosotis scorpioides—Forget-me-not
Papaver nudicaule—Iceland poppy
Penstemon cobaea—Beard-tongue
   P. glaber—Sawsepal penstemon
   P. hirsutus—Hairy beard-tongue
Phlox divaricata—Sweet William phlox
Physalis alkekengi—Chinese lantern plant
Polygonum bistorta—Snakeweed
Potentilla nepaliensis—Nepal cinquefoil
Primula capitata—Purplehead primrose
   P. chionantha—Snowblossom primrose
   P. japonica—Japanese primrose
Prunella vulgaris—Heal-all. Selfheal
Pulmonaria saccharata—Bethlehem-sage
Ranunculus asiaticus—Persian buttercup
Rhexia mariana—Meadow-beauty
Salvia rutilans—Pineapple sage
Saxifraga stolonifera—Aaron's-beard.
   Strawberry-geranium
Scabiosa columbaria—Dove scabious
Sedum spectabile—Showy sedum
Senecio doronicum—Leopard's-bane
Stachys olympica—Lamb's-ears
Stokesia laevis—Stokes'-aster
Stylophorum diphyllum—Celandine-
   poppy
Talinum paniculatum—Jewels of Opar
Trollius europaeus—Globeflower
   T. ledebouri—Ledebour globeflower
Vancouveria hexandra
Verbena canadensis—Rose vervain
Veronica latifolia—Hungarian speedwell
   V. spicata—Spike speedwell
Zauschneria californica—California-
   fuchsia

Perennials
BY HEIGHT: MEDIUM, TO 3 FEET

Acanthus spinosa—Bear's-breech
Achillea ptarmica—Sneezewort
Adenophora potaninii—Lady-bell
Alstroemeria aurantiaca—Yellow alstro-
   emeria
Amsonia tabernaemontana—Willow
   amsonia
Anaphalis margaritacea—Pearly ever-
   lasting
Anemone glaucifolia—Haller's anemone
   A. hupehensis var. japonica—Dwarf
   Japanese anemone
Anthemis sancti-johannis—St. John's-
   chamomile
   A. tinctoria—Golden marguerite
Aquilegia formosa—Sitka columbine
Arnica montana—Mountain-tobacco
Asclepias tuberosa—Butterfly-weed
Aster novi-belgii—New York aster
Astilbe x arendsii—Hybrid astilbe
   A. japonica—Japanese false goat's-
   beard
Baptisia australis—False indigo
Campanula persicifolia—Peach-leaved
   bellflower
Centranthus ruber—Red valerian
Chelone lyonii—Pink turtlehead
Chrysanthemum coccineum—Painted
   daisy. Pyrethrum
   C. parthenium—Feverfew
Chrysopsis mariana—Maryland golden-
   aster
Coreopsis verticillata—Thread-leaved
   coreopsis
Cynoglossum grande—Hound's-tongue
Delphinium grandiflorum
Dicentra spectabilis—Bleeding-heart
Dictamnus albus—Gasplant
Digitalis grandiflora—Yellow foxglove
   D. lanata—Grecian foxglove
Dracocephalum sibiricum—Dragonhead
Eryngium alpinum—Alpine sea-holly
Euphorbia corollata—Flowering spurge
Filipendula hexapetala—Dropwort
Francoa ramosa—Maiden's-wreath
Gaillardia aristata—Blanket-flower
Galega officinalis—Goat's-rue
Gilia californica—Prickly-phlox

Gypsophila paniculata—Baby's-breath
Helenium bigelovii—Bigelow sneezeweed
  H. hoopesii—Orange sneezeweed
Helichrysum bracteum—Strawflower
Hemerocallis flava—Lemon-lily
Hesperis matronalis—Sweet rocket
Hosta undulata—Wavy-leaved plantain-
  lily
  H. ventricosa—Blue plantain-lily
Hypericum androsaemum—Tutsan St.
  John's-wort
Iris germanica—German iris
Lavandula officinalis—English lavender
Limonium latifolium—Statice
Lobelia siphilitica—Blue lobelia
Lunaria rediviva—Perennial honesty
Lupinus, Russell hybrids—Lupine
Lychnis chalcedonica—Maltese-cross.
  Jerusalem-cross
  L. coronaria—Rose campion
Lysimachia clethroides—Japanese
  loosestrife
Monarda didyma—Bee-balm
  M. pectinata—Lemon-mint
Oenothera fruticosa—Sundrop
Paeonia species and varieties—Peony
Papaver orientale—Oriental poppy
Penstemon digitalis—Beard-tongue
Platycodon grandiflorum—Balloon-flower
Polemonium caeruleum—Jacob's-ladder.
  Greek-valerian
Polygonatum biflorum—Solomon's seal
Potentilla argyrophylla—Silver-leaved
  cinquefoil
  P. fruticosa—Cinquefoil
Primula bulleyana—Primrose
  P. burmanica—Burman primrose
Ranunculus lyallii—Lyall buttercup
Rudbeckia speciosa—Showy coneflower
Salvia officinalis—Garden sage
  S. pratensis—Meadow sage
Sanguisorba obtusa—Japanese bottle-
  brush flower
Saponaria officinalis—Bouncing Bet
Scabiosa caucasica—Scabious. Mourning
  bride
Sidalcea malvaeflora—Wild-hollyhock
Smilacina racemosa—False Solomon's
  seal
Stachys grandiflora—Lamb's-ears
Thalictrum aquilegifolium—Columbine

meadow-rue
Tradescantia virginiana—Virginia
  spiderwort
Veronica longifolia—Speedwell

Perennials
BY HEIGHT: MEDIUM TALL, TO 4 FEET

Acanthus mollis—Bear's-breech
Achillea filipendulina—Fernleaf yarrow
Aconitum napellus—Monkshood
Alstroemeria litgu
  Litgu hybrids
Aquilegia chrysantha—Golden-spurred
  columbine
  A. longissima—Longspur columbine
Artemisia albula—Silver king
Asphodeline lutea—Asphodel
Belamcanda chinensis—Blackberry-lily
Chrysanthemum maximum—Shasta daisy
Doronicum plantagineum—Plantain
  leopard's-bane
Echinacea purpurea—Purple coneflower
Echinops exaltatus—Russian globe-thistle
Filipendula purpurea—Meadow-sweet
Gypsophila acutifolia—Baby's-breath
Hypericum frondosum—St. John's-wort
Kniphofia uvaria—Red-hot-poker. Tri-
  toma
Liatris elegans—Pink-scale gayfeather
Lilium species and hybrids—Lily
Linaria dalmatica—Dalmatian toadflax
Papaver orientale—Oriental poppy
Penstemon barbatus—Bearded penstemon
  P. grandiflorus—Large-flowered beard-
  tongue
Phlox paniculata—Summer phlox
Physostegia virginiana—Obedient plant
Primula florindae—Tibetan primrose
Salvia azurea var. *grandiflora*—Pitcher's
  salvia
Senecio pulcher—Uruguay groundsel
Stanleya pinnata—Desert prince's-plume
Steironema ciliatum—Fringed loosestrife
Thalictrum rochebrunianum—Lavender
  mist
Verbascum phoeniceum—Purple mullein
Verbena hastata—Blue vervain

Perennials
BY HEIGHT: TALL, TO 5 FEET

Aconitum henryi—Monkshood
Anchusa azurea—Italian alkanet. Italian bugloss
Anemone tomentosa—Windflower
Artemisia lactiflora—White mugwort
Aster novae-angliae—New England aster
Astilbe chinensis var. *davidii*—Chinese false goat's-beard
  A. grandis—False goat's-beard
Boltonia asteroides—False starwort
Campanula lactiflora—Milky bellflower
Cassia marilandica—American senna
Chrysanthemum morifolium—Florists' chrysanthemum
Cimicifuga simplex—Bugbane
Delphinium cheilanthum—Garland larkspur
Echinops ritro—Globe-thistle
Epilobium angustifolium—Fireweed
Eupatorium rugosum—White snakeroot
Gilia rubra—Texas plume
Helenium autumnale—Yellow-star. Common sneezeweed
Helianthus rigidus—Stiff sunflower
Heliopsis helianthoides
Liatris pycnostachya—Kansas gayfeather
Lilium species and hybrids—Lily
Lupinus polyphyllus—Washington lupine
Lythrum salicaria—Purple loosestrife
Paeonia suffruticosa—Tree peony
Silybum marianum—St. Mary's-thistle
Thalictrum speciocissimum—Dusty meadow-rue
Thermopsis caroliniana—Aaron's-rod
Valeriana officinalis—Valerian. Garden-heliotrope

Perennials
BY HEIGHT: VERY TALL, OVER 5 FEET

Aconitum carmichaelii—Azure monkshood
Althaea rosea—Garden hollyhock
Angelica archangelica—Holy ghost
Aruncus sylvester—Goat's-beard
Astragalus alopecuroides—Milk-vetch
Campanula pyramidalis—Chimney bellflower

Cephalaria tatarica
Cimicifuga racemosa—Black snakeroot. Cohosh bugbane
Delphinium elatum—Candle larkspur
Digitalis purpurea—Foxglove
Echinops sphaerocephalus—Great globe-thistle
Eremurus robustus—Giant desert-candle
  E. x *shelfordii*—Shelford desert-candle
Eupatorium purpureum—Joe-pyeweed
Filipendula rubra—Queen-of-the-prairie
Gunnera chilensis
Helianthus tuberosus—Jerusalem-artichoke
Hemerocallis fulva—Tawny daylily
Hibiscus moscheutos—Swamp-mallow
Hypericum densiflorum—St. John's-wort
Liatris scariosa—Tall gayfeather
  L. spicata—Spike gayfeather
Lilium species and hybrids—Lily
Macleaya cordata—Plume-poppy
Penstemon spectabilis—Beard-tongue
Polygonatum commutatum—Solomon's seal
Polygonum cuspidatum—Japanese knotweed
Romneya coulteri—Matilija-poppy
Rudbeckia laciniata—Goldenglow
Solidago canadensis—Goldenrod
Thalictrum speciosissimum—Dusty meadow-rue
Verbascum olympicum—Olympian mullein
Yucca filamentosa—Adam's-needle

Perennials
BY COLOR: BLUE

Aconitum carmichaelii—Monkshood
  A. henryi
  A. napellus
Agapanthus species and hybrids—Lily-of-the-Nile
Ajuga genevensis—Geneva bugleweed. Alpine bugleweed
  A. reptans—Bugleweed. Carpet bugle
Amsonia ciliata
  A. tabernaemontana—Willow amsonia
Anchusa azurea—Italian alkanet. Italian bugloss
  A. barrelieri

Anemone coronaria—Poppy-flowered
   anemone
   A. glaucifolia—Windflower
   A. pulsatilla—European pasque-flower
Aquilegia caerulea—Colorado columbine
   A. glandulosa—Siberian columbine
   A. vulgaris—European columbine
Aster amellus var. *elegans*—Italian aster
   A. novi-belgii—New York aster
Baptisia australis—False indigo
Brunnera macrophylla
Campanula barbata—Bellflower
   C. carpatica—Carpathian bellflower
   C. elatines var. *garganica*
   C. persicifolia—Peached-leaved bell-
   flower
   C. rotundifolia—Common harebell.
   Bluebells-of-Scotland
Catananche caerulea—Blue cupidone
Centaurea maculosa—European star-
   thistle
   C. montana—Mountain bluet
Ceratostigma plumbaginoides—Leadwort.
   Plumbago
Cynoglossum grande—Hound's-tongue
Delphinium cheilanthum—Hardy garland
   larkspur
   D. elatum and hybrids—Candle lark-
   spur
Dracocephalum sibiricum—Dragonhead
Echinops exaltatus—Russian globe-thistle
   E. ritro—Globe-thistle
   E. sphaerocephalus—Great globe-thistle
Erigeron bellidifolius—Poor-robin's-
   plantain
   E. speciosus—Oregon fleabane
Eryngium planum—Flat-leaved eryngium
Eupatorium coelestinum—Mistflower
   eupatorium
Gentiana farreri—Gentian
   G. septemfida
Hepatica americana
Hosta ventricosa—Blue plantain-lily
Houstonia caerulea—Bluets
Hyssopus officinalis—Hyssop
Iris species and hybrids
Limonium latifolium—Statice
   L. sinuatum—Florists' statice
Linum alpinum—Alpine flax
   L. narbonnense

L. perenne—Garden flax
Lobelia siphilitica—Blue lobelia. Great
   lobelia
Lupinus hartwegii—Lupine
   L. polyphyllus—Washington lupine
   Russell hybrids
Mazus japonicus
Meconopsis betonicifolia var. *baileyi*—
   Blue-poppy
   M. napaulensis—Satin-poppy
   M. quintuplenervia—Harebell-poppy
MERTENSIA—Bluebells
Myosotis scorpioides—Forget-me-not
Nemophila menziesii—Baby blue-eyes
Nepeta cataria—Catnip
Penstemon glaber—Sawsepal penstemon
   P. richardsonii—Richardson penstemon
   P. unilateralis—Oneside penstemon
Phlox divaricata—Blue phlox. Wild sweet
   William
Platycodon grandiflorum—Balloon-flower
Polemonium caeruleum—Jacob's-ladder.
   Greek-valerian
Primula vulgaris varieties—Common
   primrose
Pulmonaria angustifolia—Lungwort
   P. saccharata—Bethlehem-sage
Salvia azurea var. *grandiflora*—Blue sage
   S. farinacea—Mealycup sage
Scabiosa caucasica—Scabious. Mourning
   bride
   S. columbaria
Stokesia laevis—Stokes'-aster
Veronica austriaca—Speedwell
   V. latifolia—Hungarian speedwell
   V. spicata—Spike speedwell
Vinca minor—Periwinkle. Myrtle
Viola papilionacea—Butterfly violet

Perennials
BY COLOR: ORANGE

Alstroemeria aurantiaca cultivars—Yel-
   low alstroemeria
   Litgu hybrids
Anthemis sancti-johannis—St. John's-
   chamomile
Arnica alpina—Alpine arnica
Asclepias tuberosa—Butterfly-weed

Belamcanda chinensis—Blackberry-lily
Chrysanthemum morifolium hybrids—
  Florists' chrysanthemum
Erysimum pulchellum—Rockery blister-
  cress
Geum chiloense—Chile avens
Helenium hoopesii—Orange sneezeweed
Hemerocallis hybrids—Daylily
Iris hybrids
Lilium species and hybrids—Lily
Lupinus polyphyllus—Washington lupine
  Russell hybrids
Papaver nudicaule—Iceland poppy
  P. orientale hybrids—Oriental poppy
Physalis alkekengi—Chinese lantern plant
Primula x bullesiana—Primrose
  P. bulleyana
  P. x polyantha—Polyantha primrose
Sedum aizoon var. aurantiacum—Stone-
  crop
  S. palmeri
Trollius asiaticus—Globeflower

Perennials
BY COLOR: PINK

Achillea millefolium var. rosea—Yarrow
Aethionema grandiflorum—Persian stone-
  cress
Androsace foliosa—Rock-jasmine
  A. sarmentosa
  A. sempervivoides
Anemone coronaria—Poppy-flowered
  anemone
  A. hortensis—Garden anemone
  A. hupehensis—Dwarf Japanese
    anemone
  A. narcissiflora—Narcissus windflower
  A. tomentosa—Windflower
Antennaria aprica—Pussy-toes
  A. dioica—Common pussy-toes
  A. rosea—Rose pussy-toes
Armeria maritima—Sea-pink
  A. pseud-armeria—Thrift
Asperula hirta—Woodruff
Aster cordifolius
  A. novae-angliae cultivars—New
    England aster
  A. novi-belgii cultivars—New York
    aster

Astilbe x arendsii—False goat's-beard
  A. chinensis—Chinese false goat's-beard
  A. x rosea
Bellis perennis—English daisy
Bergenia cordifolia
  B. crassifolia
  B. ligulata
Centaurea montana varieties—Mountain
  bluet
Chelone glabra—Turtlehead
Chrysanthemum coccineum—Painted
  daisy. Pyrethrum
  C. morifolium—Florists' chrysanthe-
    mum
Clematis montana rubens
  C. montana rubens superba
Convallaria majalis var. rosea—Lily-of-
  the-valley
Coreopsis rosea—Rose coreopsis
Corydalis bulbosa—Fumaria
Cyclamen europaeum
  C. neapolitanum
Delphinium elatum varieties—Candle
  larkspur
Dianthus alpinus—Alpine pink
  D. arenarius—Sand pink
  D. barbatus—Sweet William
  D. caryophyllus—Carnation. Clove pink
  D. deltoides—Maiden pink
  D. gratianopolitanus—Cheddar pink
  D. latifolius—Button pink
  D. plumarius—Cottage pink. Grass
    pink
Dicentra formosa—Pacific bleeding-heart
  D. spectabilis—Bleeding-heart
DODECATHEON—Shooting-star
Epilobium angustifolium—Fireweed
Eremurus elwesii—Elwes desert-candle
  E. robustus—Giant desert-candle
  E. x shelfordii—Shelford desert-candle
Erigeron karvinskianus—Bonytip fleabane
Filipendula purpurea—Meadow-sweet
  F. rubra—Queen-of-the-prairie
Galega officinalis varieties—Goat's-rue
Geranium argenteum—Silver-leaved
  geranium
Gilia californica—Prickly-phlox
Gypsophila acutifolia—Baby's-breath
Hemerocallis varieties—Daylily
Hesperis matronalis—Dame's rocket.

Sweet rocket
Heuchera sanguinea—Coral-bells
Hibiscus moscheutos—Swamp-mallow
Iris species and hybrids
Kniphofia uvaria varieties—Red-hot
poker. Tritoma
Lilium species and varieties—Lily
Limonium sinuatum—Florists' statice
Linaria alpina var. *rosea*—Alpine toad-
flax
Lupinus argenteus—Lupine
L. polyphyllus varieties—Washington
lupine
Russell hybrids
Lychnis alpina—Arctic campion
L. coeli-rosa—Rose-of-heaven
L. flos-jovis—Flower-of-Jove
Lythrum varieties—Loosestrife
Malva moschata—Musk mallow
Oenothera caespitosa—Tufted evening-
primrose
Oxalis acetosella var. *rosea*—Wood sorrel
O. adenophylla
Paeonia species and hybrids—Peony
Papaver orientale hybrids—Oriental
poppy
Penstemon cardwellii—Cardwell penste-
mon
P. richardsonii—Richardson penstemon
P. rupicola—Cliff penstemon
P. unilateralis—Oneside penstemon
Phlox paniculata—Summer phlox
P. pilosa—Prairie phlox
P. subulata—Ground-pink. Moss phlox
Physostegia virginiana—False dragon-
head. Obedient plant
Platycodon grandiflorum—Balloon-flower
Polygonum affine—Knotweed. Fleece-
flower
P. amplexicaule
P. bistorta—Snakeweed
Potentilla nepalensis—Nepal cinquefoil
Primula x *bullesiana*—Primrose
P. mistassinica
P. polyneura
Prunella grandiflora—Bigflower selfheal
Saponaria caespitosa—Pyrenees soapwort
S. officinalis—Bouncing Bet
Saxifraga aizoon—Saxifrage
S. umbrosa—London pride saxifrage

Sedum dasyphyllum—Leafy stonecrop
S. ewersii—Stonecrop
S. pulchellum—Texas stonecrop
S. sieboldii
Sidalacea malvaeflora—Checkerbloom.
Wild-hollyhock
Silene armeria—Sweet William-catchfly
S. caroliniana—Wild-pink. Catchfly
S. maritima var. *rosea*—Sea campion
Stachys grandiflora—Betony
Teucrium chamaedrys—Germander
Thymus serpyllum varieties—Creeping
thyme
Trillium grandiflorum—Snow trillium
Tunica saxifraga—Tunic-flower
Valeriana montana—Valerian
Verbena canadensis—Rose vervain
Veronica longifolia varieties—Speedwell
Viola odorata—Sweet violet

Perennials
BY COLOR: PURPLE

Acanthus mollis—Bear's-breech
Adenophora potaninii—Lady-bell
Aethionema cordifolium—Lebanon stone-
cress
Ajuga reptans—Bugleweed. Carpet bugle
Allium giganteum—Giant onion
A. schoenoprasum—Chives
Anemone coronaria—Poppy-flowered
anemone
A. halleri—Haller's anemone
A. hortensis—Garden anemone
Aquilegia alpina—Alpine columbine
A. vulgaris—European columbine
Aster alpinus—Rock aster
A. amellus—Italian aster
A. x *frikartii*
A. novae-angliae—New England aster
A. novi-belgii—New York aster
AUBRIETA—Rock-cress
Bergenia cordifolia var. *purpurea*
B. ligulata
Boltonia asteroides—False starwort
Callirhoe digitata—Poppy-mallow
Camassia leichtlinii—Camass
Campanula glomerata—Clustered bell-
flower
C. poscharskyana—Serbian bellflower

Centaurea cineraria—Dusty miller
C. montana—European star-thistle
Chelone lyonii—Turtlehead
Chrysanthemum species and varieties
Clematis x jackmanii
Clintonia andrewsiana—Red bead-lily
Corydalis bulbosa—Fumaria
Cynoglossum grande—Hound's-tongue
Delphinium elatum and hybrids—Candle
    larkspur
Dianthus barbatus—Sweet William
Dracocephalum sibiricum—Dragonhead
Echinacea purpurea—Purple coneflower
Epilobium angustifolium—Fireweed
Erigeron speciosus—Oregon fleabane
Erythronium dens-canis—European fawn-
    lily
Eupatorium purpureum—Joe-pyeweed
Galega officinalis—Goat's-rue
Geranium grandiflorum—Cranesbill
G. ibericum—Iberian cranesbill
Helleborus orientalis—Lenten-rose
Hesperis matronalis—Dame's rocket.
    Sweet rocket
Heuchera americana—American alum-root
Hosta decorata—Blunt-leaved plantain-
    lily
H. lancifolia—Narrow-leaved plantain-
    lily
Houstonia caerulea—Bluets. Quaker ladies
Iberis gibraltarica—Gibraltar candytuft
Iris species and varieties
Lathyrus grandiflorus—Everlasting-pea
Lavandula officinalis—English lavender
L. stoechas—French lavender
Lavatera assurgentiflora—Tree-mallow
Liatris pycnostachya—Kansas gayfeather
L. scariosa—Blazing-star
Lilium species and varieties—Lily
Limonium carolinianum—Statice
Liriope muscari—Lily-turf
Lunaria rediviva—Perennial honesty
Lupinus polyphyllus—Washington lupine
    Russell hybrids
Lythrum salicaria—Purple loosestrife
Meconopsis grandis
M. quintuplenervia—Harebell-poppy
Nepeta cataria—Catnip
Ophiopogon japonicus—Lily-turf
Penstemon calycosus
    Henry hybrids

North Platte hybrids
Phlox bifida—Sand phlox
P. paniculata—Summer phlox
Physostegia virginiana—False dragon-
    head. Obedient plant
Primula species and varieties—Primrose
PRUNELLA—Heal-all. Selfheal
Pulmonaria angustifolia—Lungwort
Ramonda pyrenaica
Rhexia mariana—Meadow-beauty
Salvia argentea—Silver sage
S. officinalis—Garden sage
Scabiosa caucasica—Scabious. Mourning
    bride
Sedum cauticolum—Stonecrop
S. ewersii
Sempervivum montanum—Houseleek
S. tectorum—Hen-and-chickens. Com-
    mon houseleek
Silene acaulis—Moss campion
S. virginica—Fire-pink. Catchfly
Stachys grandiflora—Betony
S. olympica—Lamb's-ears
Teucrium chamaedrys—Germander
Thalictrum dipterocarpum—Meadow-rue
T. rochebrunianum—Lavender-mist
Thymus herba-barona—Caraway thyme
T. vulgaris—Common thyme
Tunica saxifraga—Tunic-flower
Verbena canadensis—Rose vervain
V. pulchella—Moss vervain
V. rigida
V. tenera
Vinca minor—Periwinkle. Myrtle
Viola species and hybrids—Violet. Pansy
Yucca aloifolia—Spanish bayonet

Perennials
BY COLOR: RED

Acaena microphylla—New Zealand bur
Alstroemeria chilensis—Chilean
    alstroemeria
    Litgu hybrids
Althaea rosea—Garden hollyhock
Anemone coronaria—Poppy-flowered
    anemone
A. fulgens—Scarlet windflower
A. hortensis—Garden anemone
A. hupehensis—Dwarf Japanese
    anemone

Aquilegia canadensis—American colum-
bine
A. *formosa*—Sitka columbine
A. *skinneri*—Skinner columbine
Astilbe hybrids—False goat's-beard
Callirhoe digitata—Poppy-mallow
Centranthus ruber—Red valerian.
Jupiter's-beard
Cheiranthus cheiri—Wallflower
Cosmos diversifolius—Black cosmos
Cyclamen europaeum—European cycla-
men
Delphinium nudicaule—Red larkspur
Dianthus x *allwoodii*—Allwood pink
D. *barbatus*—Sweet William
D. *caryophyllus*—Carnation. Clove
pink
D. *plumarius*—Cottage pink
Epimedium alpinum var. *rubrum*—Red
alpine epimedium
E. x *rubrum*
Gaillardia aristata varieties—Blanket-
flower
Geranium sanguineum—Blood-red gera-
nium
Geum chiloense—Chile avens
Gilia rubra—Tree-cypress. Texas plume
Helenium autumnale var. *rubrum*—Yel-
low-star. Red common sneezeweed
Helianthemum nummularium—Sun-rose
Hemerocallis hybrids—Daylily
Heuchera sanguinea—Coral-bells
Incarvillea grandiflora—Bigflower in-
carvillea
Iris species and hybrids
Kniphofia uvaria—Red-hot-poker.
Tritoma
Lilium species and hybrids—Lily
Lobelia cardinalis—Cardinal flower
Lupinus, Russell hybrids—Lupine
Lychnis x *arkwrightii*—Campion
L. *chalcedonica*—Maltese-cross. Jeru-
salem-cross
L. *flos-cuculi*—Cuckoo-flower. Ragged
Robin
L. x *haageana*
Lythrum salicaria cultivars—Loosestrife
Monarda didyma—Bee-balm
Oxalis bowiei
Paeonia officinalis hybrids—Peony

P. *suffruticosa* hybrids—Tree peony
Papaver nudicaule—Iceland poppy
P. *orientale*—Oriental poppy
Penstemon barbatus—Bearded penstemon
P. *murrayanus*—Beard-tongue
North Platte hybrids
Phlox paniculata—Summer phlox
P. *subulata*—Ground-pink. Moss phlox
Potentilla atrosanguinea—Himalayan
cinquefoil
Primula x *bullesiana*—Primrose
Salvia rutilans—Pineapple sage
Schizostylis coccinea—Crimson-flag
Sedum spurium—Two-row stonecrop
Sempervivum arachnoideum—Cobweb
houseleek. Spiderweb houseleek
S. x *fauconnettii*
Silene virginica—Fire-pink. Catchfly
Verbena x *hybrida*—Garden verbena
Zauschneria californica—California-
fuchsia

Perennials
BY COLOR: WHITE

Acanthus mollis—Bear's-breech
Achillea clavennae—Silver yarrow
A. *ptarmica*—Sneezewort
A. *p.* var. 'Boule de Neige'
A. *p.* var. 'The Pearl'
Actaea pachypoda—White baneberry
Ajuga reptans var. *alba*—Bugleweed
Althaea rosea—Garden hollyhock
Alyssum spinosum—Spiny alyssum
Anaphalis nubegina—Pearly everlasting
Anemone alpina—Alpine anemone
A. *blanda*—Greek anemone
Antennaria species—Pussy-toes
Arabis albida—Wall rock-cress
Arenaria balearica—Corsican sandwort
Armeria maritima var. *alba*—Sea-pink
Artemisia albula—Silver king
A. *lactiflora*—White mugwort
A. *schmidtiana*
A. *s.* var. *nana*—Silvermound
Astilbe x *arendsii* cultivars—False goat's-
beard
A. *japonica*—Japanese false goat's-
beard
Boltonia asteroides—False starwort

Caltha biflora—Twinflower marsh-marigold

Campanula carpatica—Carpathian bellflower

C. *glomerata*—Clustered bellflower

C. *pyramidalis*—Chimney bellflower

Catananche caerulea—Blue cupidone

Centaurea dealbata—Persian centaurea

Centranthus ruber var. *alba*—Red valerian. Jupiter's-beard

Cerastium alpinum—Alpine chickweed

C. *tomentosum*—Snow-in-summer

Chelone glabra—White turtlehead

Chrysanthemum coreanum—Korean daisy

C. *leucanthemum*—Daisy

C. *maximum*—Shasta daisy

C. *morifolium*—Florists' chrysanthemum

C. *nipponicum*—Nippon daisy

C. *parthenium*—Feverfew

Cimicifuga racemosa—Black snakeroot. Cohosh bugbane

Claytonia virginica—Spring-beauty

Clematis recta—Ground clematis

Clintonia uniflora—Queen-cup

Convallaria majalis—Lily-of-the-valley

Cyclamen coum var. *alba*

C. *neapolitanum* var. *album*

Delphinium cheilanthum var. *moorheimii*—Garland larkspur

D. *elatum* hybrids

D. *grandiflorum* var. *alba*

Dentaria diphylla—Crinkleroot toothwort

Dianthus x *allwoodii* var. 'Helen'—Pink

D. *barbatus*—Sweet William

D. *deltoides*—Maiden pink

Dictamnus albus—Gasplant

Digitalis lanata—Grecian foxglove

D. *purpurea*—Common foxglove

Dodecatheon meadia—Shooting-star

Epimedium grandiflorum var. *album*—Mitrewort. Bishop's-hat

Eremurus elwesii var. *albus*—Elwes desert-candle

E. *himalaicus*—Himalayan desert-candle

Eupatorium rugosum—White snakeroot

Euphorbia corollata—Flowering spurge

Filipendula hexapetala—Dropwort

Galax aphylla

Galega officinalis var. *alba*—Goat's-rue

Gypsophila paniculata—Baby's-breath

G. *repens*

Helleborus niger—Christmas-rose

Hesperis matronalis—Dame's rocket. Sweet rocket

Heuchera sanguinea var. *alba*—Coralbells

Hibiscus moscheutos—Swamp-mallow

Hosta plantaginea—Fragrant plantain-lily

Iberis saxatilis—Rock candytuft

I. *sempervirens*—Evergreen candytuft

Iris cristata var. *alba*—Crested dwarf iris

I. *tectorum* var. *alba*—Roof iris

Iris hybrids

Jeffersonia diphylla—Twinleaf

Lespedeza japonica—Bush-clover

Liatris elegans—Gayfeather

Lilium candidum—Madonna lily

L. *formosanum*—Formosa lily

L. *regale*—Regal lily

Lilium hybrids

Lychnis chalcedonica varieties—Maltese-cross. Jerusalem-cross

L. *coronaria* varieties—Campion

Lysimachia clethroides—Japanese loosestrife

Maranta arundinacea—Arrowroot

Matricaria tchihatchewii—Turfing daisy

Nepeta cataria—Catnip

Oenothera speciosa—Evening-primrose

Ophiopogon jaburan—Jaburan

Oxalis montana

Pachysandra terminalis—Japanese spurge

Paeonia hybrids—Peony

Papaver alpinum—Alpine poppy

Penstemon digitalis hybrids—Foxglove beard-tongue

Phlox paniculata—Summer phlox

P. *subulata*—Ground-pink. Moss phlox

Physostegia virginiana varieties—False dragonhead. Obedient plant

Platycodon grandiflorum—Balloon-flower

Polemonium caeruleum varieties—Jacob's-ladder. Greek-valerian

POLYGONATUM—Solomon's seal

Polygonum amplexicaule—Mountain fleece-flower

P. *bistorta*

Potentilla alba—White cinquefoil

P. *fruticosa*—Bush cinquefoil

Primula chionantha—Snowblossom prim-

rose
P. japonica—Japanese primrose
P. x polyantha—Polyantha primrose
P. sieboldii—Siebold primrose
Prunella vulgaris varieties—Common self-heal
Pyrola rotundifolia—Shinleaf
Ranunculus amplexicaulis—Yellow-eye buttercup
Sagina glabra—Irish-moss. Pearlwort
S. subulata—Corsican pearlwort
Salvia azurea—Blue sage
S. patens—Gentian sage
Sanguinaria canadensis—Bloodroot
Sanguisorba minor—Burnet
Saponaria officinalis—Bouncing Bet
Saxifraga caespitosa—Saxifrage
S. hostii—Saxifrage
S. umbrosa—London pride saxifrage
Scabiosa caucasica—Scabious. Mourning bride
Sedum album—White stonecrop
S. anglicum—English stonecrop
S. telephium—Live-forever stonecrop
Shortia galacifolia—Oconee-bells
Sidalcea candida—Prairie-mallow
Silene maritima—Sea campion
Smilacina racemosa—False Solomon's-seal
Stachys grandiflora—Betony
Symphytum officinale—Comfrey
Thalictrum aquilegifolium—Meadow-rue
Thymus serpyllum var. *albus*—Creeping thyme
Tiarella cordifolia—Foamflower
Trillium nivale—Dwarf trillium
Valeriana officinalis—Valerian. Garden-heliotrope
Vancouveria hexandra
Viola blanda—Sweet white violet
V. odorata—Sweet violet
Yucca filamentosa—Adam's-needle

Perennials
BY COLOR: YELLOW

Achillea filipendulina—Fernleaf yarrow. Golden yarrow
Adonis chrysocyathus—Pheasant-eye
A. vernalis—Spring adonis

Alstroemeria aurantiaca—Yellow alstroemeria
Litgu hybrids
Althaea rosea hybrids—Garden hollyhock
Alyssum montanum—Yellow-tuft alyssum
Anthemis tinctoria—Golden marguerite
Aquilegia chrysantha—Golden-spurred columbine
Arnica montana—Mountain-tobacco
Artemisia abrotanum—Southernwood
Asphodeline lutea—Asphodel
Aurinia saxatilis—Basket-of-gold. Golden tuft
Baptisia tinctoria—False indigo
Cassia marilandica—Wild senna
Centaurea montana varieties—Mountain bluet
Cephalaria alpina
Chrysanthemum morifolium—Florists' chrysanthemum
C. segetum—Corn-marigold
Chrysogonum virginianum—Golden-star
CHRYSOPSIS—Golden-aster
Coreopsis auriculata—Eared coreopsis
C. grandiflora—Bigflower coreopsis
C. lanceolata—Lance coreopsis
C. major—Trefoil coreopsis
C. verticillata—Thread-leaved coreopsis
Corydalis cheilanthifolia—Fernleaf corydalis
C. lutea—Yellow corydalis
Digitalis grandiflora—Yellow foxglove
Doronicum caucasicum—Caucasian leopard's-bane
Epimedium pinnatum hybrids—Persian epimedium
Eremurus x shelfordii—Shelford desert-candle
Erysimum asperum—Siberian wallflower
Euphorbia epithymoides—Spurge
E. myrsinites—Myrtle euphorbia
Gaillardia aristata—Blanket-flower
Galium verum—Yellow bedstraw. Lady's bedstraw
Heleniun autumnale—Yellow-star. Common sneezeweed
H. bigelovii—Bigelow sneezeweed
Helianthus mollis—Ashy sunflower
H. rigidus—Stiff sunflower
H. salicifolius—Willow-leaved sunflower

Heliopsis helianthoides—Sunflower
heliopsis
H. scabra—Rough heliopsis
Hemerocallis hybrids—Daylily
Hypericum androsaemum—Tutsan St.
John's-wort
H. calycinum—Aaron's-beard
H. frondosum—Golden St. John's-wort
Hypoxis hirsuta—Star-grass
Inula helenium—Elecampane
Iris hybrids
Kniphofia uvaria—Red-hot-poker.
Tritoma
Ligularia clivorum—Golden-ray
L. wilsoniana—Wilson's golden-ray
Lilium species and hybrids—Lily
Limonium sinuatum—Florists' statice
Linaria dalmatica—Dalmatian toadflax
Lupinus arboreus—Tree lupine
L. luteus—Yellow lupine
L. polyphyllus—Washington lupine
Russell hybrids
Oenothera fruticosa—Sundrop
O. missouriensis—Ozark sundrop.
Missouri-primrose
O. odorata
O. perennis—Perennial sundrop
Paeonia suffruticosa hybrids—Tree peony
P. wittmanniana—Iran-gold peony
Papaver nudicaule—Iceland poppy
Potentilla argyrophylla—Silver-leaved
cinquefoil
Primula elatior—Oxlip
P. florindae—Tibetan primrose
P. x polyantha—Polyantha primrose
P. sikkimensis—Sikkim cowslip
Ranunculus asiaticus—Persian buttercup
Rudbeckia laciniata—Goldenglow
R. nitida
R. speciosa—Showy coneflower
R. submentosa—Sweet coneflower
Santolina chamaecyparissus—Lavender-
cotton
Scabiosa ochroleuca—Scabious. Pin-
cushion-flower
Sedum acre—Gold-moss stonecrop
S. aizoon—Aizoon stonecrop
S. reflexum—Jenny stonecrop
S. spathulifolium
Sempervivum soboliferum—Houseleek

Senecio aureus—Golden ragwort
Sisyrinchium boreale—Spokane blue-
eyed-grass
S. striatum—Argentine blue-eyed-grass
SOLIDAGO—Goldenrod
Stylophorum diphyllum—Celandine-
poppy
Thalictrum speciosissimum—Meadow-rue
Thermopsis caroliniana—Aaron's-rod
T. montana
Trollius species and varieties—Globe-
flower
UVULARIA—Bellwort. Merrybells
Viola pubescens—Downy violet

Perennials
BY MONTH OF FLOWERING: APRIL

Actaea spicata—Black baneberry. Herb
Christopher
Adonis amurensis—Pheasant eye
A. vernalis—Spring adonis
Alyssum species and hybrids—Madwort
Anemone species and varieties—Wind-
flower
Aquilegia canadensis—Columbine
Arabis species and varieties—Rock-cress
Arnica montana—Mountain-tobacco
Aubrieta species and varieties—Aubretia.
Rock-cress
Aurinia saxatilis—Basket-of-gold
Brunnera macrophylla—Heartleaf brun-
nera
Caltha palustris—Marsh-marigold
Corydalis bulbosa—Fumaria
Dentaria diphylla—Crinkleroot tooth-
wort
D. laciniata—Cutleaf toothwort
Dicentra cucullaria—Dutchman's-
breeches
D. spectabilis—Bleeding-heart
Doronicum caucasicum—Caucasian leop-
ard's-bane
D. plantagineum—Plantain leopard's-
bane
Eranthis hyemalis—Winter aconite
Euphorbia ephithymoides—Common
euphorbia
E. myrsinites—Myrtle euphorbia
Helleborus orientalis—Lenten-rose

Hemerocallis species and varieties—Daylily

Hepatica species and varieties—Liverleaf

Iberis saxatilis—Rock candytuft

Iris species and varieties

Jeffersonia diphylla—Twinleaf

Lychnis alpina—Arctic campion

Micromeria chamissonis—Yerba buena

Primula species and varieties—Primrose

Pulmonaria saccharata—Bethlehem-sage

Ranunculus repens—Creeping buttercup

Sanguinaria canadensis—Bloodroot

Senecio doronicum—Leopard's-bane

Shortia galacifolia—Oconee-bells

   S. soldanelloides–-Fringe-bell

Tiarella cordifolia—Foamflower

Trillium grandiflorum

Uvularia grandiflora—Bellwort. Merrybells

Viola cornuta—Horned violet. Tufted pansy

   V. odorata—Sweet violet

Perennials
BY MONTH OF FLOWERING: MAY

Actaea pachypoda—White baneberry

Aethionema grandiflorum—Persian stonecress

Ajuga genevensis—Geneva bugleweed

   A. reptans—Carpet bugle

Alyssum species and hybrids—Madwort

Amsonia tabernaemontana—Dogbane. Willow amsonia

Anaphalis margaritacea—Pearly everlasting

Anchusa barrelieri—Alkanet. Bugloss

Anemone species and varieties—Windflower

Anthemis tinctoria—Golden marguerite

Aquilegia species and varieties—Columbine

Arabis species and varieties—Rock-cress

Arenaria species and varieties—Sandwort

Armeria maritima—Sea-pink

Arnica montana—Mountain-tobacco

Asarum canadense—Wild-ginger

   A. shuttleworthii

Asperula hirta—Woodruff

   A. odorata—Sweet woodruff

Aubrieta species and varieties—Aubretia. Rock-cress

Baptisia australis—False indigo

Bellis perennis—English daisy

BERGENIA

Brunnera macrophylla

Callirhoe digitata—Poppy-mallow

Caltha palustris—Marsh-marigold

Camassia leichtlinii—Camass

Campanula species and varieties—Bellflower

Centaurea montana—Mountain bluet

Chrysogonum virginianum—Golden star

Claytonia virginica—Spring-beauty

Convallaria majalis—Lily-of-the-valley

Cyclamen coum

Delphinium nudicaule—Orange or red larkspur

Dentaria diphylla—Crinkleroot toothwort

   D. laciniata—Cutleaf toothwort

Dianthus species and varieties—Pink

Dicentra species—Bleeding-heart

Dodecatheon species—Shooting star

Doronicum caucasicum—Caucasian leopard's-bane

Epimedium species and varieties—Barrenwort

Euphorbia epithymoides—Common euphorbia

   E. myrsinites—Myrtle euphorbia

Galax aphylla

Geranium grandiflorum—Cranesbill

   G. sanguineum—Blood-red geranium

Helenium hoopesii—Orange sneezeweed

Hemerocallis hybrids—Daylily

Hesperis matronalis—Sweet rocket

Iberis gibraltarica—Gibraltar candytuft

   I. saxatilis—Rock candytuft

   I. sempervirens—Evergreen candytuft

Iris species and varieties

Jeffersonia diphylla—Twinleaf

Lilium species and varieties—Lily

Linaria rediviva—Perennial honesty

Linum species and varieties—Flax

Lupinus arboreus—Tree lupine

   L. polyphyllus—Washington lupine Russell hybrids

Lychnis viscaria—German catchfly
Mertensia virginica—Virginia bluebells
Micromeria chamissonis—Yerba buena
Mitella diphylla—Mitrewort. Bishop's-
cap
Myosotis alpestris—Forget-me-not
Oenothera caespitosa—Tufted evening-
primrose
Oxalis montana
Paeonia species and varieties—Peony
Phlox divaricata—Blue phlox. Wild
sweet William
Polemonium caeruleum—Jacob's-ladder.
Greek-valerian
POLYGONATUM—Solomon's seal
Potentilla nepalensis—Cinquefoil
Primula species and varieties—Primrose
Pulmonaria angustifolia—Lungwort
P. saccharata—Bethlehem-sage
Ranunculus amplexicaulis—Buttercup.
Crowfoot
R. asiaticus—Persian buttercup
Romneya coulteris—Matilija-poppy
Saxifraga species and varieties—Saxifrage
Sedum palmeri—Stonecrop
S. prealtum
Senecio doronicum—Leopard's-bane
Stylophorum diphyllum—Celandine-
poppy
Thalictrum aquilegifolium—Meadow-rue
Thymus serpyllum and varieties—Creep-
ing thyme. Mother-of-thyme
Tiarella cordifolia—Foamflower
Trillium grandiflorum
Trollius asiaticus—Globeflower
T. europaeus
Uvularia grandiflora—Bellwort
Veronica latifolia—Hungarian speedwell
Viola cornuta—Horned violet. Tufted
pansy
V. odorata—Sweet violet

Perennials
BY MONTH OF FLOWERING: JUNE

Achillea tomentosa—Woolly yarrow
Acorus calamus—Sweet-flag
Adonis vernalis—Spring adonis
Aethionema cordifolium—Stone-cress
Ajuga genevensis—Geneva bugleweed

A. reptans—Carpet bugle
Alyssum species and hybrids—Madwort
Amsonia tabernaemontana—Willow
amsonia. Dogbane
Anaphalis margaritacea—Pearly ever-
lasting
Anchusa azurea—Italian bugloss
A. barrelieri—Alkanet. Bugloss
Anemone species and varieties—Wind-
flower
Antennaria species and varieties—Ever-
lasting
Anthemis tinctoria—Golden marguerite
Aquilegia species and varieties—
Columbine
Arenaria species and varieties—Sand-
wort
Armeria maritima—Sea-pink
Arnica alpina
Aruncus sylvester—Goat's-beard
Asarum caudatum—Wild-ginger
A. shuttleworthii
Asclepias tuberosa—Butterfly-weed
Asperula odorata—Sweet woodruff
Asphodeline lutea—Asphodel
Astilbe x *arendsii*—Hybrid astilbe
A. japonica—Japanese false goat's-
beard
Baptisia australis—False indigo
Begonia evansiana—Hardy begonia
Bellis perennis—English daisy
Callirhoe digitata—Poppy-mallow
Caltha biflora
C. leptosepala
Camassia scilloides—Wild-hyacinth
Campanula species and varieties—Bell-
flower
Centaurea dealbata—Persian centaurea
C. montana—Mountain bluet
Centranthus ruber—Red valerian
Cephalaria tatarica
Cerastium tomentosum—Snow-in-
summer
Chrysanthemum coccineum—Painted
daisy
C. maximum—Shasta daisy
Chrysogonum virginianum—Golden star
Clematis, shrub varieties
Convallaria majalis—Lily-of-the-valley
Coreopsis auriculata var. *nana*—Dwarf
eared coreopsis

Corydalis nobilis—Siberian corydalis
Delphinium species and varieties
Dianthus species and varieties—Pink
Dicentra species—Bleeding-heart
Dictamnus albus—Gasplant
Digitalis grandiflora—Yellow foxglove
Dracocephalum sibericum—Dragonhead
Echinops ritro—Globe-thistle
Epilobium angustifolium—Fireweed
Epimedium species and varieties—Barrenwort
Eremurus elwesii—Elwes desert-candle
Erigeron speciosus—Oregon fleabane
Filipendula species and varieties—Meadow-sweet
Gaillardia aristata—Blanket-flower
Galax aphylla
Galega officinalis—Goat's-rue
Geranium ibericum—Iberian cranesbill
Geum chiloense—Avens
Gypsophila paniculata—Baby's-breath
Helenium hoopesii—Orange sneezeweed
Helianthemum nummularium—Sun-rose
Hemerocallis hybrids—Daylily
Hesperis matronalis—Sweet rocket
Heuchera sanguinea—Coral-bells
Hosta species and varieties—Plantain-lily
Iris species and varieties
Kniphofia uvaria—Red-hot-poker. Tritoma
Lilium species and varieties—Lily
Linum species and varieties—Flax
Lupinus polyphyllus—Washington lupine
Lychnis flos-jovis—Flower-of-Jove
    L. x haageana
    L. viscaria—German catchfly
Lysimachia clethroides—Japanese loosestrife
Macleaya cordata—Plume-poppy. Tree celandine
Matricaria tchihatchewii—Turfing daisy
Meconopsis betonicifolia—Blue-poppy
    M. cambrica—Welsh-poppy
    M. integrifolia—Yellow Chinese-poppy
    M. napaulensis—Satin-poppy
Mitella diphylla—Mitrewort. Bishop's-cap
Myosotis scorpioides—Forget-me-not
Nepeta cataria—Catnip. Catmint

Oenothera caespitosa—Tufted evening-primrose
    O. fruticosa—Sundrop
    O. missouriensis
    O. perennis
Oxalis acetosella—Wood-sorrel
Paeonia species and varieties—Peony
Papaver nudicaule—Iceland poppy
    P. orientale—Oriental poppy
Penstemon species and varieties, including North Platte hybrids—Beardtongue
Phlox x arendsii
    P. divaricata—Blue phlox
Polemonium caeruleum—Jacob's-ladder. Greek-valerian
Potentilla argyrophylla—Silver-leaved cinquefoil
    P. fruticosa
    P. nepalensis
Primula species and varieties—Primrose
Ranunculus amplexicaulis—Buttercup. Crowfoot
    R. asiaticus—Persian buttercup
Romneya coulteri—Matilija-poppy
Saxifraga species and varieties—Saxifrage
Sedum prealtum—Stonecrop
Sidalcea candida—Prairie-mallow
    S. malvaeflora—Checkerbloom. Wild-hollyhock
Silene maritima—Sea campion
Sisyrinchium boreale—Spokane blue-eyed-grass
    S. striatum
Steironema ciliatum—Fringed loosestrife
Stylophorum diphyllum—Celandine-poppy
Thalictrum aquilegifolium—Meadow-rue
Thermopsis caroliniana—Aaron's-rod
Thymus serpyllum and varieties—Creeping thyme. Mother-of-thyme
Tiarella cordifolia—Foamflower
Tradescantia virginiana and varieties—Virginia spiderwort
Trollius europaevs—Globeflower
    T. ledebouri
Valeriana officinalis—Valerian. Garden-heliotrope
Verbena canadensis—Rose vervain

Veronica incana—Speedwell
V. latifolia—Hungarian speedwell
V. spicata
Viola cornuta—Horned violet. Tufted
pansy
Yucca filamentosa—Adam's-needle
Y. flaccida

Perennials
BY MONTH OF FLOWERING: JULY

Acanthus mollis—Bear's-breech
Achillea species and hybrids—Yarrow
Aconitum napellus—Aconite. Monks-
hood
A. vulparia
Adenophora potaninii—Lady-bell
Adonis chrysocyathus—Pheasant eye
A. pyrenaica—Pyrenees adonis
Althaea rosea—Hollyhock
Alyssum species and hybrids—Madwort
Anchusa azurea—European pasque-
flower
Anthemis sancti-johannis—St. John's
chamomile
A. tinctoria—Golden marguerite
Aquilegia species and varieties—
Columbine
Arnica chamissonis
Artemisia lactiflora—White mugwort
Asclepias tuberosa—Butterfly-weed
Asphodeline lutea—Asphodel
Aster x frikartii
Astilbe x arendsii—Hybrid astilbe
A. japonica—Japanese false goat's-
beard
Baptisia tinctoria—False indigo
Begonia evansiana—Hardy begonia
Belamcanda chinensis—Blackberry-lily
BOLTONIA—False starwort
Callirhoe digitata—Poppy-mallow
Caltha biflora
C. leptosepala
Campanula species and varieties—Bell-
flower
Cassia marilandica—Wild senna
Catananche caerulea—Blue cupidone
Centaurea dealbata—Persian centaurea
C. montana—Mountain bluet
Centranthus ruber—Red valerian

Cephalaria tatarica
Chelone lyonii—Pink turtle-head
Chrysanthemum coccineum
C. maximum—Shasta daisy
Chrysogonum virginianum—Golden star
Chrysopsis bakeri—Baker's golden-aster
Cimicifuga racemosa—Black snakeroot.
Cohosh bugbane
Clematis recta
Coreopsis species and varieties—Tick-
seed
Cosmos diversifolius—Black cosmos
Cyclamen europaeum
Cynoglossum grande—Hound's-tongue
Delphinium species and varieties
Dianthus species and varieties—Pink
Dicentra eximia—Fringed bleeding-heart
Dictamnus albus—Gasplant
Digitalis grandiflora—Yellow foxglove
Dracocephalum sibericum—Dragonhead
Echinacea purpurea—Purple coneflower
Echinops ritro—Globe-thistle
Epilobium angustifolium—Fireweed
Eremurus species and varieties—Desert-
candle
Erigeron speciosus—Oregon fleabane
Eryngium alpinum—Alpine sea-holly
Euphorbia corollata—Flowering spurge
Filipendula species and varieties—
Meadow-sweet
Gaillardia aristata—Blanket flower
Galax aphylla
Galega officinalis—Goat's-rue
Geranium grandiflorum—Cranesbill
G. sanguineum—Blood-red geranium
Geum chiloense—Chile avens
Gypsophila paniculata—Baby's-breath
Helenium hoopesii—Orange sneezeweed
Helianthemum nummularium—Sun-rose
Heliopsis species and varieties
Hemerocallis hybrids—Daylily
Hesperis matronalis—Sweet rocket
Heuchera sanguinea—Coral-bells
Hosta species and varieties—Plantain-lily
Hunnemannia fumariaefolia—Mexican
golden-cup. Mexican tulip-poppy
Hypericum species and varieties—St.
John's-wort
Incarvillea delavayi—Hardy-gloxinia
I. grandiflora—Bigflower incarvillea
Inula helenium—Elecampane

Iris species and varieties
Kniphofia uvaria—Red-hot-poker
Lathyrus species and varieties
Lavandula officinalis—English lavender
  L. stoechas—French lavender
Lavatera assurgentiflora—Tree-mallow
Ligularia species and varieties—Golden
  ray
Lilium species and varieties—Lily
Limonium latifolium—Sea-lavender
Linaria dalmatica—Dalmatian toadflax
Linum species and varieties—Flax
Lupinus polyphyllus—Washington lupine
  Russell hybrids
Lychnis chalcedonica—Maltese-cross
  L. flos-cuculi—Cuckoo flower
Lysimachia clethroides
Lythrum salicaria—Purple loosestrife
Macleaya cordata—Plume-poppy
Malva moschata—Musk mallow
Matricaria tchihatchewii—Turfing daisy
Meconopsis betonicifolia—Blue-poppy
Micromeria chamissonis—Yerba buena
  M. rupestris
Monarda didyma—Bee-balm
Myosotis scorpioides var. *semperflorens*—
  Forget-me-not
Nepeta cataria—Catnip. Catmint
Oenothera fruticosa—Sundrop
  O. missouriensis—Evening-primrose
  O. perennis
Ophiopogon jaburan—Jaburan
Oxalis bowiei
  O. montana
Papaver nudicaule—Iceland poppy
Penstemon species and varieties, includ-
  ing North Platte hybrids—Beard-
  tongue
Phlox paniculata varieties—Summer gar-
  den phlox
Physostegia virginiana—False dragonhead.
  Obedient plant
Platycodon grandiflorum—Balloon-flower
Potentilla argyrophylla—Silver-leaved
  cinquefoil
  P. fruticosa
Primula japonica—Japanese primrose
Rhexia mariana—Meadow-beauty
  R. virginica
Romneya coulteri—Matilija-poppy. Tree-

poppy
Saxifraga aizoon—Saxifrage
Scabiosa caucasica—Scabious. Mourning
  bride
Scutellaria alpina—Skullcap
Sedum aizoon—Stonecrop
  S. a. var. *aurantiacum*
Sidalcea candida—Prairie-mallow
  S. malvaeflora—Checkerbloom. Wild-
  hollyhock
Silene maritima—Sea campion
Silphium laciniatum—Compass plant
Solidago canadensis and varieties—
  Goldenrod
Stachys olympica—Lamb's-ears
Steironema ciliatum—Fringed loosestrife
Tanacetum vulgare var. *crispum*—Tansy
Teucrium chamaedrys—Germander
Thalictrum aquilegifolium—Meadow-rue
  T. rochebrunianum—Lavender-mist
Thermopsis caroliniana—Aaron's-rod
Thymus serpyllum and varieties—Creep-
  ing thyme. Mother-of-thyme
Tiarella cordifolia—Foamflower
Tradescantia virginiana and varieties—
  Virginia spiderwort
Trollius europaeus—Globeflower
  T. ledebouri
Tunica saxifraga—Tunic-flower
Valeriana officinalis—Valerian. Garden-
  heliotrope
Verbascum olympicum—Olympian mul-
  lein
Verbena canadensis—Rose vervain
Veronica austriaca—Speedwell
  V. incana
  V. spicata
Viola cornuta—Horned violet. Tufted
  pansy
Yucca filamentosa—Adam's-needle
  Y. flaccida

Perennials
BY MONTH OF FLOWERING:
AUGUST

Acanthus mollis—Bear's-breech
Achillea species and hybrids—Yarrow
Aconitum henryi—Aconite. Monkshood
  A. napellus

Adenophora potaninii—Lady-bell
Althaea rosea—Hollyhock
Alyssum species and varieties—Madwort
Anaphalis nubegina
Anchusa azurea—Italian alkanet
Anemone hupehensis—Dwarf Japanese
    anemone
Anthemis sancti-johannis—St. John's
    chamomile
Aquilegia species and varieties—Colum-
    bine
Arnica chamissonis
    A. sachalinensis
Artemisia lactiflora—White mugwort
    A. schmidtiana var. *nana*—Silver-
      mound
    A. stelleriana—Beach wormwood
Asclepias tuberosa—Butterfly-weed
Aster species and varieties
Begonia evansiana—Hardy begonia
Belamcanda chinensis—Blackberry-lily
BOLTONIA—False starwort
Caltha biflora
    C. leptosepala
Campanula species and varieties—Bell-
    flower
Cassia marilandica—Wild senna
Catananche caerulea—Blue cupidone
Centaurea dealbata—Persian centaurea
    C. montana—Mountain bluet
Cephalaria tatarica
Ceratostigma plumbaginoides—Plumbago
Chelone lyonii—Pink turtle-head
Chrysanthemum maximum
    C. morifolium—Florists' chrysanthe-
      mum
Chrysopsis species and varieties—Golden-
    aster
Cimicifuga racemosa—Black snakeroot.
    Cohosh bugbane
Clematis, shrub varieties
Coreopsis auriculata var. *nana*—Dwarf-
    eared coreopsis
    C. lanceolata—Lance coreopsis
    C. verticillata—Thread-leaved coreopsis
Cosmos diversifolius—Black cosmos
Cyclamen europaeum
Cynoglossum grande—Hound's-tongue
Delphinium species and varieties
Dianthus barbatus—Sweet William

Dicentra eximia—Fringed bleeding-heart
Echinacea purpurea—Purple coneflower
Echinops ritro—Globe-thistle
Eryngium alpinum—Alpine sea-holly
Eupatorium purpureum—Joe-pyeweed
Euphorbia corollata—Flowering spurge
Gaillardia aristata—Blanket-flower
Galega officinalis—Goat's-rue
Gentiana species—Gentian
Gypsophila paniculata—Baby's-breath
    G. repens var. *rosea*
Helenium autumnale—Yellow-star
    H. bigelovii—Bigelow sneezeweed
Helianthus species and varieties—Sun-
    flower
Heliopsis species and varieties
Hemerocallis hybrids—Daylily
Hibiscus moscheutos—Swamp-mallow
Hosta species and varieties—Plantain-lily
Hunnemannia fumariaefolia—Mexican
    golden-cup. Mexican tulip-poppy
Hypericum species and varieties—St.
    John's-wort
Inula helenium—Elecampane
Iris species and varieties
Lathyrus species and varieties
Lavandula officinalis—English lavender
    L. stoechas—French lavender
Liatris species and varieties—Gayfeather
Ligularia species and varieties—Golden
    ray
Lilium species and varieties—Lily
Limonium latifolium—Sea-lavender
    L. sinuatum
Linaria dalmatica—Dalmatian toadflax
Linum species and varieties—Flax
Lobelia cardinalis—Cardinal flower. Scar-
    let lobelia
    L. siphilitica—Blue or great lobelia
Lythrum salicaria—Purple loosestrife
Malva moschata—Musk mallow
Matricaria tchihatchewii—Turfing daisy
Micromeria chamissonis—Yerba buena
Monarda didyma—Bee-balm
Myosotis scorpioides var. *semperflorens*—
    Forget-me-not
Oenothera perennis—Sundrop
    O. speciosa
Ophiopogon jaburan—Jaburan
Oxalis bowiei

O. montana
Papaver nudicaule—Iceland poppy
Phlox paniculata varieties—Summer garden phlox
Physalis alkekengi—Chinese lantern plant. Winter-cherry
Physostegia virginiana
Platycodon grandiflorum—Balloon-flower
Polygonum affine—Knotweed
P. amplexicaule
Potentilla fruticosa—Cinquefoil
Rhexia mariana—Meadow-beauty
R. virginica
Romneya coulteri—Matilija-poppy
Salvia farinacea—Mealycup sage
S. patens—Gentian sage. Blue sage
S. pratensis—Meadow sage
Sanguisorba obtusa—Japanese bottle-brush flower
Scabiosa caucasica—Mourning bride
Scutellaria alpina—Skullcap
Sedum spectabile—Showy sedum
S. telephium—Stonecrop
Silphium laciniatum—Compass plant
Solidago canadensis and varieties—Goldenrod
Stachys olympica—Lamb's-ears
Steironema ciliatum—Fringed loosestrife
Stokesia laevis—Stokes'-aster
Tanacetum vulgare var. crispum—Tansy
Teucrium chamaedrys—Germander
Thalictrum dipterocarpum—Meadow-rue
T. rochebrunianum—Lavender-mist
Tradescantia virginiana—Virginia spider-wort
Trollius europaeus—Globeflower
T. ledebouri
Tunica saxifraga—Tunic-flower
Verbascum olympicum—Olympian mullein
Verbena canadensis—Rose vervain
Veronica longifolia—Speedwell
V. spicata
Viola cornuta—Horned violet. Tufted pansy

Perennials
BY MONTH OF FLOWERING: SEPTEMBER

Achillea millefolium var. rosea—Pink yarrow
Aconitum carmichaellii—Azure monks-hood
A. henryi
Anemone hupehensis—Dwarf Japanese anemone
Asclepias tuberosa—Butterfly-weed
Aster species and varieties
Artemisia lactiflora—White mugwort
A. schmidtiana var. nana—Silver-mound artemisia
A. stelleriana—Beach wormwood
Begonia evansiana—Hardy begonia
Belamcanda flabellata
Bellis perennis—English daisy
BOLTONIA—False starwort
Campanula carpatica—Carpathian bellflower
Centaurea dealbata—Persian centaurea
C. montana—Mountain bluet
Ceratostigma plumbaginoides—Plumbago
Chrysanthemum maximum—Shasta daisy
C. morifolium—Florists' chrysanthemum
Chrysopsis species and varieties—Golden-aster
Coreopsis grandiflora—Bigflower coreopsis
Cosmos diversifolius—Black cosmos
Cyclamen europaeum
C. neapolitanum
Cynoglossum grande—Hound's-tongue
Eupatorium coelestinum—Mistflower eupatorium
Dicentra eximia—Fringed bleeding-heart
Gentiana species—Gentian
Gypsophila repens var. rosea—Creeping baby's-breath
Helenium autumnale—Yellow-star
H. bigelovii—Bigelow sneezeweed
Helianthus species and varieties—Sunflower
Hemerocallis hybrids—Daylily
Heuchera sanguinea—Coral-bells
Hibiscus moscheutos—Swamp-mallow

Hosta plantaginea—Fragrant plantain-lily
Iris species and varieties
Liatris species and varieties—Gayfeather
Lilium species and varieties—Lily
Lobelia cardinalis—Cardinal flower.
    Scarlet lobelia
    L. siphilitica—Blue lobelia. Great
    lobelia
LYCHNIS
Lythrum salicaria—Purple loosestrife
Monarda didyma—Bee-balm
Oenothera speciosa—Sundrop
Oxalis bowieiana
    O. melanosticta
Phlox paniculata varieties—Summer
    garden phlox
Polygonum affine—Knotweed
Potentilla fruticosa—Cinquefoil
Salvia farinacea—Mealycup sage
Scabiosa caucasica—Scabious. Mourning
    bride
Sedum sieboldii—Stonecrop
    S. spectabile
Silphium laciniatum—Compass plant
Solidago canadensis and varieties—
    Goldenrod
Stachys olympica—Lamb's-ears
Stokesia laevis—Stokes'-aster
Thalictrum dipterocarpum—Meadow-rue
    T. rochebrunianum—Lavender-mist
Trollius asiaticus—Globeflower
Viola cornuta—Horned violet. Tufted
    pansy

Perennials
THAT TOLERATE DAMP GROUND

ACORUS—Sweet-flag
ACONITUM—Monkshood
ACTAEA—Baneberry. Cohosh
AJUGA—Bugleweed
ALETRIS—Star-grass
ANEMONE—Windflower
Aruncus sylvester—Goat's-beard
ASTILBE—False goat's-beard
CALTHA—Marsh-marigold
Campanula persicifolia—Peach-leaved
    bellflower
CHELONE—Turtlehead

CIMICIFUGA—Bugbane
CLAYTONIA—Spring-beauty
CLINTONIA
Convallaria majalis—Lily-of-the-valley
DENTARIA—Toothwort
Digitalis grandiflora—Yellow foxglove
    D. lanata—Grecian foxglove
Dracocephalum sibiricum—Dragonhead
Epilobium angustifolium—Fireweed
Eupatorium, hardy species—Thorough-
    wort
Filipendula purpurea—Meadow-sweet
    F. rubra—Queen-of-the-prairie
Galax aphylla
Gentiana species and varieties—Gentian
Helleborus niger—Christmas-rose
    H. orientalis—Lenten-rose
Hemerocallis varieties—Daylily
HEUCHERA—Alum-root. Coral-bells
Hibiscus moscheutos—Swamp-mallow
HOSTA—Plantain-lily
Iris, beardless species and varieties
LIGULARIA—Golden-ray
Lobelia cardinalis—Cardinal flower
    L. siphilitica—Blue lobelia. Great
    lobelia
Lysimachia clethroides—Japanese loose-
    strife
    L. nummularia—Moneywort. Creeping
    Jenny
Lythrum alatum—Loosestrife
Meconopsis species and varieties
MERTENSIA—Bluebells
Myosotis scorpioides—Forget-me-not
OPHIOPOGON—Lily-turf
Physostegia virginiana—False dragon-
    head. Obedient plant
Primula species and varieties—Primrose
Ranunculus species and varieties—
    Buttercup. Crowfoot
Rhexia virginica—Meadow-beauty
Sanguinaria canadensis—Bloodroot
Smilacina racemosa—False Solomon's-
    seal
Steironema ciliatum—Fringed loosestrife
Stylophorum diphyllum—Celandine-
    poppy
THALICTRUM—Meadow-rue
TRILLIUM
TROLLIUS—Globeflower
UVULARIA—Bellwort

VANCOUVERIA
VINCA—Periwinkle
Viola species and varieties—Violet

Perennials
THAT TOLERATE DRY GROUND

ACHILLEA—Yarrow. Milfoil
AETHIONEMA—Stone-cress
ALYSSUM—Madwort
AMSONIA
ANAPHALIS—Pearly everlasting
Anchusa azurea—Italian alkanet. Italian
   bugloss
ANTHEMIS—Chamomile
Aquilegia species and varieties—Colum-
   bine
ARABIS—Rock-cress
ARMERIA—Thrift
Artemisia species and varieties—Worm-
   wood
Asclepias tuberosa—Butterfly-weed
ASPHODELINE—Asphodel
Aster laevis—Michaelmas daisy
   A. linariifolius—Savoryleaf aster
Aurinia saxatilis—Basket-of-gold
BAPTISIA—False indigo
BELAMCANDA—Blackberry-lily
Bergenia species and varieties
BUPHTHALMUM—Oxeye
Callirhoe species and varieties—Poppy-
   mallow
Campanula latifolia—Great bellflower
Catananche caerulea—Blue cupidone
Centaurea delabata—Persian centaurea
Centranthus ruber—Red valerian
CEPHALARIA
Cerastium tomentosum—Snow-in-
   summer
Coreopsis grandiflora—Bigflower core-
   opsis
Dianthus gratianopolitanus—Cheddar
   pink
Dictamnus albus—Gasplant
DORONICUM—Leopard's-bane
EPIMEDIUM—Barrenwort
Eryngium pulchellum—Blister-cress
Euphorbia epithymoides—Cushion
   euphorbia
   E. mammillaris

E. polygona
Gaillardia aristata—Blanket-flower
Geranium species and varieties—Cranes-
   bill
Gypsophila paniculata—Baby's-breath
Helianthus maximillianii—Sunflower
   H. mollis
HELIOPSIS
Hemerocallis varieties—Daylily
Hypoxis hirsuta—Star-grass
INULA—Elecampane
Ipomoea leptophylla—Bush morning-
   glory
Iris, bearded species and varieties
Kniphofia uvaria—Tritoma. Red-hot-
   poker
LAVANDULA—Lavender
LIATRIS—Blazing-star. Gayfeather
LIMONIUM—Sea-lavender. Statice
Linum species and varieties—Flax
Lupinus species and varieties—Lupine
Lythrum species and varieties—Loose-
   strife
Nepeta hederacea—Ground-ivy. Gill-
   over-the-ground
Oenothera missouriensis—Evening-
   primrose
   O. speciosa var. *rosea*
Origanum vulgare—Pot-marjoram
   (oregano)
Papaver nudicaule—Iceland poppy
   P. orientale—Oriental poppy
Penstemon species and varieties—Beard-
   tongue
Phlox subulata—Ground-pink. Moss
   phlox
Potentilla species and varieties—Cinque-
   foil
PRUNELLA—Heal all. Selfheal
Romneya coulteri—Matilija-poppy
Rudbeckia species and varieties—Cone-
   flower
Satureja montana—Winter savory
SEDUM—Stonecrop
SEMPERVIVUM—Hen-and-chickens.
   Houseleek
Silene maritima—Sea campion
   S. virginica—Fire-pink. Catchfly
Solidago species and varieties—Golden-
   rod
Stokesia laevis—Stokes'-aster

Thermopsis caroliniana—Aaron's-rod
Veronica spicata—Spike speedwell
Yucca filamentosa—Adam's-needle
ZAUSCHNERIA

Perennials
FOR DRIED ARRANGEMENTS

ACHILLEA—Yarrow. Milfoil
Allium karataviense—Turkestan onion
Ammobium alatum—Winged everlasting
ANAPHALIS—Pearly everlasting
ANTENNARIA—Pussy-toes. Everlasting
Artemisia albula—Silver king
ASTILBE—False goat's-beard
Atriplex hymenelytra—Desert-holly
BAPTISIA—False indigo
Catananche caerulea—Blue cupidone
CELASTRUS—Bittersweet
Echinops ritro—Globe-thistle
ERYNGIUM—Eryngo. Sea-holly
Eupatorium perfoliatum—Boneset
  E. purpureum—Joe-pyeweed
Gypsophila paniculata—Baby's-breath
Helichrysum species and varieties—
  Everlasting
HELIPTERUM—Everlasting. Immortelle
Lavandula officinalis—English lavender
LIATRIS—Gayfeather. Blazing-star
Limonium species and varieties—Sea-
  lavender. Statice
Lunaria rediviva—Perennial honesty
SOLIDAGO—Goldenrod
Stachys olympica—Lamb's-ears
Typha latifolia—Cattail

Perennials
WITH FRAGRANT FLOWERS

Acorus calamus—Sweet-flag
Anthemis nobilis—Chamomile
Aponogeton distachyus—Water-hawthorn
Aquilegia chrysantha—Golden-spurred
  columbine
ARABIS—Rock-cress
Asperula odorata—Sweet woodruff
Asphodeline lutea—Asphodel
Centranthus ruber—Red valerian
Cheiranthus cheiri—Wallflower
Chrysanthemum balsamita—Costmary
Convallaria majalis—Lily-of-the-valley

Cyclamen europaeum—European cycla-
  men
Dianthus species and varieties—Pink.
  Carnation
Dicentra canadensis—Squirrel-corn
Dictamnus albus—Gasplant
Epigaea repens—Trailing arbutus
Hemerocallis dumortieri—Early daylily
  H. flava—Lemon-lily
  H. thunbergii
Hesperis matronalis—Dame's rocket.
  Sweet rocket
Hosta plantaginea—Fragrant plantain-lily
Iris, bearded and German species and
  hybrids
Lavandula officinalis—English lavender
Leucocrinum montanum—Star-lily. Sand-
  lily
Lilium species and varieties—Lily
Lychnis alba—Evening campion
Mirabilis longiflora—Sweet four-o'clock
Monarda didyma—Bee-balm
  M. pectinata—Lemon-mint
Nymphaea lotus—White-lotus-of-Egypt
  N. odorata—Pond-lily
Oenothera caespitosa—Tufted evening-
  primrose
Paeonia officinalis hybrids—Peony
Phlox species and varieties
Primula bulleyana—Primrose
  P. chionantha—Snowblossom primrose
  P. veris—Cowslip
Romneya coulteri—Matilija-poppy. Tree-
  poppy
Saxifraga cotyledon—Saxifrage
Trillium ovatum
  T. vaseyi—Sweet trillium
Valeriana officinalis—Common valerian.
  Garden-heliotrope
Verbena teucrioides—Vervain
Viola blanda—Sweet white violet
  V. cornuta—Horned violet. Tufted
  pansy
  V. odorata—Sweet violet
YUCCA

Perennials
THAT FLOWER IN LIGHT SHADE

ACONITUM—Monkshood. Aconite
ACTAEA—Baneberry. Cohosh
AJUGA—Bugleweed
AMSONIA
ANEMONE—Windflower
AQUILEGIA—Columbine
Aruncus sylvester—Goat's-beard
ASPERULA—Woodruff
ASTER—Michaelmas daisy
ASTILBE—False goat's-beard
Begonia evansiana—Hardy begonia
Brunnera macrophylla
CALTHA—Marsh-marigold
Campanula elatines var. *garganica*—
    Bellflower
   C. lactiflora—Milky bellflower
Cephalaria tatarica
CHELONE—Turtlehead
CIMICIFUGA—Bugbane
CLAYTONIA—Spring-beauty
CLINTONIA
Convallaria majalis—Lily-of-the-valley
Corydalis bulbosa
   C. lutea—Yellow corydalis
Cynoglossum grande—Hound's-tongue
DENTARIA—Toothwort
DICENTRA—Bleeding-heart
Dictamnus albus—Gasplant
Digitalis grandiflora—Yellow foxglove
   D. lanata—Grecian foxglove
Dodecatheon meadia—Common shoot-
   ing-star
Doronicum caucasicum—Caucasian
   leopard's-bane
Dracocephalum sibiricum—Dragonhead
EPIMEDIUM—Barrenwort
FILIPENDULA—Meadow-sweet
Galax aphylla
Gentiana species and varieties—Gentian
Geranium species and varieties—Cranes-
   bill
Helleborus niger—Christmas-rose
   H. orientalis—Lenten-rose
HEMEROCALLIS—Daylily
HEPATICA—Liverleaf
HEUCHERA—Alum-root. Coral-bells
Hibiscus moscheutos—Swamp-mallow
HOSTA—Plantain-lily

Iris cristata—Crested dwarf iris
Jeffersonia diphylla—Twinleaf
LIGULARIA—Golden-ray
Lobelia cardinalis—Cardinal flower
Lunaria rediviva—Perennial honesty
Lysimachia nummularia—Moneywort.
   Creeping Jenny
MERTENSIA—Bluebells
MITELLA
Myosotis scorpioides—Forget-me-not
Oenothera fruticosa—Sundrop
OPHIOPOGON—Lily-turf
Phlox species and varieties
Physostegia virginiana—False dragonhead.
   Obedient plant
Polemonium species
Polygonatum species—Solomon's seal
Primula species and varieties—Primrose
PRUNELLA—Heal-all. Selfheal
PULMONARIA—Lungwort
Sanguinaria canadensis—Bloodroot
Saxifraga species and varieties—Saxifrage
Shortia galacifolia—Oconee-bells
Smilacina racemosa—False Solomon's-seal
Stylophorum diphyllum—Celandine-
   poppy
THALICTRUM—Meadow-rue
Tiarella cordifolia—Foamflower
TRILLIUM
TROLLIUS—Globeflower
UVULARIA—Bellwort. Merrybells
VANCOUVERIA
Veronica species and varieties—Speedwell
VINCA—Periwinkle
Viola species and varieties—Violet

Rock-garden Plants

Rock Plants
BY FLOWERING PERIOD: EARLY SPRING

Adonis amurensis—Pheasant-eye
   A. vernalis—Spring adonis
Alyssum species and varieties—Madwort
Anemone species and varieties—Wind-
   flower

Arabis albida—Wall rock-cress
AUBRIETA—Aubretia
BELLIS—English daisy
CHRYSOGONUM—Golden-star
Claytonia species—Spring-beauty
Corydalis species—Fumaria
Dicentra species—Bleeding-heart
Douglasia species—Rock-primrose
DRABA
Epigaea repens—Trailing arbutus
Erica carnea—Spring heath
GLOBULARIA
HEPATICA—Liverleaf
Iris species and varieties
Lychnis alpina—Arctic campion
Maianthemum canadense—Wild-lily-of
the-valley
Myosotis alpestris—Forget-me-not
Ranunculus species—Buttercup
Raoulia species
Rhododendron, dwarf species and varieties
Saxifraga species and varieties—Saxifrage

Rock Plants
BY FLOWERING PERIOD: MID-SPRING

Alyssum species and varieties—Madwort
ANDROMEDA—Bog-rosemary
Anemone species and varieties—Wind-
flower
ANEMONELLA—Rue-anemone
ARABIS—Rock-cress
Asperula species—Woodruff
AUBRIETA—Aubretia
Aurinia saxatilis—Basket-of-gold. Golden
tuft
BERGENIA
Cheiranthus cheiri—Wallflower
Chiogenes hispidula—Creeping snowberry
CHRYSOGONUM—Golden-star
CLINTONIA
Convallaria majalis—Lily-of-the-valley
Coptis species—Goldthread
Corydalis species—Fumaria
Cyclamen coum
Dalibarda repens—Robin-run-away
Daphne species
DENTARIA—Toothwort
Dicentra species—Bleeding-heart

Douglasia species—Rock-primrose
DRABA
DRYAS—Mountain avens
Epigaea repens—Trailing arbutus
ERYSIMUM
Erythronium species—Dogtooth-violet
Gaylussacia brachycera—Box huckleberry
Gentiana species—Gentian
HYPOXIS—Star-grass
Iris species and varieties
Isopyrum biternatum—False anemone
Kalmiopsis leachiana
Lamium amplexicaule—Henbit dead nettle
Lychnis alpina—Arctic campion
Mertensia species—Bluebells
Myosotis alpestris—Forget-me-not
Phlox species and varieties
Polygonatum species—Solomon's seal
Primula species and varieties—Primrose
Pulmonaria species—Lungwort
Ranunculus species—Buttercup
Raoulia species
Rhododendron, dwarf species and varieties
Sanguinaria canadensis—Bloodroot
Saxifraga species and varieties—Saxifrage
Sisyrinchium species and varieties—Blue-
eyed-grass
Tiarella cordifolia—Foamflower
Vaccinium vitis-idaea—Cowberry

Rock Plants
BY FLOWERING PERIOD: LATE SPRING

Achillea species and varieties—Milfoil.
Yarrow
AETHIONEMA—Stone-cress
AJUGA—Bugleweed
Allium species and varieties—Ornamental
onion
Alyssum species and varieties—Madwort
ANDROMEDA
Androsace species and varieties—Rock-
jasmine
Anemone species and varieties—Wind-
flower
ANTENNARIA—Pussy-toes
Aquilegia species and varieties—Colum-
bine
ARABIS—Rock-cress

Arctostaphylos uva-ursi—Bearberry
ARENARIA—Sandwort
ARMERIA—Thrift
Arnica montana—Mountain-tobacco
ASARUM—Wild-ginger
Asperula species—Woodruff
Astilbe species and varieties—False goat's-
beard
AUBRIETA—Aubretia
Bellis perennis—English daisy
Berberis verruculosa—Barberry
Campanula species and varieties—Bell-
flower
Carlina acaulis
Cassiope mertensiana
Cerastium tomentosum—Snow-in-summer
CHAMAEDAPHNE—Leather-leaf
CHRYSOGONUM—Golden-star
Coptis species—Goldthread
Cornus canadensis—Bunchberry dogwood
Corydalis species—Fumaria
Cotoneaster species
Cytisus x *kewensis*—Kew broom
  C. purpureus—Purple broom
Daphne species
Dianthus species—Pink
Dicentra species—Bleeding-heart
Dodecatheon meadia—Shooting-star
Douglasia species—Rock-primrose
DRYAS—Mountain avens
Empetrum nigrum—Black crowberry
EPIMEDIUM—Barrenwort
ERODIUM—Heronsbill
ERYSIMUM
Galax aphylla
GAULTHERIA
Gaylussacia brachycera—Box huckleberry
Genista pilosa—Silky-leaf woadwaxen
Gentiana species—Gentian
Geranium species—Cranesbill
GEUM—Avens
Gypsophila species—Baby's-breath
HABERLEA
HELIANTHEMUM—Sun-rose
Heuchera species—Alum-root
HOUSTONIA—Bluets
Iberis, perennial species—Candytuft
Iris species and varieties
Lamium amplexicaule—Henbit dead nettle
LEIOPHYLLUM—Sand-myrtle

Leucothoe keiskei
LEWISIA
Mahonia nervosa
  M. repens
MAZUS
Meconopsis quintuplenervia—Harebell-
poppy
Mertensia species—Bluebells
MITCHELLA—Partridge-berry. Twin-
berry
MITELLA—Mitrewort. Bishop's-cap
Myosotis alpestris—Forget-me-not
Omphalodes species—Navelwort
PERNETTYA
Phlox species and varieties
Phyllodoce empetriformis
Pieris nana—Kamchatka pieris
Polemonium reptans—Creeping pole-
monium
Primula species and varieties—Primrose
Pulmonaria species—Lungwort
Ramonda species
Ranunculus species—Buttercup
Rhododendron, dwarf species and varieties
Rosa, miniature species and varieties—
Rose
Saponaria ocymoides—Soapwort
Saxifraga species and varieties—Saxifrage
Sedum species and varieties—Stonecrop
Shortia galacifolia—Oconee-bells
Silene species and varieties—Catchfly.
Campion
Sisyrinchium species and varieties—Blue-
eyed-grass
SMILACINA—False Solomon's-seal
Thymus species and varieties—Thyme
Tiarella cordifolia—Foamflower
Vaccinium vitis-idaea—Cowberry
Viola species and varieties—Violet. Tufted
pansy
Waldsteinia fragarioides—Barren-straw-
berry

Rock Plants
BY FLOWERING PERIOD: SUMMER

ABRONIA—Sand-verbena
ACAENA

ACANTHOLIMON—Prickly-thrift
Achillea species and varieties—Milfoil. Yarrow
AETHIONEMA—Stone-cress
AJUGA—Bugleweed
Allium species and varieties—Ornamental onion
Androsace species and varieties—Rock-jasmine
Aquilegia species and varieties—Columbine
Arnica species
Aster, dwarf species and varieties
Astilbe species and varieties—False goat's-beard
BELLIUM—False daisy
Borago laxiflora—Borage
BRUCKENTHALIA—Spike-heath
CALANDRINIA—Rock-purslane
Calceolaria polyrrhiza—Slipperwort
Callirhoe involucrata—Poppy-mallow
CALLUNA—Heather
Campanula species and varieties—Bellflower
CASSIOPE
Ceratostigma plumbaginoides—Leadwort. Plumbago
CHRYSOGONUM—Golden-star
CISTUS—Rock-rose
Coptis species—Goldthread
Corydalis species—Fumaria
Cytisus albus—Portuguese broom
Daboecia cantabrica—Irish-heath
Dianthus species—Pink
Dicentra eximia—Fringed bleeding-heart
Dorotheanthus gramineus
Eriogonum species
ERODIUM—Heronsbill
ERYNGIUM—Eryngo. Sea-holly
ESCHSCHOLTZIA
Euphorbia myrsinites—Myrtle euphorbia
Gaillardia aristata cv. 'Goblin'—Dwarf blanket-flower
Galax aphylla
GALIUM—Bedstraw
GAULTHERIA
Genista pilosa—Silky-leaf woadwaxen
Gentiana species—Gentian

Geranium species—Cranesbill
Geum species—Avens
Gilia species
Gypsophila species—Baby's-breath
HELIANTHEMUM—Sun-rose
HEUCHERA—Alum-root. Coral-bells
HORMINUM
Hosta species and varieties—Plantain-lily. Funkia
Hypericum species and varieties—St. John's-wort
Ionopsidium acaule—Diamond-flower
JASIONE
Lavandula officinalis—English lavender
LAYIA
Leontopodium alpinum—Edelweiss
LEWISIA
LIMONIUM—Sea-lavender. Statice
Linaria species and varieties—Toadflax
Linnaea borealis—Twinflower
Linum species—Flax
Lithospermum diffusum—Gromwell
LOISELEURIA—Alpine-azalea
Lychnis flos-jovis—Flower-of-Jove
Lysimachia nummularia—Moneywort
Malcomia maritima—Virginia-stock
MAZUS
Mentha requienii—Corsican mint
Micromeria species
Mimulus primuloides—Monkey-flower
Moltkia petraea
Nepeta mussinii
Nierembergia species—Cup-flower
NOLANA—Chilean-bellflower
Oenothera species and varieties—Evening-primrose
Onosma species—Golden drops
Ophiopogon species and varieties—Lily-turf
Origanum vulgare—Wild-marjoram. Pot-marjoram. Oregano
OURISIA
Oxalis, hardy species
Papaver alpinum—Alpine poppy
Penstemon species—Beard-tongue
Phacelia campanularia
Phlox species and varieties
Phyla nodiflora—Creeping-lippia
Phyllodoce caerulea

P. glanduliflora
PHYTEUMA—Horned rampion
Platycodon, dwarf varieties—Balloon-
flower
PLATYSTEMON—Cream-cups
Polemonium richardsonii
Portulaca grandiflora—Rose-moss
Potentilla species—Cinquefoil
PRUNELLA—Heal-all. Selfheal
Rosa, miniature species and varieties—
Rose
Rubus arcticus—Bramble
R. fockeanus
SAGINA—Irish-moss
SANTOLINA—Lavender-cotton
Saponaria ocymoides—Soapwort
Satureja montana—Winter savory
Saxifraga species and varieties—Saxifrage
Sedum species and varieties—Stonecrop
Sempervivum species and varieties—Hen-
and-chickens. Houseleek
Silene species and varieties—Catchfly.
Campion
Teucrium chamaedrys—Germander
Thymus species and varieties—Thyme
TUNICA
Veronica species and varieties—Speedwell
Vinca species and varieties—Myrtle. Peri-
winkle
Viola species and varieties—Violet.
Tufted pansy
ZAUSCHNERIA

Rock Plants
BY FLOWERING PERIOD: AUTUMN

Aster species and varieties
Ceratostigma plumbaginoides—Leadwort.
Plumbago
Cyclamen europaeum—European cyclamen
C. neapolitanum
Daphne cneorum
Dicentra eximia—Fringed bleeding-heart
Galium verum—Yellow bedstraw
Gentiana species—Gentian
Gypsophila species—Baby's-breath
Lamium amplexicaule—Henbit dead
nettle
Linaria broussonnetia—Toadflax

Lychnis species and varieties—Catchfly.
Campion
Phyla nodiflora—Creeping-lippia
Polygonum affine—Knotweed
P. vaccinifolium
Prunella vulgaris—Heal-all. Selfheal
Rosa, miniature species and varieties—
Rose

Rock Plants
BY COLOR: BLUE

Ajuga species and varieties—Bugleweed
Allium species and varieties—Ornamental
onion
Anemone species and varieties—Wind-
flower
Aquilegia species and varieties—Colum-
bine
Aster, dwarf species and varieties
Campanula species and varieties—Bell-
flower
Ceratostigma plumbaginoides—Leadwort.
Plumbago
ERYNGIUM—Eryngo. Sea-holly
Gentiana species—Gentian
Gilia species
GLOBULARIA
Haberlea ferdinandi-coburgii
HEPATICA—Liverleaf
HOUSTONIA—Bluets
Iris species and varieties
JASIONE
Lavandula officinalis varieties—English
lavender
Limonium species—Sea-lavender
Linaria species—Toadflax
Linum species—Flax
Lithospermum diffusum—Gromwell
MAZUS
Meconopsis quintuplenervia—Harebell-
poppy
Mertensia species—Bluebells
Moltkia petraea
Myosotis alpestris—Forget-me-not
Nepeta mussinii
Nierembergia species and varieties—Cup-
flower
NOLANA—Chilean-bellflower

Omphalodes species—Navelwort
Penstemon species—Beard-tongue
Phacelia campanularia
Phlox species and varieties
PHYTEUMA—Horned rampion
Platycodon, dwarf varieties—Balloon-
flower
POLEMONIUM
Primula species and varieties—Primrose
Pulmonaria species—Lungwort
Rhododendron, dwarf species and varieties
Sisyrinchium species and varieties—Blue-
eyed-grass
Veronica species and varieties—Speedwell
Vinca species and varieties—Myrtle. Peri-
winkle

Rock Plants
BY COLOR: ORANGE

Cheiranthus cheiri—Wallflower
Erysimum perofskianum
    E. *pulchellum*—Blister-cress
Eschscholtzia species and varieties
Geum species—Avens
Helianthemum varieties—Sun-rose
Linaria species—Toadflax
Papaver alpinum—Alpine poppy
Portulaca grandiflora—Rose-moss
Primula species and varieties—Primrose
Rhododendron, dwarf species and varieties
Rosa, miniature species and varieties—
    Rose

Rock Plants
BY COLOR: PINK

Abronia umbellata—Prostrate sand-
verbena
Aethionema species and varieties—Stone-
cress
Andromeda polifolia—Bog-rosemary
Androsace species—Rock-jasmine
Antennaria species and varieties—Pussy-
toes
Arctostaphylos uva-ursi—Bearberry
ARMERIA—Thrift

Aster, dwarf species and varieties
Astilbe species and varieties—False goat's-
beard
Bellis perennis—English daisy
BERGENIA
Bruckenthalia spiculifolia—Spike-heath
Calandrinia grandiflora—Rock-purslane
Calluna species and varieties—Heather
Cassiope hypnoides
Cistus species—Rock-rose
Claytonia species—Spring-beauty
Corydalis species—Fumaria
Cotoneaster horizontalis—Rock-spray
Cyclamen species
Daphne species
Dianthus species—Pink
Dicentra species—Bleeding-heart
Dodecatheon meadia—Shooting-star
Dorotheanthus gramineus
Douglasia laevigata—Rock-primrose
Epimedium species—Barrenwort
Erica carnea varieties—Spring heath
Eriogonum arborescens
Erodium cheilanthifolium—Heronsbill
Erythronium species—Dogtooth-violet
Eschscholtzia californica hybrid—Cali-
fornia-poppy
Gaultheria species
Gaylussacia brachycera—Box huckleberry
Geranium species—Cranesbill
Gilia species
Gypsophila species—Baby's-breath
Helianthemum varieties—Sun-rose
Hepatica varieties—Liverleaf
Heuchera species and varieties—Alum-
root. Coral-bells
Lamium amplexicaule—Henbit dead nettle
Lewisia species
Limonium species—Sea-lavender. Statice
Linnaea borealis—Twinflower
LOISELEURIA—Alpine-azalea
Lychnis species—Campion
Malcomia maritima—Virginia-stock
Origanum vulgare—Wild-marjoram. Pot-
marjoram. Oregano
Oxalis, hardy species
Papaver alpinum—Alpine poppy
Penstemon species—Beard-tongue
PERNETTYA
Phlox species and varieties

Phyla nodiflora—Creeping-lippia
Phyllodoce caerulea
Platycodon, dwarf varieties—Balloon-
flower
Polygonum affine—Knotweed
P. vaccinifolium
Portulaca grandiflora—Rose-moss
Primula species and varieties—Primrose
Prunella grandiflora, selected variety
Rhododendron, dwarf species and varieties
Rosa, miniature species and varieties—
Rose
Rubus arcticus—Bramble
Saponaria ocymoides—Soapwort
Satureja montana—Winter savory
Saxifraga species and varieties—Saxifrage
Sedum species and varieties—Stonecrop
Sempervivum species and varieties—Hen-
and-chickens. Houseleek
Silene species and varieties—Catchfly.
Campion
Thymus species and varieties—Thyme
Tunica saxifraga—Tunic-flower
Vaccinium vitis-idaea—Cowberry
Veronica species and varieties—Speedwell

Rock Plants
BY COLOR: PURPLE

Aethionema species and varieties—Stone-
cress
Anemone species and varieties—Wind-
flower
Arenaria species and varieties—Sandwort
ASARUM—Wild-ginger
Aster, dwarf species and varieties
Aubrieta species and varieties—Aubretia
CALANDRINIA—Rock-purslane
Callirhoe involucrata—Poppy-mallow
Calluna species and varieties—Heather
Campanula species and varieties—Bell-
flower
Clintonia andrewsiana
Corydalis bulbosa—Fumaria
Cytisus purpureus—Purple broom
Daboecia cantabrica—Irish-heath
Daphne species
Dianthus species—Pink
Dodecatheon meadia—Shooting-star

Douglasia montana—Mountain douglasia
Empetrum nigrum—Black crowberry
Geranium species—Cranesbill
Gilia species
HORMINUM
Iris species and varieties
Kalmiopsis leachiana
Lamium amplexicaule—Henbit dead nettle
Lavandula officinalis varieties—English
lavender
Mentha requienii—Corsican mint
Micromeria species
Nierembergia species and varieties—Cup-
flower
Nolana paradoxa—Chilean-bellflower
Ophiopogon species and varieties—Lily-
turf
Origanum vulgare—Wild-marjoram. Pot-
marjoram. Oregano
Penstemon species—Beard-tongue
Phlox species and varieties
Phyla nodiflora—Creeping-lippia
Phyllodoce caerulea
P. empetriformis
Primula species and varieties—Primrose
PRUNELLA—Heal-all. Selfheal
Pulmonaria species—Lungwort
Ramonda species
Rhododendron, dwarf species and varieties
Sempervivum species and varieties—Hen-
and-chickens. Houseleek
Sisyrinchium species and varieties—Blue-
eyed-grass
Thymus species and varieties—Thyme
Tunica saxifraga—Tunic-flower
Vinca species and varieties—Periwinkle
Viola species and varieties—Violet. Tufted
pansy

Rock Plants
BY COLOR: RED

Acaena microphylla—New Zealand bur
Aquilegia species and varieties—Colum-
bine
Calandrinia umbellata—Rock-purslane
Callirhoe involucrata—Poppy-mallow
Cheiranthus cheiri—Wallflower

Cyclamen species
Dianthus species—Pink
Dodecatheon meadia—Shooting-star
Dorotheanthus gramineus
Douglasia laevigata—Rock-primrose
Epimedium species—Barrenwort
Erica carnea varieties—Spring heath
Eschscholtzia californica hybrid—California-poppy
Gaillardia aristata cv. 'Goblin'—Dwarf blanket-flower
Geranium species—Cranesbill
Geum species—Avens
Gilia species
Helianthemum varieties—Sun-rose
Heuchera species and varieties—Alum-root. Coral-bells
Lychnis alpina variety—Arctic campion
Malcomia maritima—Virginia-stock
Ourisia coccinea
Oxalis, hardy species
Penstemon species—Beard-tongue
Phlox species and varieties
Portulaca grandiflora—Rose-moss
Primula species and varieties—Primrose
Prunella grandiflora, selected variety
Rhododendron, dwarf species and varieties
Rosa, miniature species and varieties—Rose
Sempervivum species and varieties—Hen-and-chickens. Houseleek
Silene species and varieties—Catchfly. Campion
ZAUSCHNERIA

Rock Plants
BY COLOR: WHITE

Achillea clavennae—Silver yarrow
Ajuga reptans var. alba—Bugleweed
Allium species and varieties—Ornamental onion
Androsace species—Rock-jasmine
Anemone species and varieties—Windflower
Anemonella thalictroides—Rue-anemone
Antennaria species and varieties—Pussy-toes

Aquilegia species and varieties—Columbine
ARABIS—Rock-cress
Arctostaphylos uva-ursi—Bearberry
ARENARIA—Sandwort
Asperula odorata—Sweet woodruff
Aster, dwarf species and varieties
Astilbe species and varieties—False goat's-beard
Campanula species and varieties—Bellflower
Carlina acaulis
CASSIOPE
Cerastium tomentosum—Snow-in-summer
CHAMAEDAPHNE—Leather-leaf
Chiogenes hispidula—Creeping snowberry
Cistus species—Rock-rose
Claytonia species—Spring-beauty
Clintonia uniflora—Queen-cup
Convallaria majalis—Lily-of-the-valley
Coptis species—Goldthread
Cornus canadensis—Bunchberry dogwood
Corydalis nobilis—Siberian corydalis
Cotoneaster dammeri
Cyclamen species
Cytisus albus—Portuguese broom
Daboecia cantabrica var. alba—Irish-heath
Dalibarda repens—Robin-run-away
Daphne x burkwoodii—Burkwood daphne
DENTARIA—Toothwort
Dianthus species—Pink
Dicentra canadensis—Squirrel-corn
 D. cucullaria—Dutchman's-breeches
Dodecatheon meadia—Shooting-star
Dorotheanthus gramineus
DRYAS—Mountain avens
Epigaea repens—Trailing arbutus
Epimedium species—Barrenwort
Erica carnea varieties—Spring heath
Erodium species—Heronsbill
Erythronium species—Dogtooth-violet
Eschscholtzia californica hybrid—California-poppy
Galax aphylla
Galium mollugo—Wild madder
GAULTHERIA
Gaylussacia brachycera—Box huckleberry
Geranium sanguineum var. album—Cranesbill

Gilia species
Gypsophila species—Baby's-breath
Helianthemum varieties—Sun-rose
Hepatica varieties—Liverleaf
Heuchera species and varieties—Alum-root. Coral-bells
Hosta species and varieties—Plantain-lily. Funkia
Houstonia caerulea—Bluets
Iberis, perennial species—Candytuft
Ionopsidium acaule—Diamond-flower
Iris cristata var. *alba*—Crested dwarf iris
Isopyrum biternatum—False anemone
Lavandula officinalis var. *alba*—Lavender
Layia species
Leiophyllum buxifolium—Box sand-myrtle
Leontopodium alpinum—Edelweiss
Leucothoe keiskei
Lewisia species
Limonium species—Sea-lavender. Statice
Linnaea borealis—Twinflower
Lithophragma affinis—Woodland star
LOISELEURIA—Alpine-azalea
Lychnis alpina variety—Arctic campion
Maianthemum canadense—Wild-lily-of-the-valley
Malcomia maritima—Virginia-stock
Micromeria rupestris
MITCHELLA—Partridge-berry
MITELLA—Mitrewort. Bishop's-cap
NEPETA
Nierembergia species and varieties—Cup-flower
Nolana paradoxa—Chilean-bellflower
Oenothera species and varieties—Evening-primrose
Ophiopogon species and varieties—Lily-turf
Ourisia species
Oxalis, hardy species
Pachysandra species—Spurge
Papaver alpinum—Alpine poppy
Penstemon species—Beard-tongue
PERNETTYA
Phacelia campanularia var. *alba*
Phlox species and varieties
Phyla nodiflora—Creeping-lippia
Pieris nana—Kamchatka pieris
Platycodon, dwarf varieties—Balloon-flower

Polygonatum species—Solomon's seal
Portulaca grandiflora—Rose-moss
Potentilla species—Cinquefoil
Primula species and varieties—Primrose
Prunella, selected varieties
Ramonda species
Rhododendron, dwarf species and varieties
Romanzoffia species
Rosa, miniature species and varieties—Rose
Rubus fockeanus—Bramble
Sagina species—Irish-moss
Sanguinaria canadensis—Bloodroot
Saxifraga species and varieties—Saxifrage
Sedum species and varieties—Stonecrop
Sempervivum species and varieties—Hen-and-chickens. Houseleek
Shortia galacifolia—Oconee-bells
Silene species and varieties—Catchfly
Smilacina species—False Solomon's-seal
Tiarella cordifolia—Foamflower
Veronica species and varieties—Speedwell
Viola species and varieties—Violet. Tufted pansy

Rock Plants
BY COLOR: YELLOW

Achillea tomentosa—Woolly yarrow
Adonis species and varieties—Pheasant-eye
Allium species and varieties—Ornamental onion
ALYSSUM—Madwort
Aquilegia species and varieties—Colum-bine
ARNICA
Berberis verruculosa—Barberry
Cheiranthus cheiri—Wallflower
CHRYSOGONUM—Golden-star
Clintonia borealis
Coptis trifoliata—Alaska goldthread
Corydalis species—Fumaria
Cytisus albus—Portuguese broom
  C. x *kewensis*—Kew broom
Douglasia vitaliana—Rock-primrose
DRABA
Epimedium species—Barrenwort
Eriogonum umbellatum—Sulfur-flower

Erodium species—Heronsbill
Erysimum asperum—Siberian wallflower
Erythronium species—Dogtooth-violet
ESCHSCHOLTZIA
Euphorbia myrsinites—Myrtle euphorbia
Gaillardia aristata cv. 'Goblin'—Dwarf
 blanket-flower
Galium verum—Yellow bedstraw
Genista pilosa—Silky-leaf woadwaxen
Geum species—Avens
Gilia species
Helianthemum nummularium—Sun-rose
HYPERICUM—St. John's-wort
HYPOXIS—Star-grass
Layia elegans—Tidy-tips
Limonium species—Sea-lavender
Linaria species—Toadflax
Lysimachia nummularia—Moneywort
Mahonia nervosa
 M. repens
Mimulus primuloides—Monkey-flower
Oenothera species and varieties—Evening-
 primrose
Onosma species—Golden drops
Oxalis, hardy species
Papaver alpinum—Alpine poppy
Phyllodoce glanduliflora
Physaria didymocarpa
PLATYSTEMON—Cream-cups
Portulaca grandiflora—Rose-moss
Potentilla species—Cinquefoil
Primula species and varieties—Primrose
Ranunculus species—Buttercup
Raoulia species
Rhododendron, dwarf species and varieties
Rosa, miniature species and varieties—
 Rose
SANTOLINA—Lavender-cotton
Saxifraga species and varieties—Saxifrage
Sedum species and varieties—Stonecrop
Sempervivum species and varieties—Hen-
 and-chickens. Houseleek
Waldsteinia fragarioides—Barren-straw-
 berry

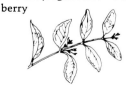

Rock Plants
FOR TERRACE CREVICES

Achillea species and varieties—Yarrow.
 Milfoil
AETHIONEMA—Stone-cress
Alyssum species—Madwort
ANTENNARIA—Pussy-toes
ARABIS—Rock-cress
ARENARIA—Sandwort
ARMERIA—Thrift
AUBRIETA—Aubretia
Campanula species—Bellflower
Cerastium tomentosum—Snow-in-summer
Ceratostigma plumbaginoides—Leadwort.
 Plumbago
Cheiranthus cheiri—Wallflower
Dianthus species—Pink
Dorotheanthus gramineus
Douglasia species—Rock-primrose
DRABA
DRYAS—Mountain avens
ERODIUM—Heronsbill
Gypsophila, creeping species—Baby's-
 breath
HELIANTHEMUM—Sun-rose
Hypericum species and varieties—St.
 John's-wort
Iberis, perennial species—Candytuft
Leontopodium alpinum—Edelweiss
LINARIA—Toadflax
Lithospermum diffusum—Gromwell
Malcomia maritima—Virginia-stock
MAZUS
Mentha requienii—Corsican mint
Nierembergia repens var. *rivularis*—Cup-
 flower
Polemonium reptans—Creeping pole-
 monium
Potentilla species—Cinquefoil
Ramonda species
SAGINA—Irish-moss
Saponaria ocymoides—Soapwort
Saxifraga species and varieties—Saxifrage
Sedum species and varieties—Stonecrop
Sempervivum species and varieties—Hen-
 and-chickens. Houseleek
Thymus species and varieties—Thyme
Vaccinium vitis-idaea—Cowberry

Veronica species and varieties—Speedwell
ZAUSCHNERIA

Rock Plants
FOR WALL CREVICES

AETHIONEMA—Stone-cress
Alyssum species—Madwort
Aquilegia species and varieties—Columbine
ARABIS—Rock-cress
Aurinia saxatilis—Basket-of-gold. Golden tuft
Campanula species and varieties—Bellflower
Cerastium tomentosum—Snow-in-summer
Cheiranthus cheiri—Wallflower
Cymbalaria muralis—Kenilworth-ivy
DRABA
DRYAS—Mountain avens
ERODIUM—Heronsbill
Euphorbia myrsinites—Myrtle euphorbia
HELIANTHEMUM—Sun-rose
HEUCHERA—Alum-root. Coral-bells
Iberis, perennial species—Candytuft
Linaria alpina—Alpine toadflax
Lysimachia nummularia—Moneywort
Malcomia maritima—Virginia-stock
MAZUS
Micromeria species
MITELLA—Mitrewort. Bishop's-cap
Nepeta mussinii
Origanum vulgare—Wild-marjoram. Pot-marjoram. Oregano
Pellaea atropurpurea—Purple-stemmed cliff-brake
Physaria didymocarpa
POLEMONIUM
Polygonum affine—Knotweed
   P. vaccinifolium
Saponaria ocymoides—Soapwort
Sedum species and varieties—Stonecrop
Sempervivum species and varieties—Hen-and-chickens. Houseleek

Rock Plants
THAT TOLERATE CONSIDERABLE SHADE

ADONIS—Pheasant-eye
ARENARIA—Sandwort
ASPERULA—Woodruff
Asplenium species—Spleenwort fern
ASTILBE—False goat's-beard
Bellis perennis—English daisy
CAMPTOSORUS—Walking fern
CASSIOPE
Cornus canadensis—Bunchberry dogwood
Corydalis species—Fumaria
CRYPTOGRAMMA—Rock-brake fern
Cyclamen species
CYSTOPTERIS—Bladder fern
Dalibarda repens—Robin-run-away
DENTARIA—Toothwort
Dicentra species—Bleeding-heart
Dodecatheon media—Shooting-star
DRYAS—Mountain avens
Epigaea repens—Trailing arbutus
EPIMEDIUM—Barrenwort
Erythronium species—Dogtooth-violet
Galax aphylla
GAULTHERIA
Gaylussacia brachycera—Box huckleberry
GLOBULARIA
HABERLEA
HEPATICA—Liverleaf
Hosta species and varieties—Plaintain-lily. Funkia
HOUSTONIA—Bluets
Iris cristata—Crested dwarf iris
   I. gracilipes—Slender iris
Isopyrum biternatum—False anemone
Linnaea borealis—Twinflower
Lithophragma affinis—Woodland star
Mahonia nervosa
   M. repens
Maianthemum canadense
Meconopsis quintuplenervia—Harebell-poppy
Mertensia species—Bluebells
Micromeria species
Mimulus primuloides—Monkey-flower
MITCHELLA—Partridge-berry
MITELLA—Mitrewort. Bishop's-cap

Myosotis alpestris—Forget-me-not
OPHIOPOGON—Lily-turf
OSMUNDA—Fern
OURISIA
PACHYSANDRA—Spurge
Pieris nana—Kamchatka pieris
POLEMONIUM
Polygonatum species—Solomon's seal
Polypodium vulgare—Common polypody
POLYSTICHUM—Fern
Primula species and varieties—Primrose
PRUNELLA—Heal-all. Selfheal
Pulmonaria species—Lungwort
Ramonda species
Rhododendron, dwarf species and varieties
Romanzoffia species
SAGINA—Irish-moss
Sanguinaria canadensis—Bloodroot
Saxifraga species and varieties—Saxifrage
Shortia galacifolia—Oconee-bells
Silene, Kruckeberg hybrids—Catchfly.
    Campion
Smilacina species and varieties—False
    Solomon's-seal
Tiarella cordifolia—Foamflower
Tsuga canadensis var. pendula—Canada
    hemlock
Viola species and varieties—Violet. Tufted
    pansy

Seaside Plants

Seaside Plants
ANNUAL FLOWERS: FOR BELT I

Arctotis species and varieties—African
    daisy
Echium creticum—Viper's-bugloss
Helianthus annus and varieties—Sun-
    flower
Lobularia maritima—Sweet-alyssum
Medicago echinus—Calvary-clover
Vinca rosea—Madagascar periwinkle

Seaside Plants
ANNUAL FLOWERS: FOR BELT II OR III

ABRONIA—Sand-verbena
Ageratum houstonianum
CALENDULA—Pot-marigold
Centaurea cyanus—Cornflower.
    Bachelor's-button
Clarkia species and varieties
Cleome species and varieties—Spider-
    flower
Cobaea scandens—Cup-and-saucer vine
Coreopsis species and varieties—
    Tickseed
COSMOS
Delphinium ajacis—Larkspur
Dianthus, annual species and varieties—
    Pink
Dolichos lablab—Hyacinth-bean
Eschscholtzia californica—California-
    poppy
Euphorbia marginata—Snow-on-the-
    mountain
Gaillardia species and varieties—Blanket-
    flower
GAZANIA
GODETIA
Gypsophila, annual species—Baby's-
    breath
Helichrysum species and varieties—
    Straw-flower
Ipomoea species and varieties—Morning-
    glory
NEMESIA
Nicotiana, annual species and varieties—
    Flowering tobacco
Nigella damascena—Love-in-a-mist
Papaver, annual species and varieties—
    Poppy
Petunia x hybrida
Phaseolus coccineus—Scarlet-runner bean
Phlox drummondii—Annual phlox
Portulaca grandiflora—Rose-moss
Reseda odorata—Mignonette
SALPIGLOSSIS—Painted-tongue
Salvia splendens—Sage
TAGETES—Marigold
Thunbergia alata—Clock-vine
TITHONIA—Mexican-sunflower

Tropaeolum species and varieties—
  Nasturtium
Verbena species and varieties—Vervain
ZINNIA

Seaside Plants
HARDY PERENNIAL FLOWERS: FOR BELT I

Achillea tomentosa—Woolly yarrow
Anthemis species and varieties—
  Chamomile
ARABIS—Rock-cress
Armeria species and varieties—Thrift.
  Sea-pink
Artemisia stelleriana—Beach wormwood
Baptisia australis—False indigo
Chrysanthemum species and varieties
Eryngium amethystinum—Eryngo. Sea-
  holly
Euphorbia myrsinites—Spurge
Glaucium species—Horned-poppy. Sea-
  poppy
Iberis sempervirens—Perennial candytuft
Lathyrus littoralis—Beach-pea
  L. maritimus—Beach-pea. Seaside-pea
Lavandula officinalis—English lavender
Liatris species and varieties—Gayfeather.
  Blazing-star
Limonium species—Sea-lavender. Statice
Oenothera species and varieties—
  Evening-primrose
Opuntia species—Prickly-pear cactus
Sempervivum species and varieties—
  Houseleek. Hen-and-chickens
Solidago species and varieties—
  Goldenrod
Stachys olympica—Lamb's-ears

Seaside Plants
**HARDY PERENNIAL FLOWERS:
FOR BELT II OR III**

Althaea officinalis—Marsh-mallow
  A. rosea—Hollyhock
Alyssum species and varieties—Madwort
Aquilegia species and varieties—
  Columbine
Arenaria species and varieties—Sandwort
Artemisia schmidtiana—Silvermound
  artemisia

Asclepias tuberosa—Butterfly-weed
Aurinia saxatilis—Basket-of-gold. Golden
  tuft
Campanula persicifolia—Peachleaf bell-
  flower
Centranthus ruber—Red-valerian
Cerastium tomentosum—Snow-in-summer
CHRYSOPSIS—Golden-aster
Coreopsis lanceolata—Tickseed
Delphinium species and varieties—
  Perennial larkspur
Doronicum caucasicum—Caucasian
  leopard's-bane
Echinacea purpurea—Coneflower
Echinops ritro—Globe-thistle
Erigeron glaucus—Beach-aster
Gaillardia aristata—Blanket-flower
Gypsophila paniculata—Baby's-breath
Hemerocallis species and hybrids—
  Daylily
Heuchera species and varieties—Coral-
  bells
Hibiscus palustris—Swamp-mallow
Iris species and varieties
Linum species and varieties—Flax
Lobelia cardinalis—Cardinal-flower
Lupinus species and varieties—Lupine
Lychnis species and varieties—Catchfly.
  Campion
Lythrum salicaria—Loosestrife
Monarda species and varieties—Bee-balm
Nepeta mussinii—Catmint
Paeonia species and varieties—Peony
Papaver orientale—Oriental poppy
Phlox paniculata—Summer phlox
Physostegia species and varieties—False
  dragonhead
Platycodon grandiflorum—Balloon-flower
Santolina chamaecyparissus—Lavender-
  cotton
Thymus species and varieties—Thyme
Veronica species and varieties—Speedwell
Yucca filamentosa—Adam's-needle

Seaside Plants
SHRUBS: FOR BELT I, NORTH (ON THE SHORE)

Amelanchier canadensis—Shadbush. Serviceberry
Arctostaphylos uva-ursi—Bearberry
Baccharis halimifolia—Groundsel bush
Berberis species—Barberry
Caragana arborescens—Siberian pea-tree
Comptonia peregrina—Sweet-fern
Cotoneaster species and varieties
Cytisus species and varieties—Broom
Elaeagnus angustifolia—Russian-olive
Halimodendron halodendron—Salt-tree
Hippophae rhamnoides—Sea-buckthorn
Juniperus species and varieties—Juniper
Lonicera species and varieties—Honeysuckle
Myrica pensylvanica—Bayberry
Pieris japonica—Japanese andromeda
Pinus mugo var. *mughus*—Mugho pine
Prunus maritima—Beach plum
Raphiolepis umbellata—Yeddo-hawthorn
Rhamnus species—Buckthorn
Rhododendron indicum
  R. *mucronatum*
Rhus species—Sumac
Robinia hispida—Rose-acacia
Rosa rugosa—Rugosa rose
Salix species—Willow
Shepherdia species—Buffalo-berry
Symphoricarpos orbiculatus—Coralberry
Tamarix species—Tamarisk

Seaside Plants
SHRUBS: FOR BELT I, SOUTH (ON THE SHORE)

Acacia species—Wattle
Acanthocereus pentagonus—Night-blooming-cereus
Ardisia paniculata—Marlberry
Atriplex species—Saltbush
Aucuba japonica and varieties—Japanese-laurel. Gold-dust plant
Baccharis halimifolia—Groundsel bush
Berberis chilensis—Chilean barberry
Buddleia species and varieties—Butterfly-bush

Callistemon species—Bottle-brush
Carissa grandiflora—Natal-plum
Casuarina species—Australian-pine
Coccolobis species—Sea-grape
Codiaeum species—Seaside croton
Coprosma baueri—Mirror plant
Cotoneaster species and varieties
Elaeagnus pungens—Japanese oleaster
Eugenia buxifolia—Box-leaf eugenia
Euonymus japonicus—Evergreen euonymus
Fuchsia magellanica
Hymenanthera species
Jacquinia species
Lavandula stoechas—Lavender
Ligustrum japonicum—Waxleaf privet. Japanese privet
  L. *lucidum*—Glossy privet
Melaleuca pubescens—Bottle-brush
Myrica cereifera—Wax myrtle
Olearia species—Daisy-bush
Pittosporum tobira—Japanese pittosporum
Raphiolepis umbellata—Yeddo-hawthorn
Rhus laurina—Laurel sumac
Rosmarinus officinalis—Rosemary
Ruscus aculeatus—Butcher's-broom
Santolina chamaecyparissus—Lavender-cotton
Suriana maritima—Bay-cedar
Synadenium species—Milk-bush
Tamarix species—Tamarisk

Seaside Plants
SHRUBS: FOR BELT I, WEST (ON THE SHORE)

Acacia longifolia—Sydney golden wattle
  A. *verticillata*
Arbutus unedo—Strawberry-tree
Arctostaphylos hookeri—Hooker manzanita
Atriplex breweri—Brewer saltbush
Aucuba japonica and varieties—Japanese-laurel. Gold-dust plant
Banksia ericifolia—Heath-leaved banksia
Berberis species—Barberry
Butia capitata—Pindo palm
Callistemon species—Bottle-brush
Carissa grandiflora—Natal-plum

Ceanothus griseus—Carmel ceanothus
Coprosma repens—Mirror plant
Cotoneaster species and varieties
Cytisus species and varieties—Broom
Elaeagnus angustifolia—Russian-olive
  E. pungens—Japanese oleaster
Erythea armata—Mexican blue palm
Euonymus species and varieties—Spindle-tree
Gaultheria shallon—Salal
Heteromeles arbutifolia—Toyon
Juniperus species and varieties—Juniper
Lantana species and varieties
Lavatera assurgentiflora—Tree-mallow
Ligustrum japonicum—Waxleaf privet.
  Japanese privet
Lonicera species and varieties—Honey-suckle
Melaleuca species—Bottle-brush
Myrica californica—Pacific wax myrtle
Olearia species—Daisy-bush
Pinus mugo var. mughus—Mugho pine
Pittosporum tobira—Japanese pitto-sporum
Prunus laurocerasus—Cherry-laurel
  P. l. var. zabeliana—Zabel-laurel
Rhus glabra—Smooth sumac
  R. integrifolia—Lemonade-berry
  R. ovata—Sugar bush
Rosa rugosa—Rugosa rose
Salix desertorum—Desert willow
Tamarix species—Tamarisk
Trachycarpus fortunei—Windmill palm
Vitex species and varieties—Chaste-tree

Empetrum nigrum—Crowberry
Erica carnea—Heath
Forsythia intermedia var. spectabilis
Hippophae rhamnoides—Sea-buckthorn
Hydrangea arborescens var. grandiflora—
  Hills-of-snow
  H. paniculata var. grandiflora
  H. quercifolia—Oak-leaved hydrangea
HYPERICUM—St. John's-wort
Hyssopus officinalis—Hyssop
Ilex glabra—Inkberry
  I. opaca—American holly
Juniperus chinensis and varieties—
  Juniper
Kolkwitzia amabilis—Beauty-bush
Leiophyllum buxifolium—Box sand-myrtle
Leucothoe species
Ligustrum amurense—Amur privet
Lindera benzoin—Spicebush
Pieris floribunda—Mountain-andromeda
Potentilla fruticosa—Cinquefoil
Pyracantha coccinea var. lalandii—
  Firethorn
Rhododendron schlippenbachii
Rosa species and varieties—Rose
Salix purpurea var. nana—Dwarf arctic
  willow
Schizophragma hydrangeoides—Japanese
  hydrangea-vine
Shepherdia canadensis—Russet buffalo-berry
Spiraea species and varieties—Spirea
Syringa vulgaris—Lilac
Vaccinium corymbosum—Blueberry
Viburnum dentatum—Arrowwood
  V. opulus

Seaside Plants
SHRUBS: FOR COLD SHORES, BELT II OR III

Abelia grandiflora—Glossy abelia
Amorpha canescens—Lead-plant
Andromeda glaucophylla—Bog-rosemary
Aronia arbutifolia—Chokeberry
Artemisia tridentata—Sagebrush
Calluna vulgaris and varieties—Heather
Chaenomeles japonica—Flowering-quince
Clematis species and varieties
Clethra alnifolia—Summersweet
Cornus sericea—Red osier dogwood

Seaside Plants
SHRUBS: FOR WARM SHORES, BELT II OR III

Cordyline species
Escallonia species
Lagerstroemia indica—Crape-myrtle
Lupinus arboreus—Tree lupine
Myrtus communis—Myrtle
Nerium oleander—Oleander
Romneya coulteri—Matilija-poppy
Trachelospermum jasminoides—Star-jasmine

Seaside Plants
TREES: FOR BELT I, COLD SHORES

Acer platanoides—Norway maple
  A. pseudoplatanus—Sycamore maple
Alnus glutinosa—Black alder
Caragana arborescens—Siberian pea-tree
Elaeagnus angustifolia—Russian-olive
Fraxinus americana—White ash
Juniperus chinensis var. *keteleeri*—
  Keteleer juniper
  J. virginiana var. 'Canaert'—Canaert
  juniper
Picea abies and varieties—Norway spruce
Pinus species and varieties—Pine
Platanus acerifolia—London plane tree
Populus alba and varieties—Silver or
  white poplar
  P. tremula—European aspen
Prunus serotina—Wild black cherry
  P. spinosa—Blackthorn
Quercus ilex—Holly oak
Robinia pseudoacacia—Black locust. Yel-
  low locust
Salix alba—White willow
  S. caprea—Goat willow
Taxus baccata and varieties—English yew
Tilia cordata—Small-leaved linden

Seaside Plants
TREES: FOR BELT I, WARM SHORES

Acacia species—Wattle
Araucaria excelsa—Norfolk Island-pine
Casuarina species—Australian-pine
Cocos nucifera—Coconut
Cupressus macrocarpa—Monterey cypress
Eucalyptus species and varieties—Gum
  tree
Ficus macrophylla—Moreton Bay fig
  F. rubiginosa—Rusty fig
Ilex paraguariensis—Paraguay-tea
Melia azedarach—Chinaberry. China tree
Metrosideros tomentosa—Iron-tree
Phoenix dactylifera—Date palm
Pittosporum crassifolium—Karo
Sabal palmetto—Cabbage palm
Washingtonia robusta—Washington palm

Seaside Plants
VINES: FOR BELT I,
NORTH (ON THE SHORE)

Celastrus scandens—Bittersweet
Lonicera japonica var. *halliana*—Hall's
  honeysuckle
Lycium halimifolium—Matrimony-vine
Parthenocissus quinquefolia—Virginia
  creeper

Shrubs

Shrubs
WITH DECIDUOUS FOLIAGE:
BY HEIGHT: DWARF, TO 3 FEET

Artemisia frigida—Fringed wormwood
  A. stelleriana—Beach wormwood
Berberis buxifolia var. *nana*—Dwarf
  Magellan barberry
  B. candidula
  B. concinna
  B. thunbergii var. 'Crimson Pygmy'—
  Japanese barberry
Caryopteris x *clandonensis*—Bluebeard
Chaenomeles japonica—Flowering-quince
Cotoneaster species and varieties
Cytisus species and varieties—Broom
Daphne genkwa—Lilac daphne
  D. giraldii
Diervilla lonicera—Dwarf bush-
  honeysuckle
Dryas species and varieties—Mountain
  avens
Forsythia 'Arnold Dwarf'
  F. viridissima var. *bronxensis*
Fothergilla gardenii—Dwarf fothergilla
Fuchsia magellanica
Gaylussacia baccata—Black huckleberry
Genista cinerea—Broom
  G. hispanica—Spanish broom
  G. tinctoria—Dyers'-greenweed
Holodiscus microphyllus
Hydrangea arborescens var. *grandiflora*—
  Hills-of-snow hydrangea
Hypericum species and varieties—St.
  John's-wort
Indigofera incarnata—Indigo

Ligustrum vulgare var. *lodense*—Privet
Lonicera alpigena var. *nana*—Honeysuckle
  L. prostrata
  L. pyrenaica
  L. tatarica var. *nana*
Moltkia petraea
Punica granatum var. *nana*—Dwarf
  pomegranate
Ribes species and varieties—Currant.
  Gooseberry
Rosa carolina—Pasture rose
  R. chinensis var. *minima*—Miniature
  rose
  R. spinossima—Scotch rose
  R. wichuraiana—Memorial rose
Salix repens—Creeping willow
  S. tristis—Dwarf gray willow
Salvia greggii—Autumn sage
Spiraea species and varieties—Spirea
Suaeda fruticosa
Symphoricarpos species and varieties—
  Snowberry
Teucrium chamaedrys—Germander
Vaccinium angustifolium—Blueberry
  V. pallidum—Dryland blueberry
  V. stamineum—Common deerberry
Viburnum davidii
  V. farreri var. *nanum*—Fragrant
  viburnum
  V. opulus var. *nanum*—European cran-
  berry bush
  V. wrightii var. *hessei*
Weigela florida var. *variegata nana*
Xanthorhiza simplicissima—Yellow-root

Shrubs
WITH DECIDUOUS FOLIAGE:
BY HEIGHT: LOW, 3 TO 6 FEET

Abelia species and varieties
Abeliophyllum distichum—Korean abelia-
  leaf
Acer campestre var. *compactum*—Hedge
  maple
  A. ginnala var. 'Durand Dwarf'—Amur
  maple
Amelanchier stolonifera—June-berry
Amorpha canescens—Lead plant
Aronia melanocarpa—Black chokeberry
Atriplex species—Salt-bush

Berberis concinna—Dainty barberry
  B. koreana—Korean barberry
Callicarpa japonica—Beauty-berry
Caragana maximowicziana—Pea-tree
Cassia marilandica—Wild senna
Ceanothus species and varieties
Ceratostigma willmottianum
Chaenomeles japonica—Japanese-quince
Clerodendrum species—Glory-bower
Colutea species and varieties—Bladder-
  senna
Comptonia peregrina—Sweet-fern
Corylopsis pauciflora—Winter-hazel
Cotoneaster divaricata—Spreading
  cotoneaster
  C. multiflora—Flowering cotoneaster
Cytisus nigricans—Spike broom
  C. purgans—Provence broom
Daphne mezereum—February daphne
Deutzia gracilis—Slender deutzia
  D. lemoinei—Lemoinei deutzia
  D. scabra var. *plena*—'Pride of
  Rochester' deutzia
Diervilla sessilifolia—Southern bush-
  honeysuckle
Dirca palustris—Leatherwood
Elsholtzia stauntonii
Enkianthus perulatus—White enkianthus
Euonymus species and varieties—Spindle-
  tree
Forsythia ovata
Fothergilla gardenii—Dwarf fothergilla
  F. monticola—Alabama fothergilla
Fuchsia species and varieties
Genista species and varieties—Broom
Hamamelis vernalis—Ozark witch-hazel
Hydrangea quercifolia—Oak-leaved
  hydrangea
Hypericum kalmianum—Kalm St. John's-
  wort
Ilex species and varieties—Holly
Indigofera species and varieties—Indigo
Kerria japonica
Lonicera x *bella-candida*—Belle honey-
  suckle
  L. thibetica—Tibetan honeysuckle
Lyonia mariana—Stagger-bush
Malus sargentii—Apple
Myrica gale—Sweet-gale
Neillia sinensis—Chinese neillia

Neviusia alabamensis—Snow-wreath
Paeonia suffruticosa—Tree peony
Philadelphus x lemoinei—Avalanche
    mock-orange
Physocarpus species and varieties—
    Ninebark
Potentilla fruticosa—Cinquefoil
Prunus glandulosa—Dwarf flowering
    almond
    P. maritima—Beach plum
Rhododendron species and varieties,
    including azalea
Rhodotypos tetrapetala—Jetbead
Rhus aromatica—Fragrant sumac
Ribes species and varieties—Currant.
    Gooseberry
Robinia hispida—Rose-acacia
Rosa species and varieties—Rose
Rubus deliciosus—Rocky Mountain
    flowering raspberry
    R. odoratus—Flowering raspberry
    R. parviflora
Salix purpurea var. nana—Purple osier
Sorbaria sorbifolia—Ural false spirea
Spiraea species and varieties—Spirea
Symphoricarpos albus var. laevigatus—
    Garden snowberry
    S. x chenaultii—Chenault coralberry
Syringa persica—Persian lilac
Tamarix hispida and varieties—Kashgar
    tamarisk
    T. odessana
Viburnum acerifolium—Dockmackie.
    Mapleleaf viburnum
    V. carlesii—Fragrant viburnum
Weigela species and varieties
ZENOBIA

Shrubs
WITH DECIDUOUS FOLIAGE:
BY HEIGHT: MEDIUM, 6 TO 12 FEET

Abelia triflora
Acanthopanax species and varieties
Aesculus parviflora—Dwarf horse-
    chestnut
Aronia arbutifolia—Red chokeberry
Atriplex species—Salt-bush

Baccharis halimifolia—Groundsel-bush
Berberis darwinii—Darwin barberry
    B. thunbergii—Japanese barberry
Buddleia alternifolia—Fountain buddleia
    B. davidii—Butterfly-bush. Summer-
    lilac
Callicarpa species—Beauty-berry
Calycanthus floridus—Common sweet-
    shrub
Caragana microphylla—Littleleaf pea-tree
Cephalanthus occidentalis—Button-bush
Chimonanthus praecox—Wintersweet
Clerodendrum species—Glory-bower
Clethra alnifolia—Sweet pepperbush
Colutea species and varieties—Bladder-
    senna
Cornus alba var. sibirica—Coral dogwood
    C. racemosa—Gray dogwood
    C. sericea—Red osier dogwood
Corylus americana—American hazelnut
    C. cornuta—Beaked filbert
Cotoneaster species and varieties
Cytisus x praecox—Warminster broom
    C. scoparius—Scotch broom
Deutzia scabra var. plena—'Pride of
    Rochester' deutzia
Dirca palustris—Leatherwood
DISANTHUS
Elaeagnus species and varieties
Enkianthus cernuus
    E. perulatus—White enkianthus
Euonymus yedoensis—Yeddo euonymus
Exochorda giraldii—Wilson pearl-bush
Forsythia species and varieties
Fothergilla monticola—Alabama fother-
    gilla
Hamamelis virginiana—Common witch-
    hazel
Hibiscus syriacus—Shrub althea
Holodiscus dumosus
Hydrangea arborescens var. grandiflora—
    Hills-of-snow hydrangea
    H. macrophylla
Ilex verticillata—Winterberry
Itea virginica—Virginia sweetspire
Kerria japonica var. pleniflora—Double
    kerria
Kolkwitzia amabilis—Beauty-bush
Lespedeza species and varieties—Bush-

clover
Leucothoe racemosa—Sweetbells
Ligustrum obtusifolium var. regelianum—
    Border privet
Lindera benzoin—Spicebush
Lonicera species and varieties—Honey-
    suckle
Lycium species and varieties—Box-thorn
Magnolia liliflora
Myrica pensylvanica—Bayberry
Philadelphus coronarius—Sweet mock-
    orange
    P. x virginalis—Virginal mock-orange
Photinia villosa—Oriental photinia
Physocarpus species and varieties—
    Ninebark
PRINSEPIA
Prunus tomentosa—Manchu cherry
    P. triloba—Flowering almond
Rhamnus cathartica—Common buckthorn
Rhododendron arborescens—Sweet azalea
    R. calendulaceum—Flame azalea
    R. roseum—Roseshell azalea
    R. schlippenbachii—Royal azalea
Robinia species—Locust
Rosa eglanteria—Sweetbrier
    R. hugonis—Father Hugo rose
    R. rubrifolia—Red-leaved rose
Rubus phoenicolasius—Wineberry
    R. x tridel 'Benenden'—Bramble
Salix species and varieties—Willow
Sambucus pubens—American red elder.
    Scarlet elder
Shepherdia canadensis
Sorbaria aitchisonii—Kashmir false
    spirea
Spartium junceum—Spanish-broom
Spiraea species and varieties—Spirea
STACHYURUS
Staphylea trifolia—American bladdernut
Stephanandra incisa—Cutleaf steph-
    anandra
Stewartia ovata—Mountain stewartia
Syringa chinensis—Chinese lilac
    S. reflexa—Nodding lilac
Tamarix species and varieties—Tamarisk
Vaccinium species and varieties—
    Blueberry

Viburnum species and varieties
Vitex agnus-castus—Chaste-tree
Weigela species and varieties

Shrubs
WITH DECIDUOUS FOLIAGE:
BY HEIGHT: TALL, 12 TO 18 FEET

Buddleia alternifolia—Fountain buddleia
    B. davidii—Butterfly-bush. Summer-
    lilac
Caragana arborescens—Pea-tree
Chionanthus retusa—Fringetree
Cornus racemosa—Gray dogwood
Corylopsis species—Winter-hazel
Corylus species—Hazelnut
Cotinus coggygria—Smoketree
DISANTHUS
Elaeagnus umbellatus—Autumn elaeagnus
Enkianthus campanulatus—Redvein
    enkianthus
Euonymus species and varieties—Spindle-
    tree
Franklinia alatamaha
Hamamelis virginiana—Common witch-
    hazel
Holodiscus discolor—Rock-spirea
Hydrangea paniculata—Panicle hydrangea
Lagerstroemia indica—Crape-myrtle
Ligustrum ovalifolium—California privet
Lindera benzoin—Spicebush
Lonicera maackii—Amur honeysuckle
Photinia villosa—Oriental photinia
Prunus species and varieties
Punica granatum—Pomegranate
Rhamnus cathartica—Common buckthorn
Rhododendron vaseyi—Pinkshell azalea
    R. viscosum—Swamp-honeysuckle
Rhus species—Sumac
Salix species—Willow
Sambucus pubens—American red elder.
    Scarlet elder
Shepherdia argentea—Buffalo-berry
Sorbaria species and varieties—False
    spirea
Staphylea trifolia—American bladdernut
Stewartia ovata—Mountain stewartia
Syringa chinensis—Chinese lilac
    S. reflexa—Nodding lilac
    S. vulgaris—Common lilac

Tamarix species and varieties—Tamarisk
Vaccinium corymbosum—High-bush
  blueberry
Viburnum lantana—Wayfaring-tree
  V. macrocephalum—Chinese snowball
Vitex species and varieties

Shrubs
WITH DECIDUOUS FOLIAGE: BY
HEIGHT: VERY TALL, OVER 18 FEET

Alnus species and varieties—Alder
Amelanchier oblongifolia—Thicket
  shadblow
CHILOPSIS—Desert-willow
Chionanthus virginica—Fringetree
Clethra barbinervis—White-alder
Corylus heterophylla—Hazelnut
Cotinus americanus—Smokebush
CYRILLA—Leatherwood
Elaeagnus species and varieties
Enkianthus species and varieties
Euonymus species and varieties
Hamamelis mollis—Chinese witch-hazel
HIPPOPHAE—Sea-buckthorn
Hydrangea paniculata—Panicle hydrangea
Ilex species and varieties—Holly
Lagerstroemia indica—Crape-myrtle
Rhamnus species—Buckthorn
Rhus species and varieties—Sumac
Salix species and varieties—Willow
Sambucus species and varieties—Elder
Syringa species and varieties—Lilac
Viburnum species and varieties

Shrubs
WITH EVERGREEN FOLIAGE:
BY HEIGHT: DWARF, TO 3 FEET

Andromeda polifolia—Bog-rosemary
Arctostaphylos species—Bearberry
Ardisia crispa—Coral-berry
  A. japonica
Bruckenthalia spiculifolia—Spike-heath

Buxus microphylla varieties—Boxwood
  B. sempervirens varieties
Calluna vulgaris—Heather
Ceanothus americanus—New Jersey-tea
  C. ovatus
Chamaecyparis obtusa var. *pygmaea*—
  Falsecypress
Coprosma petriei
Cornus canadensis—Bunchberry dogwood
Cotoneaster dammeri
Daboecia cantabrica—Irish-heath
Danae racemosa—Alexandrian-laurel
Daphne cneorum—Garland-flower
  D. collina
  D. odora—Winter daphne
Empetrum nigrum—Black crowberry
Erica species and varieties—Heath
Euonymus fortunei var. 'Berryhill'—
  Wintercreeper
  E. nanus
Gaultheria miqueliana—Miquel winter-
  green
  G. procumbens—Wintergreen
  G. veitchiana—Veitch wintergreen
Gaylussacia brachycera—Box huckleberry
Ilex crenata varieties—Japanese holly
Juniperus chinensis var. *sargentii*—
  'Sargent' juniper
  J. conferta—Shore juniper
  J. horizontalis varieties—Creeping
  juniper
  J. procumbens
Kalmia angustifolia—Sheep-laurel
  K. polifolia—Bog kalmia
Kalmiopsis leachiana
Lavandula officinalis—English lavender
Ledum groenlandicum—Labrador-tea
  L. palustre—Wild-rosemary
Leiophyllum buxifolium—Box sand-
  myrtle
Leucothoe fontanesiana—Drooping
  leucothoe
Loiseleuria procumbens—Alpine-azalea
Mahonia aquifolium var. *compacta*—
  Oregon-grape
  M. a. var. 'Maham Strain'
  M. repens
Pachistima canbyi
Pernettya mucronata
Philesia magellanica

Phoradendron flavescens—American mistletoe
Picea abies varieties—Spruce
Pieris nana—Kamchatka pieris
Pinus mugo var. *pumilio*—Pine
   P. m. var. *slavinii*
Rhododendron species and varieties, including azalea
Ruscus aculeatus—Butcher's-broom
Sabal minor—Dwarf palmetto
Santolina chamaecyparissus—Lavender-cotton
Sarcococca hookeriana var. *humilis*
Serenoa repens—Saw-palmetto
Skimmia reevesiana
Taxus baccata var. *nana*—Yew
   T. b. var. *pygmaea*
   T. cuspidata var. *aurescens*
Thuja occidentalis varieties—Arborvitae
Zamia integrifolia

Shrubs
WITH EVERGREEN FOLIAGE:
BY HEIGHT: LOW, 3 TO 6 FEET

Arctostaphylos species—Bearberry
Aucuba japonica var. *nana*—Japanese-laurel
Bauhinia acuminata
Berberis candidula—Paleleaf barberry
   B. triacanthophora—Three-spine barberry
Buxus species and varieties—Boxwood
Calluna vulgaris—Heather
Carissa species and varieties—Natal-plum
Cassia artemisioides—Senna
Ceanothus species and varieties
Cestrum parqui—Willow-leaved-jessamine
Chamaecyparis obtusa varieties—False-cypress
CHAMAEDAPHNE—Leather-leaf
Cistus species and varieties—Rock-rose
Cotoneaster microphylla
Cytisus canariensis—Canary broom
   C. x *racemosus*
Daphne x *burkwoodii*—Burkwood daphne. Somerset daphne
Erica species and varieties—Heath
Escallonia species and varieties

Euonymus fortunei—Wintercreeper
Gardenia species and varieties
Gaultheria species and varieties
Hebe species and varieties
Hypericum species and varieties—St. John's-wort
Ilex crenata—Japanese holly
Juniperus chinensis var. *pfitzeriana*—'Pfitzer' juniper
Kalmia cuneata
Ledum glandulosum
Leucothoe fontanesiana—Drooping leucothoe
Lonicera species and varieties—Honeysuckle
Mahonia species and varieties
Pieris floribunda—Mountain-andromeda
Prunus laurocerasus var. *schipkaensis*—Schipka cherry-laurel
Raphiolepis indica—India-hawthorn
Rhamnus species and varieties—Buckthorn
Rhododendron species and varieties
Rosmarinus officinalis—Rosemary
Skimmia japonica
Taxus species and varieties—Yew
Thuja species and varieties—Arborvitae
Viburnum davidii—David viburnum

Shrubs
WITH EVERGREEN FOLIAGE:
BY HEIGHT: MEDIUM, 6 TO 12 FEET

Abelia floribunda—Mexican abelia
Acacia farnesiana—Popinac. Sweet acacia
Arctostaphylos species and varieties—Bearberry
Aucuba japonica—Japanese-laurel
Berberis darwinii—Darwin barberry
Camellia sasanqua
Carissa species and varieties—Natal-plum
CARPENTERIA—Evergreen mock-orange
Cassia species and varieties—Senna
Ceanothus species and varieties
Cestrum species and varieties
Choisya ternata—Mexican-orange
Cistus species and varieties—Rock-rose
Clerodendrum species—Glory-bower

Cotoneaster salicifolia var. floccosa—
    Willowleaf cotoneaster
Cycas species
Elaeagnus pungens—Thorny elaeagnus
Escallonia species and varieties
Euonymus kiautschovicus—Spindle-tree
x Fatshedera lizei
Gardenia species and varieties
Garrya elliptica—Silk-tassel bush
    G. fremontii
Hebe species and varieties
HETEROMELES—Toyon
Ilex species and varieties—Holly
Itea ilicifolia
Juniperus species and varieties—Juniper
Kalmia latifolia—Mountain-laurel
Ligustrum species and varieties—Privet
Lonicera fragrantissima—Winter
    honeysuckle
Loropetalum chinense
Mahonia species and varieties
Melianthus major—Honey-bush
Myrtus communis—Myrtle
NANDINA—Heavenly-bamboo
Nerium indicum—Sweet-scented oleander
Olearia species and varieties—Tree-aster
Osmanthus species and varieties
Phillyrea species
Photinia species
Pieris japonica—Japanese-andromeda
Pittosporum heterophyllum
    P. tobira—Japanese pittosporum
Pyracantha species and varieties—
    Firethorn
Raphiolepis umbellata—Yeddo-hawthorn
Rhamnus species and varieties—Buck-
    thorn
Rhododendron species and varieties
Taxus species and varieties—Yew
THUJA species and varieties—Arborvitae
Vaccinium species and varieties—
    Blueberry
Viburnum species and varieties

Shrubs
WITH EVERGREEN FOLIAGE:
BY HEIGHT: TALL, 12 TO 18 FEET

Arctostaphylos diversifolia—Bearberry
Camellia species

Carissa species and varieties—-Natal-
    plum
Ceanothus species
Cephalotaxus harringtonia—Japanese
    plum-yew
Cocculus laurifolius—Snailseed
Coprosma baueri
Cotoneaster salicifolia var. floccosa—
    Willowleaf cotoneaster
Cycas species
Elaeagnus pungens—Thorny elaeagnus
Euonymus japonicus—Evergreen
    euonymus
Fatsia japonica—Japan fatsia
Garrya laurifolia—-Silk-tassel bush
Ilex crenata—Japanese holly
Leptospermum species and varieties
Michelia figo—Banana-shrub
Myrtus species and varieties—Myrtle
Nerium oleander—Oleander
Olearia species and varieties—Tree-aster
Osmanthus ilicifolius—Holly osmanthus
Phillyrea species
Photinia species and varieties
Pieris formosa—Himalayan-andromeda
Pittosporum species and varieties
Prunus species and varieties
Pyracantha coccinea var. lalandii—Laland
    firethorn
Rhamnus species and varieties—
    Buckthorn
Rhododendron minus—Piedmont
    rhododendron
    R. smirnowii—Smirnow rhododendron
Stranvaesia davidiana—Chinese
    stranvaesia
Taxus species and varieties—Yew
Thuja species and varieties—Arborvitae
Viburnum species and varieties

Shrubs
WITH EVERGREEN FOLIAGE: BY
HEIGHT: VERY TALL, OVER 18 FEET

Bauhinia species
Buxus sempervirens—Common box
Callistemon species and varieties—
    Bottle-brush
Camellia japonica—Common camellia
Ceanothus species and varieties

Clethra arborea—White-alder
Erica species and varieties—Heath
Ilex species and varieties—Holly
Juniperus species and varieties—Juniper
Ligustrum lucidum—Glossy privet
Myrica species and varieties
Nerium oleander—Oleander
Olearia species and varieties—Tree-aster
Osmanthus species and varieties
Photinia species and varieties
Pittosporum species and varieties
Prunus species and varieties
Rhododendron maximum—Rosebay
  rhododendron

Shrubs
WITH DECORATIVE FLOWERS: BY COLOR: BLUE

Amorpha canescens—Lead-plant
Callicarpa americana—Beauty-berry
CARYOPTERIS—Bluebeard
Ceanothus species and varieties
Ceratostigma plumbaginoides—Leadwort.
  Plumbago
Hydrangea species and varieties
Lagerstroemia indica variety—Crape-
  myrtle
Rhododendron species and varieties
Rosmarinus officinalis—Rosemary
Teucrium chamaedrys—Germander

Shrubs
WITH DECORATIVE FLOWERS: BY COLOR: ORANGE

Abutilon x hybridum—Flowering-maple
Berberis darwinii—Barberry
Chaenomeles species and varieties—
  Flowering-quince
Enkianthus species and varieties
Rhododendron species and varieties, in-
  cluding azalea

Shrubs
WITH DECORATIVE FLOWERS: BY COLOR: PINK

Abelia floribunda—Mexican abelia
Abutilon x hybridum—Flowering-maple

Andromeda species
Arctostaphylos species—Manzanita. Bear-
  berry
Bauhinia species
BRUCKENTHALIA—Spike-heath
Callicarpa species—Beauty-berry
Callistemon species and varieties—Bottle-
  brush
Calluna vulgaris varieties—Heather
Camellia species and varieties
Cercis species and varieties—Redbud
Chaenomeles species and varieties—
  Flowering-quince
Cistus species and varieties—Rock-rose
Clerodendrum species—Glory-bower
Cotoneaster species and varieties
Daboecia cantabrica var. pallida—Irish-
  heath
Daphne species and varieties
Deutzia species and varieties
Erica species and varieties—Heath
Escallonia species
Fuchsia species and varieties
Hebe species and varieties
Hibiscus syriacus—Shrub-althea
Hydrangea species and varieties
Kalmia species and varieties—Lambkill.
  Mountain-laurel
KALMIOPSIS
KOLKWITZIA—Beauty-bush
Lagerstroemia species and varieties—
  Crape-myrtle
Leiophyllum species—Sand-myrtle
LOISELEURIA—Alpine-azalea
Lonicera species and varieties—Honey-
  suckle
Lyonia mariana—Staggerbush
Melaleuca species—Bottle-brush
Myrtus ugni—Chilean-guava
Neillia sinensis
Paeonia suffruticosa—Peony
Pernettya species
Physocarpus species and varieties—Nine-
  bark
Raphiolepis indica—India raphiolepis
Rhododendron species and varieties, in-
  cluding azalea
Robinia species and varieties—Locust
Rosa species and varieties—Rose
Spiraea species and varieties—Spirea

Symphoricarpos species—Snowberry
Syringa species and varieties—Lilac
Tamarix species and varieties—Tamarisk
Teucrium species—Germander
Vaccinium species and varieties—Blue-
berry
Viburnum species and varieties
Weigela species and varieties

Shrubs
WITH DECORATIVE FLOWERS:
BY COLOR: PURPLE

Abutilon x *hybridum*—Flowering-maple
Buddleia species and varieties—Butterfly-
bush
Callistemon species and varieties—Bottle-
brush
Calluna vulgaris varieties—Heather
Cercis species and varieties—Redbud
Chilopsis linearis—Desert-willow
Cistus species and varieties—Rock-rose
Clerodendrum species—Glory-bower
Cytisus purpureus—Purple broom
Daboecia cantabrica var. *atropurpurea*—
Irish-heath
Daphne species and varieties
DISANTHUS
ELSHOLTZIA
Empetrum nigrum—Black crowberry
Erica species and varieties—Heath
Fuchsia species and varieties
Hibiscus syriacus—Shrub-althea
Hydrangea species and varieties
Kalmia species and varieties—Lambkill.
Mountain-laurel
KALMIOPSIS
Lagerstroemia species and varieties—
Crape-myrtle
LEPTODERMIS
Lespedeza species—Bush-clover
Lycium chinense—Chinese wolfberry
Nerium oleander—Oleander
Pittosporum crassifolium—Karo
Rhododendron species and varieties, in-
cluding azalea
Robinia species and varieties—Locust
Syringa species and varieties—Lilac
Vitex species and varieties—Chaste-tree
Weigela species and varieties

Shrubs
WITH DECORATIVE FLOWERS:
BY COLOR: RED

Abutilon x *hybridum*—Flowering-maple
Bauhinia punctata
Callistemon species and varieties—Bottle-
brush
Calycanthus species—Sweet shrub
Camellia species and varieties
Cestrum species
Chaenomeles species and varieties—
Flowering-quince
Clerodendrum species and varieties—
Glory-bower
Colutea arborescens—Bladder-senna
Enkianthus species and varieties
Erica species and varieties—Heath
Escallonia species
Fuchsia species and varieties
Hakea laurina—Sea-urchin
Lagerstroemia species and varieties—
Crape-myrtle
Lonicera species and varieties—Honey-
suckle
Melaleuca species—Bottle-brush
Melianthus major—Large honey-bush
Nerium oleander—Oleander
Pittosporum crassifolium—Karo
Punica granatum—Pomegranate
Rhododendron species and varieties, in-
cluding azalea
Ribes species and varieties—Currant.
Gooseberry
Rosa species and varieties—Rose
RUSSELIA
Spiraea species and varieties—Spirea
Weigela species and varieties

Shrubs
WITH DECORATIVE FLOWERS:
BY COLOR: WHITE

Abelia species and varieties
ABELIOPHYLLUM
Abutilon x *hybridum*—Flowering-maple
Aesculus parviflora—Dwarf horse-
chestnut
AMELANCHIER—Serviceberry. Shadblow

Arctostaphylos species—Manzanita. Bear-
berry
ARDISIA
ARONIA—Chokeberry
Bauhinia acuminata
Calluna vulgaris varieties—Heather
Camellia species and varieties
Carissa grandiflora—Natal-plum
Carpenteria californica—Evergreen mock-
orange
Ceanothus americanus—New Jersey-tea
C. ovatus—Inland ceanothus
Cephalanthus occidentalis—Button-bush
Cestrum species
Chaenomeles species and varieties—
Flowering-quince
CHIONANTHUS—Fringetree
Choisya ternata—Mexican-orange
Cistus species and varieties—Rock-rose
Clerodendrum species—Glory-bower
CLETHRA—White-alder
Cornus species and varieties—Dogwood
Cotoneaster species and varieties
Cyrilla racemiflora—American cyrilla
Cytisus species and varieties—Broom
Daboecia cantabrica var. *alba*—Irish-heath
Daphne species and varieties
Deutzia species and varieties
Elaeagnus pungens—Thorny elaeagnus
Enkianthus species and varieties
Erica species and varieties—Heath
Eurya ochnacea—Sakaki
EXOCHORDA—Pearl-bush
FOTHERGILLA
FRANKLINIA
GARDENIA
GAULTHERIA—Wintergreen
GAYLUSSACIA—Huckleberry
Hakea suaveolens—Sweet hakea
Hebe species and varieties
HETEROMELES—Christmas-berry
Hibiscus syriacus—Shrub-althea
HOLODISCUS—Ocean spray
Hydrangea species and varieties
ITEA—Sweetspire
Jasminum species and varieties—Jasmine
Kalmia species and varieties—Lambkill
Lagerstroemia species and varieties—
Crape-myrtle
Ledum groenlandicum—Labrador-tea

LEIOPHYLLUM—Sand-myrtle
LEUCOTHOE
Ligustrum species and varieties—Privet
Lonicera species and varieties—Honey-
suckle
LOROPETALUM
LYONIA
Magnolia species and varieties
Malus sargentii—Sargent crab apple
Melaleuca species—Bottle-brush
Myrtus communis—Myrtle
NANDINA—Heavenly-bamboo
Neillia species
Nerium oleander—Oleander
NEVIUSIA—Snow-wreath
Olearia haastii—New Zealand daisy-bush
Osmanthus species
Paeonia suffruticosa—Peony
PERNETTYA
Philadelphus species and varieties—Mock-
orange
PHILLYREA
PHOTINIA
Physocarpus species and varieties—Nine-
bark
PIERIS
Pittosporum species
Prunus species and varieties
Pyracantha species and varieties—Fire-
thorn
Raphiolepis umbellata—Yeddo-hawthorn
Rhododendron species and varieties, in-
cluding azalea
RHODOTYPOS—Jetbead
Robinia leucantha—Locust
Rosa species and varieties—Rose
Rubus species and varieties—Raspberry.
Blackberry
Sambucus species—Elder. Elderberry
SARCOCOCCA
SIPHONOSMANTHUS
SKIMMIA
SORBARIA—False spirea
Spiraea species and varieties—Spirea
STEWARTIA
STYRAX—Storax
Symphoricarpos species and varieties—
Snowberry
Syringa species and varieties—Lilac

TRIPETALEIA
Vaccinium species and varieties—Blue-
berry
Viburnum species and varieties
Weigela species and varieties
XANTHOCERAS
Yucca species and varieties—Adam's-
needle
ZENOBIA

Shrubs
WITH DECORATIVE FLOWERS:
BY COLOR: YELLOW

Abutilon x *hybridum*—Flowering-maple
Acacia species and varieties—Wattle
Berberis species and varieties—Barberry
Callistemon species and varieties—Bottle-
brush
Caragana species and varieties—Pea-tree
Cassia species and varieties—Senna
Cestrum species
Chimonanthus praecox—Wintersweet
Colutea arborescens—Bladder-senna
Cornus species and varieties—Dogwood
CORYLOPSIS—Winter-hazel
Cytisus species and varieties—Broom
Diervilla species—Bush-honeysuckle
DIRCA—Leatherwood
Elaeagnus species
Enkianthus species and varieties
Forsythia species and varieties
Gamolepis chrysanthemoides
Garrya species—Silk-tassel bush
GENISTA—Woadwaxen
Hamamelis species and varieties—Witch-
hazel
HIPPOPHAE—Sea-buckthorn
Hypericum species and varieties—St.
John's-wort
Jasminum species and varieties—Jasmine
Kerria species and varieties
Lindera benzoin—Spicebush
Mahonia species and varieties
Michelia figo—Banana-shrub
Nerium oleander—Oleander
Pittosporum species
Potentilla fruticosa—Cinquefoil
PRINSEPIA

Rhododendron species and varieties, in-
cluding azalea
Rhus species—Sumac
Rosa species and varieties—Rose
Spartium junceum—Spanish-broom
STACHYURUS

Shrubs
WITH DECORATIVE FLOWERS:
BY FLOWERING PERIOD:
EARLY SPRING

ABELIOPHYLLUM—Korean abelia-leaf
Acer circinatum—Vine maple
Alnus incana—Speckled alder
  A. rugosa—Hazel alder
Aucuba japonica—Japanese-laurel
Buxus microphylla—Littleleaf box
Camellia species and varieties
Ceanothus x *delilianus* and varieties
Chaenomeles species and varieties—
Flowering-quince
Chimonanthus praecox—Wintersweet
Cornus mas—Cornelian-cherry
  C. officinalis—Dogwood
Corylopsis species—Winter-hazel
Corylus species—Filbert
Daphne genkwa
  D. mezereum—February daphne
Dirca palustris—Leatherwood
Erica carnea—Spring heath
Exochorda species—Pearl-bush
FORSYTHIA
Hamamelis intermedia—Witch-hazel
  H. japonica
  H. mollis
Hippophae species—Sea-buckthorn
Jasminum nudiflorum—Winter jasmine
KALMIOPSIS
Lindera benzoin—Spicebush
Lonicera species and varieties—Honey-
suckle
Loropetalum chinense
Magnolia species and varieties
Melianthus species—Honey-bush
Myrica gale—Sweet-gale
Osmanthus fragrans—Sweet-olive
Pieris floribunda—Mountain-andromeda
  P. japonica—Japanese-andromeda

Poncirus trifoliata—Hardy-orange
Prinsepia species
Prunus tomentosa—Manchu cherry
    P. triloba—Flowering almond
Rhododendron species and varieties, in-
    cluding azalea
Rhus species—Sumac
Rosmarinus officinalis—Rosemary
Shepherdia argentea—Buffalo-berry
Siphonosmanthus delavayi
Stachyurus praecox
Viburnum farreri—Fragrant viburnum

Shrubs
WITH DECORATIVE FLOWERS:
BY FLOWERING PERIOD:
MID-SPRING

ABELIOPHYLLUM—Korean abelia-leaf
Acer palmatum—Japanese maple
Amelanchier species and varieties—
    Serviceberry. Shadblow
Arctostaphylos species—Bearberry
Ardisia crispa—Coral ardisia
Berberis species and varieties—Barberry
Calycanthus floridus—Sweet shrub
Camellia species and varieties
Caragana species and varieties—Pea-tree
Ceanothus species and varieties
Cercis chinensis—Chinese Judas-tree
Cestrum species
Chaenomeles species and varieties—
    Flowering-quince
CHAMAEDAPHNE—Leatherleaf
Chimonanthus praecox—Wintersweet
CHOISYA—Mexican-orange
Corylopsis species—Winter-hazel
Cotoneaster species and varieties
Cytisus species and varieties—Broom
Daphne altaica
    D. caucasica
    D. cneorum—Garland-flower
Deutzia species and varieties
Elaeagnus multiflora—Gumi
    E. umbellatus
Empetrum nigrum—Black crowberry
Enkianthus campanulatus
    E. perulatus
Erica species and varieties—Heath

Euonymus alatus—Corkbush. Winged
    euonymus
    E. latifolius
Exochorda species—Pearl-bush
Forsythia species and varieties
Fothergilla species
Gaultheria species
Gaylussacia baccata—Black huckleberry
Genista species—Woadwaxen
Jasminum species—Jasmine
KALMIOPSIS
Kerria japonica
Ledum groenlandicum—Labrador-tea
LEIOPHYLLUM—Sand-myrtle
Leucothoe species and varieties
Lonicera species and varieties—Honey-
    suckle
Magnolia species and varieties
Mahonia species
Malus sargentii—Sargent crab apple
Michelia figo—Banana-shrub
Myrica pensylvanica—Bayberry
NEVIUSIA—Snow-wreath
Osmanthus species and varieties
Photinia species and varieties
Pieris species and varieties
Potentilla fruticosa—Cinquefoil
Prinsepia sinensis
    P. uniflora
Prunus species and varieties
RAPHIOLEPIS
Rhododendron species and varieties, in-
    cluding azalea
Rhus aromatica—Fragrant sumac
Ribes alpinum—Mountain currant
    R. odoratum—Clove currant
    R. sanguineum—Winter currant
Robinia species—Locust
Rosmarinus officinalis—Rosemary
Rubus species and varieties—Bramble
Sambucus pubens—Scarlet elder
SKIMMIA
Spiraea x arguta—Garland spirea
    S. thunbergii—Spirea
Syringa species and varieties—Lilac
Vaccinium angustifolium—Low-bush
    blueberry
Viburnum species and varieties
Weigela species and varieties
Xanthorhiza simplicissima—Yellow-root

Shrubs

WITH DECORATIVE FLOWERS:
BY FLOWERING PERIOD:
LATE SPRING

Acer ginnala—Amur maple
Aesculus species and varieties—Horse-chestnut. Buckeye
Amorpha fruticosa—False indigo
Andromeda species and varieties
Arctostaphylos species—Bearberry
Aronia species—Chokeberry
Berberis species and varieties—Barberry
Berchemia racemosa—Japanese supple-jack
BRUCKENTHALIA—Spike-heath
Buddleia alternifolia—Butterfly-bush
Callistemon species and varieties—Bottle-brush
Caragana maximowicziana—Pea-tree
Castanea pumila—Allegheny chinquapin
Ceanothus americanus—New Jersey-tea
  C. ovatus
Cestrum species
Chionanthus retusus—Chinese fringetree
  C. virginicus—Fringetree
CHOISYA—Mexican-orange
Cistus species—Rock-rose
Clerodendrum species—Glory-bower
COLUTEA—Bladder-senna
Cornus species and varieties—Dogwood
Cotinus coggygria—Smokebush
  C. obovatus
Cotoneaster species and varieties
Cytisus species and varieties—Broom
Daphne giraldii
  D. pontica
Decaisnea fargesii
Deutzia species and varieties
Diervilla species and varieties—Bush-honeysuckle
Elaeagnus angustifolia—Russian-olive
Enkianthus species
Erica species and varieties—Heath
Euonymus bungeanus—Winterberry euonymus
  E. europaeus—European spindle-tree
  E. fortunei var. *vegetus*—Wintercreeper
Exochorda species—Pearl-bush

Fontanesia fortunei
Fuchsia species and varieties
Gardenia species and varieties
Gaultheria species
Gaylussacia baccata—Black huckleberry
Genista hispanica—Woadwaxen
  G. pilosa—Silky-leaf woadwaxen
  G. tinctoria—Dyers' greenweed
Halimodendron halodendron—Salt-tree
Helianthemum nummularium—Sun-rose
HETEROMELES—Christmas-berry
Hydrangea anomala var. *petiolaris*
Hypericum species and varieties—St. John's-wort
Ilex species and varieties—Holly
Indigofera species and varieties—Indigo
Jasminum species—Jasmine
Kalmia species
KALMIOPSIS
Kerria japonica
Kolkwitzia amabilis—Beauty-bush
Laburnum anagyroides—Golden-chain tree
Leptospermum species—Australian tea-tree
Leucothoe fontanesiana—Drooping leucothoe
  L. racemosa—Sweetbells
Ligustrum species and varieties—Privet
Lonicera species and varieties—Honeysuckle
Lyonia species
Magnolia species and varieties
Mahonia species
Michelia figo—Banana-shrub
Neillia sinensis
NEVIUSIA—Snow-wreath
Osmanthus species
Paeonia suffruticosa—Tree peony
PERNETTYA
Philadelphus species and varieties—Mock-orange
Phillyrea species
Photinia villosa
Physocarpus species—Ninebark
Pittosporum species and varieties
Potentilla fruticosa—Cinquefoil
Prunus species and varieties
Pyracantha species and varieties—Firethorn

RAPHIOLEPIS
Rhamnus cathartica—Common buckthorn
    R. davurica
    R. frangula—Alder buckthorn
Rhododendron species and varieties,
    including azalea
Rhodotypos tetrapetala—Jetbead
Robinia species and varieties—Locust
Rosa species and varieties—Rose
Rubus deliciosus—Rocky Mountain
    raspberry
    R. phoenicolasius—Wineberry
Sambucus nigra—Black elder
SKIMMIA
Spiraea species and varieties—Spirea
Staphylea pinnata—Bladder-nut
Stephanandra incisa
Styrax species—Storax
Symphoricarpos albus var. laevigatus—
    Snowberry
Syringa species and varieties—Lilac
Tamarix parviflora—Small-flowered
    tamarisk
Vaccinium corymbosum—High-bush
    blueberry
    V. stamineum
Viburnum species and varieties
Weigela species and varieties
Wisteria species and varieties
Zenobia pulverulenta—Dusty zenobia

Shrubs
WITH DECORATIVE FLOWERS:
BY FLOWERING PERIOD: SUMMER

Abelia x grandiflora—Glossy abelia
    A. schumannii
Acanthopanax sieboldianus—Fiveleaf-
    aralia
Aesculus parviflora—Dwarf horse-
    chestnut
Amorpha canescens—Lead-plant
Aralia elata—Japanese angelica-tree
    A. spinosa—Devil's-walking-stick
Buddleia davidii—Butterfly-bush
Callicarpa species and varieties
Callistemon species and varieties
Calluna vulgaris—Heather
Carissa grandiflora—Natal-plum

Carpenteria californica—Evergreen
    mock-orange
Caryopteris incana
Cassia species and varieties—Senna
Ceanothus pallidus
Cephalanthus occidentalis—Button-bush
Ceratostigma species—Leadwort
Cestrum species
Chilopsis linearis—Desert-willow
Cistus ladaniferus—Rock-rose
Clerodendrum trichotomum—Harlequin
    glory-bower
Clethra species—White-alder
COLUTEA—Bladder-senna
Cotoneaster salicifolia
CYRILLA—Leatherwood
Cytisus decumbens—Broom
    C. nigricans—Spike broom
DABOECIA—Irish-heath
Deutzia scabra
Diervilla sessilifolia—Bush-honey-
    suckle
Elsholtzia species
Erica species and varieties—Heath
Escallonia species
Gardenia species and varieties
Gaultheria species
Genista species—Woadwaxen
Hebe species and varieties
HETEROMELES—Christmas-berry
Hibiscus syriacus—Shrub-althea
Holodiscus discolor—Rock-spirea
Hydrangea species and varieties
Hypericum species and varieties
Indigofera species—Indigo
Itea virginica—Virginia sweetspire
Jasminum species—Jasmine
Lagerstroemia indica—Crape-myrtle
Leptodermis oblonga
Lespedeza species—Bush-clover
Ligustrum quihoui—Quihou privet
LOISELEURIA—Alpine-azalea
Lonicera species and varieties
Lycium species—Box thorn
Myrtus communis—Myrtle
Nandina domestica—Heavenly-bamboo
Neillia sinensis
Olearia species—Tree-aster
Osmanthus ilicifolius

Oxydendrum arboreum—Sour-wood
Potentilla fruticosa—Cinquefoil
Punica granatum—Pomegranate
Rhododendron species and varieties,
    including azalea
Rhodotypos tetrapetala—Jetbead
Rhus copallina—Shining sumac
    R. *glabra*—Smooth sumac
    R. *typhina*—Staghorn sumac
Rosa species and varieties—Rose
Rubus odoratus—Flowering raspberry
Russelia equisetiformis—Coral plant
Sambucus canadensis—Sweet elder
Sorbaria sorbifolia—False spirea
Spartium junceum—Spanish broom
Spiraea species and varieties—Spirea
Stewartia species
Symphoricarpos species
Tamarix species—Tamarisk
Tripetaleia paniculata
Viburnum setigerum var. *aurantiacum*—
    Tea viburnum
Vitex species—Chaste-tree

Shrubs
WITH DECORATIVE FLOWERS:
BY FLOWERING PERIOD: AUTUMN

Abelia species and varieties
Camellia sasanqua
Carissa grandiflora—Natal-plum
Caryopteris species and varieties—
    Bluebeard
Chilopsis linearis—Desert-willow
Disanthus cercidifolius
Elaeagnus pungens—Thorny elaeagnus
Elsholtzia stauntonii
Escallonia species
Fatsia japonica—Japan fatsia
Franklinia alatamaha
Hamamelis virginiana—Witch-hazel
Hakea species
Lespedeza japonica—Japanese bush-
    clover

Shrubs
WITH DECORATIVE FLOWERS:
BY FLOWERING PERIOD: WINTER

Acacia species and varieties—Wattle
Bauhinia species

Camellia species and varieties
Escallonia species
Garrya elliptica—Silk-tassel bush
Hakea species
Hamamelis vernalis—Vernal witch-hazel

Shrubs
WITH DECORATIVE FRUIT:
BY COLOR: BLACK

Aronia melanocarpa—Black chokeberry
Berberis species and varieties—Barberry
Cocculus laurifolius—Snailseed
Cotoneaster lucida—Hedge cotoneaster
Empetrum nigrum—Black crowberry
Eurya japonica
Gaylussacia baccata—Black huckleberry
Ilex crenata—Japanese holly
    I. *glabra*—Inkberry. Winterberry
Ligustrum species and varieties—Privet
Lonicera species—Honeysuckle
Mahonia aquifolium—Oregon-grape
Myrtus communis—Myrtle
Osmanthus species
Phillyrea species
Prunus species and varieties
Raphiolepis umbellata—Yeddo-hawthorn
Rhamnus species and varieties—Buckthorn
Rhodotypos tetrapetala—Jetbead
Ribes species and varieties—Currant
Rubus species and varieties—Bramble
Sambucus species—Elder. Elderberry
Sarcococca hookeriana
Siphonosmanthus delavayi
Vaccinium species and varieties—Blue-
    berry
Viburnum species and varieties

Shrubs
WITH DECORATIVE FRUIT:
BY COLOR: BLUE

Berberis species—Barberry
CHIONANTHUS—Fringetree
Clerodendrum trichotomum—Glory-bower
Coprosma petriei
Cornus species—Dogwood
Fatsia japonica—Japan fatsia
Gaultheria veitchiana—Veitch wintergreen
Gaylussacia brachycera—Box huckleberry

Juniperus species and varieties—Juniper
Ligustrum species and varieties—Privet
Mahonia nervosa
Myrtus communis—Myrtle
Raphiolepis species
Sambucus caerulea—Blue elder
Symplocos paniculata—Asiatic sweetleaf
Vaccinium species and varieties—Blue-
berry
Viburnum species

Shrubs
WITH DECORATIVE FRUIT:
BY COLOR: ORANGE

Coprosma baueri
Hippophae rhamnoides—Sea-buckthorn
Pyracantha varieties—Firethorn
Rhus chinensis—Sumac

Shrubs
WITH DECORATIVE FRUIT:
BY COLOR: PINK

Cotinus coggygria—Smokebush
Euonymus species and varieties—Spindle-
tree

Shrubs
WITH DECORATIVE FRUIT:
BY COLOR: PURPLE

Amelanchier species—Serviceberry. Shad-
blow
Aronia prunifolia—Purple-fruited choke-
berry
Berberis species—Barberry
CALLICARPA—Beauty-berry
Coprosma petriei
Garrya elliptica—Silk-tassel bush
Gaultheria shallon—Salal
Myrica californica—California bayberry
Myrtus communis—Myrtle
Pernettya mucronata var. *atrococcinea*—
Chilean pernettya
Prinsepia sinensis
Prunus species
Raphiolepis species
Rubus deliciosus—Boulder raspberry
  R. x *loganobaccus*—Loganberry

Shrubs
WITH DECORATIVE FRUIT:
BY COLOR: RED

Arctostaphylos species and varieties—
Manzanita. Bearberry
Ardisia crispa—Coral ardisia
Aronia arbutifolia—Red chokeberry
Aucuba japonica—Japanese aucuba
Berberis species and varieties—Barberry
Carissa grandiflora—Natal-plum
Cestrum fasciculatum
  C. purpureum—Red cestrum
Cocculus carolinus—Carolina moonseed
Cornus species and varieties—Dogwood
Cotoneaster species and varieties
Daphne mezereum—February daphne
Elaeagnus multiflora—Gumi
  E. umbellata—Autumn elaeagnus
Euonymus species and varieties—Spindle-
tree
Eurya ochnacea
Gaultheria procumbens—Wintergreen.
Checkerberry
Heteromeles arbutifolia—Toyon. Christ-
mas-berry
Ilex species and varieties—Holly
Lindera benzoin—Spicebush
Lonicera species and varieties—Honey-
suckle
Lycium chinense—Box thorn. Matrimony-
vine
Magnolia stellata—Star magnolia
Malus sargentii—Sargent crab apple
Nandina domestica—Heavenly-bamboo
Pernettya mucronata var. *coccinea*
  P. m. var. *speciosa*
PHOTINIA
Prunus tomentosa—Beach plum
Punica granatum—Pomegranate
Pyracantha species and varieties—Fire-
thorn
Rhamnus crocea—Red-berry
Rhus species and varieties—Sumac
Ribes species and varieties—Currant.
Gooseberry

Rosa species and varieties—Rose
Rubus species and varieties—Bramble
Ruscus aculeatus—Butcher's-broom
Sambucus species and varieties—Elder.
  Elderberry
Sarcococca ruscifolia
Shepherdia canadensis
Skimmia japonica
Stranvaesia davidiana
Symphoricarpos x chenaultii—Chenault
  coralberry
Taxus species and varieties—Yew
Viburnum species and varieties

Shrubs
WITH DECORATIVE FRUIT:
BY COLOR: WHITE

Baccharis halimifolia—Groundsel-bush
Cestrum aurantiacum—Orange cestrum
  C. nocturnum—Night-jessamine
Cornus species and varieties—Dogwood
Daphne genkwa
Gaultheria miqueliana—Miquel winter-
  green
Myrica pensylvanica—Bayberry
Nandina domestica var. alba—Heavenly-
  bamboo
Pernettya mucronata var. alba
Symphoricarpos albus var. laevigatus—
  Snowberry
  S. orbiculatus var. leucocarpus—Coral-
  berry. Indian-currant

Shrubs
WITH DECORATIVE FRUIT:
BY COLOR: YELLOW

Chaenomeles species and varieties—
  Flowering-quince
Coprosma baueri
Elaeagnus angustifolia—Russian-olive
Prunus maritima var. flava—Yellow beach
  plum
Punica granatum—Pomegranate
Ribes uva-crispa variety—English goose-
  berry
Stachyurus praecox
Viburnum dilatatum var. xanthocarpum—
  Yellow linden viburnum

Shrubs
WITH CONSPICUOUSLY COLORED
AUTUMN FOLIAGE: RED

Acer circinatum—Vine maple
  A. ginnala—Amur maple
  A. palmatum—Japanese maple
Amelanchier species and varieties
Aronia arbutifolia—Red chokeberry
Berberis species and varieties—
  Barberry
Cercis occidentalis—California redbud
Cornus species and varieties—Dogwood
Cotinus coggygria—Smokebush
  C. obovatus—American smoketree
Cotoneaster species and varieties
Disanthus cercidifolius
ENKIANTHUS
Euonymus alatus—Winged euonymus
Fothergilla species and varieties
Franklinia alatamaha
Hydrangea quercifolia—Oak-leaved
  hydrangea
Itea virginica—Virginia sweetspire
Lagerstroemia indica—Crape-myrtle
Leucothoe racemosa—Sweetbells
NANDINA—Heavenly-bamboo
Pernettya mucronata
Photinia villosa—Oriental photinia
Rhododendron calendulaceum—Flame
  azalea
  R. schlippenbachii—Royal azalea
  R. vaseyi—Pinkshell azalea
Rhus species and varieties—Sumac
Rosa rugosa—Rugosa rose
  R. setigera—Prairie rose
  R. virginiana—Virginia rose
Spiraea prunifolia—Bridalwreath spirea
Stephanandra incisa—Cutleaf steph-
  anandra
Stewartia ovata var. grandiflora—Showy
  stewartia
Symphoricarpos orbiculatus—Indian-
  currant
Syringa oblata var. dilatata—Korean early
  lilac
Vaccinium species and varieties—
  Blueberry
Viburnum species and varieties

Shrubs
WITH CONSPICUOUSLY COLORED AUTUMN FOLIAGE: YELLOW

Acer circinatum—Vine maple
  A. palmatum—Japanese maple
Aesculus parviflora—Dwarf horse-chestnut
Amelanchier species and varieties—Serviceberry. Shadblow
Berberis thunbergii—Barberry
Callicarpa species and varieties—Beauty-berry
Cercis occidentalis—California redbud
Chionanthus virginicus—Fringetree
Clethra alnifolia—Summersweet
Cotinus obovatus—American smoketree
Enkianthus perulatus
Euonymus atropurpureus—Eastern wahoo
FOTHERGILLA
Hamamelis species and varieties—Witch-hazel
Lagerstroemia indica—Crape-myrtle
Lindera benzoin—Spice-bush
Prinsepia sinensis—Cherry prinsepia
Rhododendron schlippenbachii—Royal azalea

Shrubs
WITH BLUISH OR SILVERY FOLIAGE

Artemisia pontica—Roman wormwood
Convolvulus cneorum—Glorybind
Cytisus battandieri—Broom
Elaeagnus species and varieties
Eriogonum arborescens
  E. giganteum
Hippophae rhamnoides—Common sea-buckthorn
Juniperus species and varieties—Juniper
Lavandula officinalis—English lavender
Melianthus major—Honey-bush
Santolina chamaecyparissus—Lavender-cotton
Senecio greyii—Groundsel
Shepherdia argentea—Buffalo-berry
Teucrium fruticans—Germander
Zauschneria californica—California-fuchsia
Zenobia pulverulenta—Dusty zenobia

Shrubs
WITH DECORATIVE BARK

Clethra alnifolia—Summersweet
Cornus species and varieties—Dogwood
Lagerstroemia indica—Crape-myrtle
Stewartia ovata var. *grandiflora*—Showy stewartia

Shrubs
WITH FRAGRANT FLOWERS

Boronia megastigma—Sweet boronia
Bouvardia longiflora var. 'Albatross'
Buddleia alternifolia—Garland butterfly-bush
  B. davidii—Butterfly-bush
Buxus species—Boxwood
Carissa grandiflora—Natal-plum
Carpenteria californica—Evergreen mock-orange
Ceanothus species
Cestrum species
Chilopsis linearis—Desert-willow
Chimonanthus praecox—Wintersweet
Chionanthus virginica—Fringetree
Choisya ternata—Mexican-orange
Citrus species and varieties
Clerodendrum fragrans—Glory-bower
  C. trichotomum—Harlequin glory-bower
Clethra alnifolia—Summersweet
Cytisus battandieri—Morocco broom
Daphne species and varieties
Elaeagnus species and varieties
Elliottia racemosa—Southern-plume
Epigaea repens—Trailing arbutus
Gardenia species and varieties
Halimodendron halodendron—Salt-tree
Hamamelis mollis—Chinese witch-hazel
  H. vernalis—Vernal witch-hazel
Jasminum species and varieties—Jasmine
Lavandula officinalis—English lavender
Ligustrum species and varieties—Privet
Lonicera species and varieties—Honey-suckle
Magnolia species and varieties
Mahonia bealei—Leatherleaf mahonia
Malus baccata and hybrids—Siberian crab apple

Michelia figo—Banana-shrub
Mitchella repens—Partridge-berry
Nerium indicum—Sweet-scented oleander
Olearia haastii—New Zealand daisy-bush
Osmanthus species
Philadelphus coronarius and hybrids—
　Mock-orange
　P. microphyllus and hybrids—Mock-
　　orange
Pittosporum tobira—Japanese pittosporum
Plumeria rubra—Red-jasmine
Prunus, fruiting species and varieties—
　Apricot. Cherry. Peach. Plum
　P. mume—Japanese apricot
Rhododendron arborescens—Sweet azalea
　R. fortunei—Fortune rhododendron
　R. mucronatum—Snow azalea
　R. roseum—Roseshell azalea
　R. viscosum—Swamp azalea
　R. hybrids: Exbury, Ghent, Knap Hill,
　　Mollis, Ilam
Ribes odoratum—Buffalo currant
Rosa species and varieties—Rose
Rubus odoratus—Flowering raspberry
Sarcococca ruscifolia
Siphonosmanthus delavayi
Spartium junceum—Spanish-broom
Symplocos paniculata—Asiatic sweetleaf
Syringa species and varieties—Lilac
Viburnum species and varieties
Vitex agnus-castus—Chaste-tree
Wisteria species and varieties

Shrubs
WITH AROMATIC FOLIAGE

Artemisia species—Sagebrush. Wormwood
Buxus species—Boxwood
Calycanthus species—Sweet shrub
Choisya ternata—Mexican-orange
Coleonema album
Comptonia peregrina—Sweet-fern
Gaultheria procumbens—Wintergreen
Hypericum calycinum—Aaron's-beard
Juniperus species and varieties—Juniper
Laurus nobilis—Laurel. Sweet bay
Lavandula officinalis—English lavender
Lindera benzoin—Spicebush
Lippia citriodora—Lemon-verbena

Myrica species
Myrtus communis—Myrtle
Orixa japonica—Japanese orixa
Rhus aromatica—Fragrant sumac
Rosa eglanteria—Sweetbrier rose
Rosmarinus officinalis—Rosemary
Santolina chamaecyparissus—Lavender-
　cotton
Teucrium chamaedrys—Germander
Viburnum sieboldii—Siebold viburnum
Vitex agnus-castus—Chaste-tree

Shrubs
WITH EDIBLE FRUIT

AMELANCHIER—Serviceberry. Shadblow
Carissa grandiflora—Natal-plum
CHAENOMELES—Flowering-quince
Cornus canadensis—Bunchberry dogwood
　C. mas—Cornelian-cherry
Corylus species and varieties—Hazelnut.
　Filbert
Elaeagnus multiflorus—Cherry elaeagnus
Feijoa selloviana—Pineapple-guava
Gaylussacia baccata—Black huckleberry
Malus sargentii—Sargent crab apple
Myrtus ugni—Chilean-guava
Prunus species and varieties
Punica granatum—Pomegranate
Ribes species and varieties—Currant.
　Gooseberry
Rosa rugosa—Rugosa rose
Rubus species and varieties—Blackberry.
　Raspberry
Sambucus canadensis—American elder
Shepherdia argentea—Buffalo-berry
Vaccinium species and varieties—Blue-
　berry
Viburnum prunifolium—Black haw
　V. trilobum—American cranberry bush

Shrubs
WITH FRUIT ATTRACTIVE TO BIRDS

Amelanchier species—Serviceberry. Shad-
　blow
Arbutus species
Arctostaphylos species—Bearberry
Ardisia crispa—Coral ardisia

Aucuba japonica—Japanese aucuba
Berberis species and varieties—Barberry
Carissa grandiflora—Natal-plum
Chionanthus virginicus—Fringetree
Cocculus laurifolius—Laurel-leaf snail-
seed
Cornus species and varieties—Dogwood
Cotoneaster species and varieties
Elaeagnus species
Empetrum nigrum—Black crowberry
Eriobotrya japonica—Loquat
Euonymus species and varieties—Spindle-
tree
Feijoa sellowiana—Strawberry-guava
Garrya species—Silk-tassel bush
Gaylussacia brachycera—Box huckleberry
Heteromeles arbutifolia—Toyon. Christ-
mas-berry
Lantana species and varieties
Lonicera species and varieties—Honey-
suckle
Mahonia species
Malus sargentii—Sargent crab apple
Myrica species—Bayberry. Wax-myrtle
Myrtus communis—Myrtle
Pernettya mucronata
Photinia species
Prunus species and varieties
Pyracantha species and varieties—Fire-
thorn
Rhus species—Sumac
Ribes species—Currant. Gooseberry
Rosa multiflora—Japanese rose
Rubus species and varieties—Bramble
Sambucus species—Elder. Elderberry
Stranvaesia davidiana
Symphoricarpos species
Vaccinium species and varieties—Blue-
berry
Viburnum species and varieties

Shrubs
THAT TOLERATE CONSIDERABLE SHADE

Abelia species and varieties
Acanthopanax sieboldianus—Fiveleaf-
aralia
Acer circinatum—Maple

Alnus species—Alder
Amelanchier species and varieties—
Serviceberry. Shadblow
Ardisia crispa—Coral ardisia
  A. japonica—Japanese ardisia
Aronia species—Chokeberry
Aucuba japonica—Japanese aucuba
Azara microphylla—Boxleaf azara
Berberis species and varieties—Barberry
Brunfelsia species—Raintree
Buxus species and varieties—Boxwood
Calycanthus floridus—Carolina allspice
Camellia japonica—Common camellia
Cephalanthus occidentalis—Button-bush
Cercis chinensis—Chinese Judas-tree
Chamaecyparis obtusa varieties—Hinoki-
cypress
Chimonanthus praecox—Wintersweet
Chionanthus virginicus—Fringetree
Clethra alnifolia—Summersweet
Cocculus laurifolius—Laurel-leaf
snailseed
Colutea arborescens—Bladder-senna
Comptonia peregrina—Sweet-fern
Coprosma baueri
Cornus species and varieties—Dogwood
Corylopsis species—Winter-hazel
Corylus species—Hazelnut
Cotoneaster salicifolia var. *floccosa*
Daphne mezereum—February daphne
  D. odora—Winter daphne
Diervilla sessilifolia—Southern bush-
honeysuckle
Euonymus fortunei var. *carrierei*—Glossy
wintercreeper
  E. japonicus—Evergreen euonymus
Fatsia japonica—Japan fatsia
Ficus elastica and varieties—Fig
Fothergilla species
Fuchsia magellanica
Gaultheria shallon—Salal
Gaylussacia brachycera—Box huckleberry
Griselinia lucida
Hamamelis species—Witch-hazel

Hardenbergia comptoniana—Compton
  coral-pea
Hydrangea macrophylla
  H. quercifolia—Oak-leaved hydrangea
Hypericum species—St. John's-wort
Ilex species and varieties—Holly
Illicium floridanum—Florida anise-tree
Itea virginica—Virginia sweetspire
Jacobinia species—Plume-flower
Kalmia species—Mountain-laurel
Laurus nobilis—Sweet bay. Laurel
Leucothoe fontanesiana
Ligustrum species and varieties—Privet
Lindera benzoin—Spicebush
Lonicera species and varieties—Honey-
  suckle
Lyonia mariana—Stagger-bush
Magnolia virginiana—Sweet-bay
Mahonia species and varieties
Michelia figo—Banana-shrub
Myrica species—Bayberry. Wax-myrtle
Nandina domestica—Heavenly-bamboo
Osmanthus fragrans—Sweet osmanthus
Pachistima canbyi
Pachysandra terminalis—Japanese spurge
Philesia magellanica—Magellan box-lily
Phillyrea latifolia
Photinia species
Pieris species and varieties—Andromeda
Pittosporum tobira—Japanese pittosporum
Pyracantha species and varieties—
  Firethorn
Raphiolepis umbellata—Yeddo-
  hawthorn
Rhamnus species—Buckthorn
Rhododendron species and varieties,
  including azalea
Rhodotypos tetrapetala—Jetbead
Rubus odoratus—Flowering raspberry
Ruscus aculeatus—Butcher's-broom
Sabal minor—Dwarf palmetto
Sambucus caerulea—Blue elder
  S. pubens—Scarlet elder
Sarcococca species
Sasa palmata—Bamboo
Severinia buxifolia—Chinese box-orange
Skimmia japonica—Japanese skimmia
Sorbaria species and varieties—False
  spirea
Stachyurus praecox

Symphoricarpos species—Coralberry.
  Snowberry
Taxus species and varieties—Yew
Thea sinensis—Tea
Thuja species and varieties—Arborvitae
Torreya species
Tsuga canadensis varieties—Hemlock
Vaccinium species and varieties—
  Blueberry
Viburnum species and varieties
Xanthorhiza simplicissima—Yellow-root
Zamia integrifolia—Coontie
Zenobia pulverulenta—Dusty zenobia

Shrubs
THAT TOLERATE DAMP GROUND

Abutilon species and varieties—Flower-
  ing-maple
Alnus species—Alder
Amelanchier species—Serviceberry.
  Shadblow
Andromeda species
Aronia arbutifolia—Red chokeberry
  A. melanocarpa—Black chokeberry
Calluna vulgaris—Heather
Cephalanthus occidentalis—Button-bush
Chaenomeles species and varieties—
  Flowering-quince
Chamaedaphne calyculata—Leatherleaf
Clethra alnifolia—Summersweet
Cocculus laurifolius—Laurel-leaf
  snailseed
Cornus sericea—Red osier dogwood
Dirca palustris—Leatherwood
Enkianthus species
FOTHERGILLA
Franklinia alatamaha
Gaultheria shallon—Salal
Gaylussacia brachycera—Box huckle-
  berry
Hippophae rhamnoides—Sea-buckthorn
Hydrangea species and varieties
Ilex cassine—Dahoon holly
  I. glabra—Inkberry
  I. verticillata—Winterberry
Itea virginica—Virginia sweetspire
Kalmia species—Lambkill. Mountain-
  laurel

Ledum groenlandicum—Labrador-tea
Leiophyllum buxifolium—Box sand-
  myrtle
Leucothoe davisiae
  L. fontanesiana—Drooping leucothoe
Ligustrum species and varieties—Privet
Lindera benzoin—Spicebush
Loiseleuria procumbens—Alpine-azalea
Lyonia mariana—Staggerbush
Lysimachia clethroides—Japanese
  loosestrife
Myrica species—Bayberry. Wax-myrtle
Nandina domestica—Heavenly-bamboo
Nerium oleander—Oleander
Rhododendron arborescens—Sweet azalea
  R. canadense—Rhodora
  R. maximum—Rosebay rhododendron
  R. nudiflorum—Pinxterbloom
  R. vaseyi—Pinkshell azalea
  R. viscosum—Swamp azalea
Rosa palustris—Swamp rose
Sabal minor—Dwarf palmetto
Salix caprea—Goat willow
  S. discolor—Pussy willow
  S. purpurea—Purple osier
Sambucus canadensis—Sweet elder
SORBARIA—False spirea
Spiraea tomentosa—Hardhack
STEWARTIA
Tetrapanax papyriferum—Chinese paper
  plant
Thuja occidentalis varieties—American
  arborvitae
Vaccinium corymbosum—High-bush
  blueberry
  V. macrocarpon—American cranberry
Viburnum cassinoides—Withe-rod
Xanthorhiza simplicissima—Yellow-root
Zamia integrifolia—Coontie
Zenobia pulverulenta—Dusty zenobia

Shrubs
THAT TOLERATE DRY GROUND

Acanthopanax sieboldiana—Fiveleaf-
  aralia
Acer ginnala—Amur maple
Amorpha canescens—Lead-plant
Arctostaphylos uva-ursi—Bearberry
Atriplex species—Salt-bush

Baccharis halimifolia—Groundsel-bush
Berberis x mentorensis—Mentor barberry
  B. thunbergii
Buddleia alternifolia—Fountain buddleia
Callistemon lanceolatus—Lemon bottle-
  brush
Calluna vulgaris—Heather
Caragana species and varieties—Pea-tree
Cassia species—Senna
Ceanothus americanus—New Jersey-tea
Chaenomeles species and varieties—
  Flowering-quince
Cistus species and varieties—Rock-rose
Colutea arborescens—Bladder-senna
Comptonia peregrina—Sweet-fern
Corema conradii—Broom-crowberry
Cornus racemosa—Gray dogwood
Cotinus coggygria—Smoketree
Cytisus species and varieties—Broom
Diervilla lonicera—Dwarf bush-honey-
  suckle
Elaeagnus angustifolia—Russian-olive
Gaylussacia baccata—Black huckleberry
Genista species—Woadwaxen
Hamamelis virginiana—Witch-hazel
Hebe species
HIPPOPHAE—Sea-buckthorn
Hypericum species and varieties—St.
  John's-wort
Indigofera species—Indigo
Juniperus species and varieties—Juniper
Ligustrum species and varieties—Privet
Myrica pensylvanica—Bayberry
Myrtus communis—Myrtle
Nerium oleander—Oleander
PACHISTIMA
Physocarpus species—Ninebark
Pittosporum species
Potentilla fruticosa—Cinquefoil
Prunus besseyi—Western sand cherry
  P. maritima—Beach plum
Rhamnus species—Buckthorn
Rhus species—Sumac
Robinia species—Locust
Rosa species and varieties—Rose
Rosmarinus officinalis—Rosemary
Ruscus aculeatus—Butcher's-broom
Santolina chamaecyparissus—Lavender-
  cotton
Shepherdia canadensis—Buffalo-berry

Sophora davidii—Vetch sophora
Spartium junceum—Spanish-broom
Spiraea latifolia—Meadow-sweet
Symphoricarpos species
Tamarix species and varieties—Tamarisk
Teucrium chamaedrys—Germander
Vaccinium pallidum—Dryland blueberry
Viburnum lentago—Nannyberry
Vitex agnus-castus—Chaste-tree
Yucca species—Adam's-needle

Trees

Trees
WITH DECIDUOUS FOLIAGE:
BY HEIGHT: SMALL, UNDER 20 FEET

Acer species and varieties—Maple
Aesculus pavia—Red buckeye
Albizia lophantha—Plume albizia
Carpinus caroliniana—American horn-
    beam. Ironwood. Blue beech
Castanea pumila—Chinquapin
Cercidiphyllum japonicum—Katsura tree
Cercis canadensis var. 'Wither's Pink
    Charm'—Eastern redbud cultivar
Chionanthus retusus—Chinese fringetree
Clethra acuminata—White-alder
    C. barbinervis—White-alder
Cornus officinalis—Dogwood
Crataegus species and varieties—Haw-
    thorn. Thornapple
Cydonia oblonga—Quince
Elaeagnus angustifolia—Russian-olive
Erythrina crista-gallii—Cockspur coral
    tree
Euonymus species and varieties—Spindle-
    tree
Lagerstroemia indica—Crape-myrtle
Malus species and varieties—Apple
Mespilus germanica—Medlar
Paliurus spina-christi—Christ-thorn
Parrotia jacquemontiana
    P. persica
Prunus nipponica
    P. spinosa—Blackthorn
Punica granatum—Pomegranate
Rhamnus cathartica—Common buckthorn
Salix discolor—Pussy willow

Sambucus pubens—American red elder.
    Scarlet elder
Syringa amurensis—Lilac
    S. x chinensis—Lilac
Tamarix parviflora—Tamarisk

Trees
WITH DECIDUOUS FOLIAGE:
BY HEIGHT: MEDIUM, 20 TO 40 FEET

Acer species and varieties—Maple
Aesculus species and varieties—Horse-
    chestnut. Buckeye
Albizia julibrissin—Silk-tree
Alnus rugosa—Hazel alder
    A. serrulata—Smooth alder
Amelanchier species and varieties—
    Serviceberry. Shadblow
Aralia spinosa—Devil's-walking-stick.
    Hercules'-club
Asimina triloba—Papaw
Bauhinia variegata—Mountain ebony.
    Orchid tree
Betula populifolia—Gray birch
Broussonetia papyrifera—Paper-mulberry
Carpinus japonica—Japanese hornbeam
    C. orientalis—Oriental hornbeam
Castanea crenata—Japanese chestnut
Catalpa ovata—Chinese catalpa
Chionanthus virginicus—Fringetree
Cladrastis lutea—American yellow-wood
Cornus species and varieties—Dogwood
Cotinus obovatus
Crataegus species and varieties—Haw-
    thorn. Thornapple
Cyrilla racemiflora—American cyrilla
Delonix regia—Royal poinciana
Diospyros kaki—Persimmon
Ficus carica—Common fig
    F. lyrata—Fiddleleaf fig
Franklinia alatamaha
Fraxinus ornus—Flowering ash. Manna
    ash
Halesia carolina—Silver-bell. Snowdrop
    tree
Hamamelis japonica—Witch-hazel
    H. mollis—Witch-hazel
Ilex decidua—Possum-haw
    I. verticillata—Winterberry

Koelreuteria paniculata—Golden-rain tree
Laburnum species and varieties
Magnolia species and varieties
Malus species and varieties—apple
Melia azedarach—Chinaberry. China tree
Morus nigra—Mulberry
Paulownia tomentosa—Empress tree
Phellodendron chinense—Cork tree
Pistacia vera—Pistachio
Poncirus trifoliata—Hardy-orange
Prunus species and varieties
Pyrus salicifolia—Willowleaf pear
Rhamnus davurica—Buckthorn
   R. purshiana—Buckthorn
Robinia species and varieties—Locust
Salix species and varieties—Willow. Osier
Sambucus caerulea—Blue elder
Sophora tetraptera
Sorbus species and varieties—Mountain
   ash
Stewartia pseudo-camellia
Styrax japonica—Japanese snowbell
   S. obassia—Storax
Syringa amurensis var. *japonica*—Lilac
Tamarix aphylla—Athel tamarisk. Salt
   tree
Zizyphus jujuba—Jujube

Trees
WITH DECIDUOUS FOLIAGE:
BY HEIGHT: TALL, 40 TO 60 FEET

Acer species and varieties—Maple
Ailanthus altissima—Tree-of-heaven
Alnus cordata—Italian alder
   A. hirsuta—Manchurian alder
Aralia elata—Japanese angelica-tree
Brachychiton populneum—Bottletree
Carpinus betulus—European hornbeam
   C. tchonoskii—Hornbeam
Castanea mollissima—Chinese chestnut
Catalpa bignonioides—Indian bean tree
Celtis sinensis—Hackberry
Cladrastis platycarpa—Yellow-wood
Cornus controversa—Giant dogwood
Davidia involucrata—Dove tree
Firmiana simplex—Chinese parasol-tree.
   Phoenix tree
Fraxinus pennsylvanica—Red ash

F. velutina—Velvet ash
Ginkgo biloba—Maidenhair tree
Halesia monticola—Silver-bell. Snowdrop
   tree
Juglans sieboldiana—Walnut
Koelreuteria formosana
Larix laricina—American larch. Tamarack.
   Hackmatack
Maclura pomifera—Osage-orange
Magnolia species and varieties
Malus species and varieties—Apple
Morus alba—White mulberry
   M. rubra—Red mulberry. American
   mulberry
Ostrya virginiana—Ironwood. American
   hop hornbeam
Oxydendrum arboreum—Sour-wood. Sor-
   rel tree
Phellodendron amurense—Cork tree
Pistacia chinensis—Pistache
Populus x *berolinensis*—Poplar. Aspen
Prunus maackii
   P. maritima—Beach plum
Pterostyrax hispida—Epaulette tree
Pyrus species and varieties—Pear
Quercus coccinea—Scarlet oak
   Q. phellos—Willow oak
Robinia pseudoacacia var. *decaisneana*—
   Black locust. Yellow locust. False
   acacia
Salix pentandra—Laurel willow
Sassafras albidum
Sorbus alnifolia—Korean mountain ash
   S. aria—Whitebeam tree
Tilia x *euchlora*—Crimean linden
Ulmus rubra—Slippery elm

Trees
WITH DECIDUOUS FOLIAGE: BY
HEIGHT: VERY TALL, OVER 60 FEET

Acer species and varieties—Maple
Aesculus species and varieties—Horse-
   chestnut. Buckeye
Alnus species and varieties—Alder
Betula species and varieties—Birch
Brachychiton acerifolium—Flame bottle-
   tree

Carya species and varieties—Hickory.
Pecan
Castanea dentata—American chestnut
C. sativa—Spanish chestnut
Catalpa speciosa—Western catalpa
Celtis species and varieties—Hackberry
Cornus nuttallii—Pacific dogwood
Diospyros virginiana—Common persimmon
Fagus species and varieties—Beech
Fraxinus species and varieties—Ash
Gleditsia triacanthos—Common honey
locust. Sweet locust
Gymnocladus dioica—Kentucky coffeetree
Juglans species and varieties—Walnut
Kalopanax pictus
Larix species and varieties—Larch
Liquidambar styraciflua—Sweet gum
Liriodendron tulipifera—Tulip-tree
Magnolia species and varieties
Metasequoia glyptostroboides—Dawn-redwood
Nyssa aquatica—Cotton gum. Tupelo gum
N. sylvatica—Black gum. Pepperidge.
Sour gum
Platanus species and varieties—Plane tree
Populus species and varieties—Poplar.
Aspen
Prunus avium—Sweet cherry
P. sargentii
P. serotina—Wild black cherry
Pseudolarix amabilis—Golden larch
Quercus species and varieties—Oak
Robinia pseudoacacia—Black locust. Yellow locust. False acacia
Salix alba—White willow
Sassafras albidum
Sophora japonica—Japanese pagoda tree.
Chinese scholar tree
Taxodium distichum—Bald-cypress
T. mucronatum—Ahuwhuete
Tilia species and varieties—Linden. Basswood. Lime
Ulmus species and varieties—Elm
Zelkova carpinifolia
Z. serrata

Trees
WITH EVERGREEN FOLIAGE:
BY HEIGHT: SMALL, UNDER 20 FEET

Acacia longifolia—Sydney golden wattle
Cephalotaxus harringtonia—Japanese
plum-yew
Chamaecyparis species and varieties—
False cypress
Citrus species and varieties
Clethra arborea—White-alder
Crinodendron hookerianum
Eriobotrya japonica—Loquat
Eucalyptus species and varieties—Gum
tree
Grevillea banksii
Ilex species and varieties—Holly
Juniperus species and varieties—Juniper
Melaleuca ericifolia—Bottle-brush
Pittosporum phillyraeoides
Podocarpus alpina
Prunus ilicifolia—Holly-leaved cherry
P. laurocerasus—Cherry-laurel
Schinus molle—California peppertree
Taxus species and varieties—Yew

Trees
WITH EVERGREEN FOLIAGE:
BY HEIGHT: MEDIUM, 20 TO 40 FEET

Acacia baileyana
A. pendula—Weeping myall
Arbutus unedo—Strawberry-tree
Callistemon species and varieties—Bottlebrush
Camellia japonica—Common camellia
Casimiroa edulis—White sapote
Casuarina stricta—Beefwood. She-oak.
Australian-pine
Cephalotaxus harringtonia—Japanese
plum-yew
Crinodendron patagua
Cryptomeria japonica var. elegans
Cunninghamia lanceolata—China-fir
Cupressus species and varieties—Cypress
Eucalyptus species and varieties—Gum
tree
Eugenia species and varieties
Ficus lyrata—Fiddleleaf fig

Hippophae rhamnoides—Sea-buckthorn
Hoheria angustifolia
Ilex species and varieties—Holly
Juniperus species and varieties—Juniper
Lagunaria patersonii
Laurus nobilis—Bay. Bay tree
Leptospermum laevigatum—Australian
  tea-tree
  L. scoparium
Leucadendron argenteum—Silver tree
Ligustrum lucidum—Privet
Macadamia ternifolia—Queensland nut
Maytenus boaria
Melaleuca leucadendron—Cajeput tree
  M. styphelioides—Bottle-brush
Myrica californica—California bayberry
  M. cerifera—Wax-myrtle
Olea europaea—Common olive
Parkinsonia aculeata—Jerusalem-thorn
Photinia serrulata
Pinus mugo—Swiss mountain pine. Mugho
  pine
Pittosporum species and varieties
Podocarpus elongatus
Prunus lusitanica—Portugal-laurel
Sapindus saponaria—Soapberry
Schinus terebinthifolius—Christmas-berry
  tree. Brazilian peppertree
Sciadopitys verticillata—Umbrella-pine
Taxus baccata var. dovastonii—English
  yew
Thuja standishii—Japanese arborvitae

Trees
WITH EVERGREEN FOLIAGE:
BY HEIGHT: TALL, 40 TO 60 FEET

Abies balsamea—Balsam fir
  A. koreana—Korean fir
Acacia decurrens—Green wattle
  A. pruinosa
Austrocedrus chilensis—Chilean-cedar
Castanospermum australe—Moreton Bay-
  chestnut
Casuarina cunninghamiana—Cunningham
  beefwood
Ceratonia siliqua—Carob. St. John's-bread
Cupressus arizonica—Arizona cypress
  C. macrocarpa—Monterey cypress

Ficus species and varieties—Fig
Gordonia lasianthus—Loblolly-bay
Hymenosporum flavum
Ilex x altaclarensis—Holly
  I. opaca—American holly
Juniperus species and varieties—Juniper
Pinus species and varieties—Pine
Podocarpus macrophyllus
Taxus species and varieties—Yew
Thuja occidentalis—American arborvitae
  T. orientalis—Chinese arborvitae
Thujopsis dolabrata—False arborvitae
Torreya taxifolia—Stinking-cedar

Trees
WITH EVERGREEN FOLIAGE: BY
HEIGHT: VERY TALL, OVER 60 FEET

Abies species and varieties—Fir
Araucaria species and varieties
Arbutus menziesii—Madrone. Madroña
Calocedrus decurrens—Incense-cedar
Castanopsis chrysophylla—Giant chin-
  quapin
Casuarina equisetifolia—Horsetail beef-
  wood
Cedrus species and varieties—Cedar
Chamaecyparis species and varieties—
  False cypress
Cryptomeria japonica
Cupressus sempervirens—Italian cypress
Eucalyptus species and varieties—Gum
  tree
Ficus macrophylla—Moreton Bay fig
Grevillea robusta—Silk-oak
Ilex latifolia—Lusterleaf holly
  I. rotunda—Holly
Lithocarpus densiflora—Tanbark-oak
Magnolia grandiflora—Bull-bay
Metrosideros tomentosa—New Zealand
  Christmas tree
Picea species and varieties—Spruce
Pinus species and varieties—Pine
Pittosporum rhombifolium—Queensland
  pittosporum
Pseudotsuga menziesii—Douglas-fir
Sequoiadendron giganteum—Big tree
Sequoia sempervirens—Redwood

Thuja plicata—Giant arborvitae
Torreya californica—California-nutmeg
  T. nucifera
Tsuga species and varieties—Hemlock

Trees
WITH DECORATIVE FLOWERS:
BY COLOR: BLUE

Jacaranda mimosifolia
Lagerstroemia indica—Crape-myrtle
Sophora secundiflora—Mescal-bean.
  Texas mountain-laurel

Trees
WITH DECORATIVE FLOWERS:
BY COLOR: PINK

Albizia julibrissin—Silk-tree
Amelanchier x grandiflora var. rubes-
  cens—Shadblow. Serviceberry
Arbutus unedo—Strawberry-tree
Bauhinia monandra—Butterfly bauhinia.
  Butterfly-flower. Jerusalem-date
Brachychiton discolor—Pink flame bottle-
  tree
Camellia japonica—Common camellia
Cercis species and varieties—Redbud
Citrus limonia—Lemon
Cornus florida—Flowering dogwood
Crataegus oxyacantha—English hawthorn.
  May tree
Eucalyptus species and varieties—Gum
  tree
Lagerstroemia indica—Crape-myrtle
Lagunaria patersonii
Magnolia species and varieties
Malus species and varieties—Apple
Prunus species and varieties
Pyrus communis—Common pear
  P. ussuriensis—Pear
Robinia viscosa—Locust
Tamarix aphylla—Athel tamarisk. Salt
  tree
  T. parviflora—Tamarisk

Trees
WITH DECORATIVE FLOWERS:
BY COLOR: PURPLE

Bauhinia variegata—Mountain-ebony.
  Orchid tree
Eucalyptus leucoxylon var. purpurea—
  White ironbark
Lagerstroemia speciosa—Queen's-crape-
  myrtle. Queen's flower
Magnolia x soulangeana—Saucer
  magnolia
Melia azedarach—Chinaberry. China
  tree
Paulownia tomentosa—Empress tree
Robinia x idaho—Locust

Trees
WITH DECORATIVE FLOWERS:
BY COLOR: RED

Acer rubrum—Red maple. Swamp maple
Aesculus species and varieties—Horse-
  chestnut. Buckeye
Brachychiton acerifolium—Flame bottle-
  tree
Callistemon lanceolatus—Lemon bottle-
  brush
  C. speciosus—Bottle-brush
Camellia japonica—Common camellia
Cornus florida var. 'Cherokee Chief'—
  Flowering dogwood
Crataegus oxyacantha—English hawthorn.
  May tree
Crinodendron hookerianum
Delonix regia—Royal poinciana
Erythrina crista-gallii—Cockspur coral
Eucalyptus species and varieties—Gum
  tree
Grevillea banksii
Lagerstroemia indica—Crape-myrtle
Malus x atrosanguinea—Carmine crab
  apple
  M. floribunda—Japanese flowering crab
  apple
  M. x purpurea var. lemoinei—Apple
Metrosideros tomentosa—New Zealand
  Christmas tree
Punica granatum—Pomegranate

Trees
WITH DECORATIVE FLOWERS: BY COLOR: WHITE

Aesculus species and varieties—Horse-chestnut. Buckeye
Albizia julibrissin—Silk-tree
Amelanchier species and varieties—Shadblow. Serviceberry
Aralia elata—Japanese angelica-tree
   A. spinosa—Devil's-walking-stick. Hercules'-club
Arbutus menziesii—Madrone. Madroña
   A. unedo—Strawberry-tree
Camellia japonica—Common camellia
Castanopsis chrysophylla—Giant chinquapin
Catalpa species and varieties
Cercis canadensis var. *alba*—Eastern redbud
Chionanthus retusus—Chinese fringetree
   C. virginicus—Fringetree
Citrus species and varieties
Cladrastis lutea—American yellow-wood
Clethra acuminata—White-alder
   C. barbinervis—White-alder
Cornus florida—Flowering dogwood
   C. kousa—Japanese dogwood
Crataegus species and varieties—Hawthorn. Thornapple
Crinodendron patagua
Cyrilla racemiflora—American cyrilla
Davidia involucrata—Dove tree
Eriobotrya japonica—Loquat
Eugenia species and varieties
Franklinia alatamaha
Fraxinus ornus—Flowering ash
Gordonia lasianthus—Loblolly-bay
Halesia carolina—Silver-bell. Snowdrop tree
   H. monticola—Silver-bell. Snowdrop tree
Hoheria angustifolia
Lagerstroemia indica—Crape-myrtle
Leptospermum laevigatum—Australian tea-tree
   L. scoparium
Ligustrum lucidum—Privet
Macadamia ternifolia—Queensland nut
Magnolia species and varieties

Malus species and varieties—Apple
Melaleuca leucadendron—Cajeput tree
Oxydendrum arboreum—Sourwood. Sorrel tree
Photinia serrulata
Pittosporum rhombifolium—Queensland pittosporum
   P. undulatum—Victorian-laurel
Poncirus trifoliata—Hardy-orange
Prunus species and varieties
Pterostyrax hispida—Epaulette-tree
Pyrus species and varieties—Pear
Robinia pseudoacacia—Black locust. Yellow locust
Sambucus caerulea—Blue elder
Sophora japonica—Japanese pagoda tree. Chinese scholar tree
Sorbus aucuparia—European mountain-ash. Rowan tree
Stewartia pseudo-camellia
Styrax japonica—Japanese snowbell
   S. obassia—Storax
Symplocos paniculata—Asiatic sweetleaf
Syringa amurensis var. *japonica*—Japanese tree lilac
Tilia cordata—Small-leaved linden

Trees
WITH DECORATIVE FLOWERS: BY COLOR: YELLOW

Acacia decurrens—Green wattle
Acer opalus—Italian maple
Aesculus species and varieties—Horse-chestnut. Buckeye
Callistemon speciosus—Bottle-brush
Castanospermum australe—Moreton Bay-chestnut
Elaeagnus angustifolia—Russian-olive
Eucalyptus species and varieties—Gum tree
Grevillea robusta—Silk-oak
Hamamelis species and varieties—Witch-hazel
Hymenosporum flavum
Koelreuteria paniculata—Golden-rain tree
Laburnum anagyroides—Golden-chain tree
Liriodendron tulipifera—Tulip-tree
Magnolia cordata

Melaleuca ericifolia—Bottle-brush
Parkinsonia aculeata—Jerusalem-thorn
Pittosporum eugenioides—Tarata
Sassafras albidum
Sophora tetraptera
Tilia x euchlora—Crimean linden

Trees
**WITH DECORATIVE FLOWERS: BY
FLOWERING PERIOD: EARLY SPRING**

Amelanchier species and varieties—
    Shadblow. Serviceberry
Bauhinia monandra—Butterfly bauhinia.
    Butterfly-flower. Jerusalem-date
    B. variegata—Mountain-ebony. Orchid
    tree
Camellia japonica—Common camellia
Cercis species and varieties—Redbud
Grevillea banksii
    G. robusta—Silk-oak
Hamamelis species and varieties—Witch-
    hazel
Magnolia species and varieties
Parkinsonia aculeata—Jerusalem-thorn
Prunus yedoensis—Yoshino cherry
Pyrus kawakamii—Evergreen pear
Sophora secundiflora—Mescal-bean.
    Texas mountain-laurel

Trees
**WITH DECORATIVE FLOWERS: BY
FLOWERING PERIOD: MID-SPRING**

Acacia decurrens—Green wattle
Acer species and varieties—Maple
Aesculus species and varieties—Horse-
    chestnut. Buckeye
Fraxinus ornus—Flowering ash
Halesia carolina—Silver-bell. Snowdrop
    tree
    H. monticola—Silver-bell. Snowdrop
    tree
Leptospermum laevigatum—Australian
    tea-tree
    L. scoparium
Macadamia ternifolia—Queensland nut
Magnolia species and varieties
Malus species and varieties—Apple

Melia azedarach—Chinaberry. China
    tree
Parkinsonia aculeata—Jerusalem-thorn
Paulownia tomentosa—Empress tree
Photinia serrulata
Poncirus trifoliata—Hardy-orange
Prunus species and varieties
Punica granatum—Pomegranate
Pyrus species and varieties—Pear
Sophora tetraptera
Sassafras albidum

Trees
**WITH DECORATIVE FLOWERS: BY
FLOWERING PERIOD: LATE SPRING**

Aesculus chinensis—Chinese horse-
    chestnut
    A. x mutabilis—Horse-chestnut.
    Buckeye
Albizia julibrissin—Silk-tree
Arbutus menziesii—Madrone. Madroña
Brachychiton discolor—Pink flame bottle-
    tree
Callistemon species and varieties—Bottle-
    brush
Chionanthus retusus—Chinese fringetree
    C. virginicus—Fringetree
Cladrastis lutea—American yellow-wood
Cornus species and varieties—Dogwood
Crataegus species and varieties—
    Hawthorn. Thornapple
Crinodendron hookerianum
    C. patagua
Davidia involucrata—Dove tree
Elaeagnus angustifolia—Russian-olive
Erythrina crista-gallii—Cockspur coral
Eugenia species and varieties
Fraxinus ornus—Flowering ash
Jacaranda mimosifolia
Laburnum anagyroides—Golden-chain
    tree
Lagunaria patersonii
Liriodendron tulipifera—Tulip-tree
Magnolia sieboldii
Parkinsonia aculeata—Jerusalem-thorn
Photinia serrulata
Pittosporum species and varieties
Prunus serotina—Wild black cherry
Pterostyrax hispida—Epaulette tree

Robinia species and varieties—Locust
Sorbus aucuparia—European mountain-
ash. Rowan tree
Styrax japonica—Japanese snowbell
S. obassia—Storax
Symplocos paniculata—Asiatic sweetleaf
Tamarix aphylla—Athel tamarisk. Salt
tree
T. parviflora—Tamarisk

Trees
WITH DECORATIVE FLOWERS: BY FLOWERING PERIOD: SUMMER

Aralia elata—Japanese angelica-tree
A. spinosa—Devil's-walking-stick.
Hercules'-club
Brachychiton acerifolium—Flame bottle-
tree
Callistemon species and varieties—Bottle-
brush
Castanopsis chrysophylla—Giant chin-
quapin
Castanospermum australe—Moreton Bay-
chestnut
Catalpa species and varieties
Clethra acuminata—White-alder
C. barbinervis—White-alder
Cyrilla racemiflora—American cyrilla
Delonix regia—Royal poinciana
Erythrina crista-gallii—Cockspur coral
Eucalyptus torquata—Coral gum
Eugenia pecies and varieties
Gordonia lasianthus—Loblolly-bay
Hoheria angustifolia
Hymenosporum flavum
Jacaranda mimosifolia
Koelreuteria paniculata—Golden-rain tree
Lagerstroemia indica—Crape-myrtle
L. speciosa—Queen's crape-myrtle
Queen's flower
Lagunaria patersonii
Ligustrum lucidum—Privet
Melaleuca species and varieties—Bottle-
brush
Metrosideros tomentosa—New Zealand
Christmas tree
Oxydendrum arboreum—Sourwood.
Sorrel tree
Pittosporum species and varieties

Sambucus caerulea—Blue elder
Sophora japonica—Japanese pagoda tree.
Chinese scholar tree
Stewartia pseudo-camellia
Syringa amurensis var. japonica—
Japanese tree lilac
Tilia cordata—Small-leaved linden
T. x euchlora—Crimean linden

Trees
WITH DECORATIVE FLOWERS: BY FLOWERING PERIOD: AUTUMN

Arbutus unedo—Strawberry-tree
Eriobotrya japonica—Loquat
Eugenia species and varieties
Franklinia alatamaha
Hamamelis virginiana—Witch-hazel

Trees
WITH DECORATIVE FLOWERS: BY FLOWERING PERIOD: WINTER

Bauhinia monandra—Butterfly bauhinia.
Butterfly-flower. Jerusalem-date
B. variegata—Mountain-ebony. Orchid
tree
Camellia japonica—Common camellia
Citrus species and varieties
Eucalyptus species and varieties—Gum
tree

Trees
WITH CONSPICUOUSLY COLORED AUTUMN FOLIAGE: RED

Acer species and varieties—Maple
Amelanchier species—Serviceberry. Shad-
blow
Carpinus caroliniana—American horn-
beam
Cercidiphyllum japonicum—Katsura-tree
Cornus florida—Flowering dogwood
C. mas—Cornelian-cherry
Cotinus coggygria—Smokebush
C. obovatus—American smoketree
Crataegus lavallei—Lavalle hawthorn
C. phaenopyrum—Washington thorn
Cyrilla racemiflora—American cyrilla

Diospyros species and varieties—
Persimmon
Enkianthus campanulatus—Redvein
enkianthus
Franklinia alatamaha
GORDONIA
Liquidambar styraciflua—Sweet-gum
Malus species and varieties—Apple
Nyssa sylvatica—Tupelo
Oxydendrum arboreum—Sourwood
Parrotia persica
Prunus maximowiczii—Miyama cherry
P. sargentii—Sargent cherry
Pyrus species and varieties—Pear
Quercus alba—White oak
Q. coccinea—Scarlet oak
Q. imbricaria—Shingle oak
Q. rubra—Red oak
Rhus copallina—Shining sumac
R. typhina—Staghorn sumac
Sassafras albidum
Sorbus aucuparia—European mountain-
ash
Stewartia koreana—Korean stewartia

Trees
WITH CONSPICUOUSLY COLORED AUTUMN FOLIAGE: YELLOW

Acer species and varieties—Maple
AESCULUS—Horse-chestnut. Buckeye
Amelanchier species—Serviceberry
Asimina triloba—Papaw
Betula species and varieties—Birch
CARPINUS—Hornbeam
Castanea species and varieties—Chestnut
Cercis canadensis—Eastern redbud
Chionanthus virginicus—Fringe-tree
Cladrastis lutea—American yellow-wood
Diospyros species and varieties—
Persimmon
Fagus sylvatica—European birch
Fraxinus species and varieties—Ash
Ginkgo biloba—Maidenhair tree
Halesia species and varieties—Silver-bell.
Snowdrop tree
Hamamelis species—Witch-hazel
Larix species and varieties—Larch
LIRIODENDRON—Tulip-tree
Malus halliana var. *spontanea*—Crab

apple
Ostrya virginiana—Hop-hornbeam
Parrotia persica
Populus species and varieties—Aspen.
Poplar
Pseudolarix amabilis—Golden-larch

Trees
WITH BLUISH OR SILVERY FOLIAGE: DECIDUOUS

Acer saccharinum and varieties—Silver
maple
Elaeagnus angustifolia—Russian-olive
Hippophae rhamnoides—Sea-buckthorn
Populus alba variety—Silver poplar
Salix species and varieties—Willow
Tilia tomentosa—Silver linden

Trees
WITH BLUISH OR SILVERY FOLIAGE: EVERGREEN

Abies species and varieties—Fir
Acacia species and varieties—Wattle
Cedrus atlantica var. *glauca*—Blue Atlas
cedar
Chamaecyparis species and varieties—
Falsecypress
Cupressus lusitanica—Mexican cypress
Erythea armata—Mexican blue palm
Eucalyptus species and varieties—
Gum tree
Juniperus species and varieties—Juniper
Leucadendron argenteum—Silver-tree
OLEA—Olive
Picea species and varieties—Spruce
Pittosporum tenuifolium var. 'Silver
Queen'
Tabebuia argentea—Silver-tree
Thuja species and varieties—Arborvitae

Trees
WITH DECORATIVE BARK

Acer species and varieties—Maple
Arbutus menziesii—Pacific madrone.
Madroña
A. unedo—Strawberry-tree
Betula species and varieties—Birch
Broussonetia papyrifera—Paper-mulberry
CALOCEDRUS

Cladrastis lutea—Yellow-wood
Cornus species and varieties—Dogwood
Eucalyptus species and varieties—Gum tree
Fagus species and varieties—Beech
Lagerstroemia indica—Crape-myrtle
LEPTOSPERMUM
PHELLODENDRON—Cork-tree
Pinus bungeana—Lace-bark pine
PLATANUS—Plane-tree. Sycamore
Prunus species and varieties
Quercus variabilis—Oriental oak
STEWARTIA
Syringa amurensis var. *japonica*—Japanese tree lilac
Taxodium distichum—Baldcypress

Trees
WITH FRAGRANT FLOWERS

(Including treelike shrubs.)

Acacia species and varieties—Wattle
Acer ginnala—Amur maple
Aesculus californica—California buckeye
Albizia julibrissin—Silk-tree
Buddleia globosa—Globe butterfly-bush
Chionanthus virginicus—Fringe-tree
Choisya ternata—Mexican-orange
Citrus species and varieties—Grapefruit. Lemon. Lime. Orange
Cladrastis lutea—Yellow-wood
Clethra alnifolia—Sweet pepperbush
  C. barbinervis—White-alder
Crataegus oxyacantha—English hawthorn
Crinodendron patagua
Elaeagnus angustifolia—Russian-olive
  E. commutata—Silver-berry
  E. multiflora—Cherry elaeagnus
Eriobotrya japonica—Loquat
Eugenia jambos—Rose-apple
  E. uniflora—Surinam-cherry
Fraxinus ornus—Flowering ash
Gordonia lasianthus—Loblolly-bay
Hamamelis species and varieties—Witch-hazel
Hymenosporum flavum—Sweet-shade
Ligustrum species—Privet
Magnolia species and varieties
Malus species and varieties—Apple

Melia azedarach—Chinaberry. China tree
Michelia figo—Banana-shrub
Nerium indicum—Sweet-scented oleander
Osmanthus fragrans—Sweet-olive
Parkinsonia hymenosporum var. *flavum*—Sweetshade
Paulownia tomentosa—Empress-tree
PITTOSPORUM
Poncirus trifoliata—Hardy-orange
Prunus species and varieties—Apricot. Cherry. Peach. Plum
Pterostyrax hispida—Fragrant epaulette-tree
Robinia pseudoacacia—Black locust. Yellow locust
Salix caprea—Goat willow. French pussy willow
Sassafras albidum
Styrax grandifolia—Storax. Snowball
  S. obassia
Symplocos paniculata—Asiatic sweetleaf
Syringa species and varieties—Lilac
Tilia species and varieties—Linden
Vitex agnus-castus—Chaste-tree

Trees
THAT TOLERATE CONSIDERABLE SHADE

Acer circinatum—Vine maple
  A. pensylvanicum—Moosewood. Striped maple
  A. spicatum—Mountain maple
Amelanchier laevis—Allegheny shadblow
ASIMINA
Betula populifolia—Gray birch
Camellia japonica varieties—Common camellia
Cercis canadensis—Eastern redbud
Clethra alnifolia—Summersweet
Cornus florida—Flowering dogwood
Crataegus species and varieties—Hawthorn
Euonymus species and varieties—Spindle-tree
Ficus species and varieties—Fig
Ilex opaca—American holly
Laburnum species and varieties—Golden-chain tree
Nyssa sylvatica—Tupelo

Podocarpus species and varieties
Prunus pensylvanica—Pin cherry
Rhododendron maximum—Rosebay
Taxus species and varieties—Yew
Thuja occidentalis—American arbor-
vitae
Tsuga canadensis—Canada hemlock

Trees
THAT TOLERATE DAMP GROUND

Acer rubrum—Red maple. Swamp maple
Alnus species—Alder
Amelanchier laevis—Allegheny shadblow
Betula nigra—Black birch
Calocedrus decurrens—California incense-
cedar
Carya illinoensis—Pecan
CASUARINA—Beefwood
Cercidiphyllum japonicum—Katsura-tree
Eucalyptus leucoxylon—White ironbark
Fraxinus nigra—Black ash
Ilex opaca—American holly
Larix laricina—Eastern larch
LIQUIDAMBAR—Sweet-gum
Magnolia species and varieties
Melaleuca leucadendra—Cajeput-tree
Nyssa sylvatica—Tupelo
Populus simonii var. *fastigiata*—Poplar.
Aspen
Quercus bicolor—Swamp white oak
Salix species and varieties—Willow
Stewartia species and varieties
Taxodium distichum—Baldcypress
Thuja occidentalis—American arbor-
vitae
Thujopsis dolobrata—False arborvitae

Trees
THAT TOLERATE DRY GROUND

Acer negundo—Box-elder
Ailanthus altissima—Tree-of-heaven
Albizia julibrissin—Silk-tree
Amelanchier canadensis—Shadbush.
Serviceberry
Aralia elata—Japanese angelica-tree
Arbutus menziesii—Pacific madrone.
Madroña
Betula populifolia—Gray birch

Broussonetia papyrifera—Paper-mulberry
Carya glabra—Pignut
Cedrus atlantica—Atlas cedar
Celtis occidentalis—Common hackberry
Cladrastis lutea—Yellow-wood
Corylus species—Filbert
Crataegus species and varieties—
Hawthorn
Cupressus macrocarpa—Monterey cypress
Elaeagnus angustifolia—Russian-olive
Eucalyptus species and varieties—Gum
tree
Fraxinus velutina—Arizona ash
Gleditsia triacanthos—Honey locust
Gymnocladus dioicus—Kentucky coffee-
tree
Juniperus species and varieties—Juniper
Koelreuteria paniculata—Golden-rain tree
Lagerstroemia indica—Crape-myrtle
Maclura pomifera—Osage-orange
Malus species and varieties—Crab apple
Melia azedarach—Chinaberry. China tree
Morus species and varieties—Mulberry
Olea species—Olive
Ostrya virginiana—Hop-hornbeam.
Ironwood
Parkinsonia aculeata—Jerusalem-thorn
Phellodendron amurense—Amur cork-tree
Pinus species and varieties—Pine
Platanus x *acerifolia*—London plane-tree
Populus alba and varieties—White poplar
Pyrus calleryana—Callery pear
Quercus species and varieties—Oak
Robinia species and varieties—Locust
Salix pentandra—Laurel willow
Sassafras albidum
SCHINUS—Pepper-tree
Sophora japonica—Japanese pagoda tree.
Chinese scholar tree
Sorbus species and varieties—Mountain-
ash
Tilia cordata—Small-leaved linden
T. tomentosa—Silver linden
Ulmus parvifolia—Chinese elm
U. pumila—Siberian elm
Zelkova serrata—Japanese zelkova

Trees
THAT GROW RAPIDLY

Acer negundo—Box-elder
  A. saccharinum—Silver maple
Ailanthus altissima—Tree-of-heaven
Alnus species and varieties—Alder
Betula species and varieties—Birch
CASUARINA—Beefwood
Catalpa speciosa—Western catalpa
CELTIS—Hackberry
Eriobotrya deflexa—Loquat
Euonymus bungeanus var. 'North Platte'—
  Spindle-tree
Firmiana simplex—Chinese parasol-tree
Fraxinus americana—White ash
  F. pennsylvanica var. lanceolata—
  American ash
Gleditsia triacanthos—Honey locust
Grevillea robusta—Silk-oak
Gymnocladus dioica—Kentucky coffee-
  tree
Hymenosporum flavum—Sweet-shade
Larix decidua—European larch
  L. leptolepis—Japanese larch
Ligustrum lucidum—Privet
Liriodendron tulipifera—Tulip-tree
Maclura pomifera—Osage-orange
Magnolia veitchii
Malus species and varieties, especially
  crab apple
Melaleuca leucadendra—Cajeput-tree
Melia azedarach—Chinaberry. China tree
Morus alba, fruitless forms—Mulberry
Paulownia tomentosa—Empress-tree
Phellodendron sachalinense—Sakhalin
  cork-tree
Picea abies—Norway spruce
Pinus species and varieties—Pine
Pistacia chinensis—Pistache
Platanus orientalis—Oriental plane-tree
Populus deltoides—Cottonwood
  P. maximowiczii—Japanese poplar
  P. nigra var. italica—Lombardy poplar
Prunus serotina—Black cherry
PYRUS—Pear
Quercus palustris—Pin oak
  Q. rubra—Red oak
Robinia pseudoacacia—Black locust. Yel-
  low locust
Salix alba—White willow

S. vitellina—Golden willow
SCHINUS—Pepper-tree
Sequoia sempervirens—Coast redwood
Sorbus aucuparia—European mountain-
  ash
Tipuana tipu—Pride-of-Bolivia
Ulmus parvifolia—Chinese elm
  U. pumila—Siberian elm

Vines

Vines
BY FLOWERING PERIOD: SPRING

Akebia quinata
Aristolochia durior—Dutchman's-pipe
Arrabidaea magnifica—Purple funnel-vine
Beaumontia grandiflora—Easter-lily-vine
Bignonia capreolata—Cross-vine
BOUGAINVILLEA—Paper-flower
Clematis species and varieties
Clerodendrum thomsoniae—Bleeding-
  heart-vine
CLYTOSTOMA—Violet trumpet-vine
COBAEA—Cup-and-saucer vine
Convolvulus cneorum—Bindweed
DOXANTHA—Cat-claw
GELSEMIUM—Carolina-jessamine
HARDENBERGIA—Lilac-vine
Jasminum species and varieties—Jasmine
Lathyrus species and varieties
MENISPERMUM—Moonseed
Petra volubilis—Queen's-wreath
PHAEDRANTHUS—Blood trumpet-vine
SOLANDRA—Chalice-vine
Solanum seaforthianum
STAUNTONIA
Trachelospermum jasminoides—Confed-
  erate-jasmine
WISTERIA

Vines
BY FLOWERING PERIOD: SUMMER

ACTINIDIA
Adlumia fungosa—Mountain-fringe
Akebia trifoliata
Antigonon leptopus—Coral-vine
ARAUJIA
ARGYREIA
Aristolochia species—Birthwort
Arrabidaea magnifica—Purple funnel-vine
ARTABOTRYS—Ylang-ylang
Asparagus species
Bauhinia corymbosa
Beaumontia grandiflora—Easter-lily-vine
Benincasa hispida—Wax-gourd
BOMAREA
BOUGAINVILLEA—Paper-flower
Boussingaultia gracilis—Madeira-vine
Bryonopsis laciniosa—Marble-vine
Calonyction aculeatum—Moonflower
CAMPSIS—Trumpetcreeper
Cardiospermum halicacabum—Balloon-vine
Clematis species and varieties
Clerodendrum thomsoniae—Bleeding-heart-vine
Clitoria ternatea—Butterfly-pea
COBAEA—Cup-and-saucer vine
Cocculus carolinus—Carolina moonseed
Convolvulus cneorum—Bindweed
  C. japonicus—California-rose
CRYPTOSTEGIA—Rubber-vine
CUCURBITA—Gourd
Dipladenia splendens
DISTICTIS—Vanilla-trumpet-vine
Dolichos lablab—Hyacinth-bean
ECCREMOCARPUS—Glory-flower
Echinocystis lobata—Wild mock-cucumber
FREYCINETIA
GLORIOSA—Climbing-lily
Hibbertia volubilis—Gold Guinea-vine
Hoya carnosa—Wax-plant
Hydrangea petiolaris—Climbing hydrangea
Ipomoea species and varieties—Morning-glory
JACQUEMONTIA
Jasminum species and varieties—Jasmine

Kadsura japonica
Lagenaria species—Gourd
LAPAGERIA—Chilean-bellflower
Lathyrus species and varieties
Lonicera species and varieties—Honey-suckle
Manettia species—Firecracker vine
Maurandia species
MOMORDICA
Oxera pulchella—Royal-climber
Pandorea species
Passiflora species and varieties—Passion-flower
PERIPLOCA—Silk-vine
PHAEDRANTHUS—Blood trumpetvine
Phaseolus, ornamental species—Bean
Polygonum aubertii—Silver-lace-vine
PUERARIA—Kudzu
Pyrostegia ignea—Flame-vine
QUAMOCLIT—Star-glory
Rhodochiton volubile—Purple bell-vine
Schizophragma hydrangeoides—Hydrangea-vine
STAUNTONIA
Stephanotis floribunda—Madagascar-jasmine
Thunbergia species and varieties—Clock-vine
Trachelospermum jasminoides—Confederate-jasmine
Tropaeolum species—Nasturtium

Vines
BY FLOWERING PERIOD: AUTUMN

Antigonon leptopus—Coral-vine
Boussingaultia gracilis—Madeira-vine
Clematis species and varieties
Convolvulus japonicus—California-rose
Dipladenia splendens
DISTICTIS—Vanilla-trumpet-vine
Pandorea species
PHAEDRANTHUS—Blood trumpetvine
Pileostegia viburnoides—Tanglehead
Polygonum aubertii—Silver-lace-vine

Vines
FOR QUICK EFFECTS

ACTINIDIA
Adlumia fungosa—Mountain-fringe
Akebia quinata
AMPELOPSIS
Antigonon leptopus—Coral-vine
ARAUJIA
ARGYREIA
ARISTOLOCHIA—Birthwort
Benincasa hispida—Wax-gourd
Boussingaultia gracilis—Madeira-vine
Bryonopsis laciniosa—Marble-vine
Calonyction aculeatum—Moonflower
CAMPSIS—Trumpetcreeper
Cardiospermum halicacabum—Balloon-vine
COBAEA—Cup-and-saucer vine
CRYPTOSTEGIA—Rubber-vine
Cucurbita species and varieties—Gourd
DIOSCOREA—Yam. Cinnamon-vine
Dolichos lablab—Hyacinth-bean
DOXANTHA—Cat-claw
ECCREMOCARPUS—Glory-flower
Echinocystis lobata—Wild mock-cucumber
Humulus japonicus—Japanese hop
Ipomoea species and varieties—Morning-glory
Lagenaria species—Gourd
Lathyrus species and varieties
Lonicera species and varieties—Honey-suckle
MENISPERMUM—Moonseed
MOMORDICA
Pandorea species
Passiflora species and varieties—Passion-flower
PERIPLOCA—Silk-vine
Phaseolus, ornamental species—Bean
Polygonum aubertii—Silver-lace-vine
PUERARIA—Kudzu
Pyrostegia ignea—Flame-vine
QUAMOCLIT—Star-glory
Smilax megalantha—Greenbrier
Thunbergia species and varieties—Clock-vine
Trachelospermum jasminoides—Confed-erate-jasmine
Vitis species and varieties—Grape
WISTERIA

Vines
WITH EVERGREEN FOLIAGE

ARAUJIA
Bauhinia corymbosa
Beaumontia grandiflora—Easter-lily-vine
Bignonia capreolata—Cross-vine
CISSUS
Clematis armandii
Clerodendrum thomsoniae—Bleeding-heart-vine
CLYTOSTOMA—Violet trumpet-vine
CRYPTOSTEGIA—Rubber-vine
Dipladenia splendens
DISTICTIS—Vanilla-trumpet-vine
DOXANTHA—Cat-claw
Euonymus species—Wintercreeper
Ficus pumila—Creeping fig
FREYCINETIA
GELSEMIUM—Carolina-jessamine
HARDENBERGIA—Lilac-vine
HEDERA—Ivy
Hibbertia volubilis—Gold Guinea-vine
Jasminum species and varieties—Jasmine
Kadsura japonica
LAPAGERIA—Chilean-bellflower
Lonicera species and varieties—Honey-suckle
Lygodium species—Climbing fern
Manettia species—Firecracker-vine
MONSTERA
Oxera pulchella—Royal-climber
Pandorea species
PHAEDRANTHUS—Blood trumpetvine
Philodendron species
Pileostegia viburnoides—Tanglehead
Pyrostegia ignea—Flame-vine
Smilax megalantha—Greenbrier
SOLANDRA— Chalice-vine
STAUNTONIA
Trachelospermum jasminoides—Confed-erate-jasmine

Wild Flowers

Wild Flowers
BY FLOWERING PERIOD: EARLY SPRING

Anemone caroliniana—Carolina wind-
flower
Anemonella thalictroides—Rue-anemone
Asarum canadense—Wild-ginger
   A. shuttleworthii—Mottled wild-ginger
CLAYTONIA—Spring-beauty
Dentaria laciniata—Cutleaf toothwort
Epigaea repens—Trailing arbutus
HEPATICA—Liverleaf
Iris cristata—Crested dwarf iris
Mitella diphylla—Mitrewort. Bishop's-cap
Sanguinaria canadensis—Bloodroot
Saxifraga virginiensis—Virginia saxifrage
Shortia galacifolia—Oconee-bells
Symplocarpus foetidus—Skunk-cabbage

Wild Flowers
BY FLOWERING PERIOD: MID-SPRING

Aegopodium podagraria—Bishop's-weed
Anemone canadensis—Meadow anemone
Anemonella thalictroides—Rue-anemone
Aplectrum hyemale—Putty-root. Adam-
and-Eve
Aquilegia canadensis—Wild columbine
Arctostaphylos uva-ursi—Bearberry
Arisaema triphyllum—Jack-in-the-pulpit
Caulophyllum thalictroides—Blue cohosh
Clintonia andrewsiana—Red bead-lily
Cornus canadensis—Bunchberry dogwood
Corydalis sempervirens—Fumaria
Dentaria diphylla—Crinkleroot toothwort
Dicentra cucullaria—Dutchman's-breeches
Drosera rotundifolia—Sundew
ERYTHRONIUM—Dogtooth-violet
Galax aphylla
Geranium maculatum—Wild geranium
Helonias bullata—Swamp-pink
HOUSTONIA—Bluets
Hydrastis canadensis—Goldenseal
Iris pseudacorus—Yellow iris
Jeffersonia diphylla—Twinleaf
Leiophyllum buxifolium—Box sand-
myrtle

Lupinus perennis—Wild lupine
MAIANTHEMUM—Wild-lily-of-the-
valley
Mertensia virginica—Virginia bluebells
Mitchella repens—Partridge-berry
Phlox species
Podophyllum peltatum—May-apple
Polemonium reptans—Creeping pole-
monium
Polygala paucifolia—Fringed milkwort
POLYGONATUM—Solomon's seal
Sarracenia flava—Trumpets
Senecio aureus—Golden ragwort
Silene caroliniana—Wild-pink. Catchfly
Tiarella cordifolia—Foamflower
Trientalis borealis—Star-flower
TRILLIUM
UVULARIA—Bellwort. Merrybells
Vaccinium vitis-idaea—Cowberry
Viola species—Violet
Waldsteinia fragarioides—Barren-straw-
berry

Wild Flowers
BY FLOWERING PERIOD: LATE SPRING

Acorus calamus—Sweet-flag
Actaea pachypoda—White baneberry
Anaphalis species—Pearly everlasting
Anemone canadensis—Meadow anemone
Aplectrum hyemale—Putty-root. Adam-
and-Eve
Aquilegia caerulea—Colorado colum-
bine
Arenaria caroliniana—Sandwort
Aruncus sylvester—Goat's-beard
Baptisia australis—False indigo
Calopogon pulchellus—Grass-pink orchid
Caltha palustris—Marsh-marigold
Camassia scilloides—Wild-hyacinth
Campanula rotundifolia—Harebell. Blue-
bells-of-Scotland
Chimaphila maculata—Spotted winter-
green
Chiogenes hispidula—Creeping snow-
berry
Convallaria majalis—Lily-of-the-valley
COPTIS—Goldthread
Corydalis sempervirens—Fumaria
Cypripedium acaule—Lady's-slipper.
Moccasin-flower

C. arietinum—Ram's-head lady's-
slipper
Dicentra eximia—Wild bleeding-heart
Dodecatheon meadia—Common shooting-
star
Galax aphylla
Gaultheria procumbens—Wintergreen.
Checkerberry
Geranium species—Cranesbill
Heuchera americana—American alum-
root
Hypoxis hirsuta—Star-grass
Iris missouriensis—Blue flag
Lilium species—Lily
Linnaea borealis—Twinflower
Orchis spectabilis—Showy orchis
Phlox amoena
Pogonia ophioglossoides—Snakemouth
Polygonatum species—Solomon's seal
Pontederia cordata—Pickerel-weed
Potentilla tridentata—Cinquefoil
Sedum ternatum—Stonecrop
Silene virginica—Fire-pink. Catchfly
Sisyrinchium angustifolium—Blue-eyed-
grass
Smilacina racemosa—False Solomon's-seal
Streptopus roseus—Twisted stalk
Stylophorum diphyllum—Celandine-
poppy
Thalictrum dioicum—Meadow-rue
Trientalis borealis—Star-flower
Veratrum viride—White-hellebore
XEROPHYLLUM—Turkey-beard

Wild Flowers
BY FLOWERING PERIOD: SUMMER

Aconitum uncinatum—Wild monkshood
Aletris farinosa—Star-grass
Althaea officinalis—Marsh-mallow
Aquilegia formosa—Sitka columbine
Aralia racemosa—American spikenard
Artemisia lactiflora—White mugwort
  A. stelleriana—Beech wormwood
Aruncus sylvester—Goat's-beard
Asclepias tuberosa—Butterfly-weed
Aster species
Callirhoe species—Poppy-mallow
Campanula rotundifolia—Common hare-
bell. Bluebells-of-Scotland
Chelone species—Turtlehead
CHRYSOPSIS—Golden-aster

Cimicifuga americana—Bugbane
  C. racemosa—Black snakeroot. Cohosh
bugbane
Collinsonia canadensis—Citronella horse-
balm
COPTIS—Goldthread
Coreopsis species—Tickseed
Cypripedium reginae—Showy lady's-slip-
per
Dicentra eximia—Fringed bleeding-heart
Echinacea purpurea—Purple coneflower
Epilobium angustifolium—Fireweed
ERIGERON—Fleabane
Eupatorium species—Thoroughwort.
Boneset
Euphorbia corollata—Flowering spurge
Filipendula rubra—Queen-of-the-prairie
Gaillardia aristata—Blanket-flower
Geranium species—Cranesbill
Goodyera pubescens—Rattlesnake-
plantain
  G. repens
HABENARIA—Fringed or rein orchis
Helenium species—Sneezeweed
Helianthus species—Sunflower
HELIOPSIS
Heuchera species—Alum-root
Hibiscus moscheutos—Swamp-mallow
Inula helenium—Elecampane
Lathyrus maritimus—Seaside-pea. Beach-
pea
LIATRIS—Gayfeather. Blazing-star
Lilium species—Lily
LIPARIS—Twayblade
Lobelia species
Loiseleuria procumbens—Alpine-azalea
Lythrum species—Loosestrife
Monarda species—Horse-mint. Bee-balm.
Oswego-tea. Bergamot
Monotropa uniflora—Indian-pipe
Oenothera species—Evening-primrose
Opuntia compressa—Prickly-pear cactus
Peltandra virginica—Arrow-arum
Penstemon species—Beard-tongue
Phlox paniculata—Summer garden phlox
Physostegia virginiana—False dragon-
head. Obedient plant
Pinguicula vulgaris—Butterwort
Pogonia ophioglossoides—Snakemouth.
Rose pogonia
Pontederia cordata—Pickerel-weed
PYROLA—Shinleaf

RHEXIA—Meadow-beauty
Rudbeckia hirta—Black-eyed Susan
Sagittaria latifolia—Arrowhead
Sanguisorba canadensis—Burnet
Sarracenia purpurea—Common pitcher
plant
Sedum telephium—Stonecrop
Sidalcea candida—Prairie-mallow
S. malvaeflora—Checkerbloom. Wild-
hollyhock
Silene virginica—Fire-pink. Catchfly
SOLIDAGO—Goldenrod
SPIRANTHES—Ladies'-tresses
Steironema ciliatum—Fringed loosestrife
Thalictrum polygamum—Tall meadow-
rue
Thermopsis càroliniana—Aaron's-rod
Tradescantia virginiana—Virginia spider-
wort
Verbena hastata—Blue vervain
Vernonia noveboracensis—New York
ironweed

Wild Flowers
BY FLOWERING PERIOD: AUTUMN

Aconitum uncinatum—Wild monkshood
Aster species
Cacalia atriplicifolia—Pale Indian-
plantain
CHRYSOPSIS—Golden-aster
Cimicifuga simplex—Bugbane
Erigeron pulchellus—Poor-robin's-
plantain
EUPATORIUM—Thoroughwort
Gentiana crinita—Fringed gentian
Geranium robertianum—Herb Robert.
Red robin
Habenaria ciliaris—Yellow fringed orchis
Helenium species—Sneezeweed
Helianthus species—Sunflower
Heliopsis helianthoides—Oxeye
LIATRIS—Gayfeather. Blazing-star
Phlox paniculata—Summer garden phlox
Silene virginica—Fire-pink. Catchfly
SOLIDAGO—Goldenrod
SPIRANTHES—Ladies'-tresses
Vernonia altissima—Tall ironweed
V. noveboracensis—New York iron-
weed

Wild Flowers
THAT GROW BEST IN DAMP GROUND

ACORUS—Sweet-flag
Aletris farinosa—Star-grass
Anemonella thalictroides—Rue-anemone
Aplectrum hyemale—Putty-root
Arisaema dracontium—Dragon-root
A. triphyllum—Jack-in-the-pulpit
Aruncus sylvester—Goat's-beard
ASARUM—Wild-ginger
Asclepias incarnata—Swamp milkweed
Calopogon pulchellus—Grass-pink orchid
Caltha palustris—Marsh-marigold
Caulophyllum thalictroides—Blue cohosh
Chelone species—Turtlehead
Cimicifuga racemosa—Black snakeroot
Claytonia species—Spring-beauty
CLINTONIA—Bead-lily. Queen-cup
Collinsonia canadensis—Citronella horse-
balm
COPTIS—Goldthread
Cypripedium species—Lady's-slipper
Drosera rotundifolia—Sundew
Erythronium species—Dogtooth-violet
EUPATORIUM—Thoroughwort
Gaultheria procumbens—Wintergreen.
Checkerberry
Gentiana species—Gentian
Geranium robertianum—Herb Robert.
Red robin
Habenaria species—Fringed orchis. Rein
orchis
Helianthus angustifolius—Swamp sun-
flower
Helonias bullata—Swamp-pink
Hibiscus moscheutos—Swamp-mallow
HOUSTONIA—Bluets
Hydrastis canadensis—Goldenseal.
Orange-root
Inula helenium—Elecampane
Iris pseudacorus—Yellow flag
Linnaea borealis—Twinflower
Lobelia cardinalis—Cardinal-flower
LYCOPODIUM—Club-moss
MAIANTHEMUM—Wild-lily-of-the-
valley
Menyanthes trifoliata—Common bogbean
Mertensia virginica—Virginia bluebells

Orchis spectabilis—Showy orchis
Peltandra virginica—Arrow-arum
Pinguicula vulgaris—Common butterwort
Pogonia ophioglossoides—Snakemouth.
  Rose pogonia
Polygala paucifolia—Fringed milkwort.
  Gay-wings
Pontederia cordata—Pickerel-weed
RHEXIA—Meadow-beauty
Sagittaria latifolia—Arrowhead
Sanguinaria canadensis—Bloodroot
Sanguisorba canadensis—Burnet
Senecio aureus—Golden ragwort
Shortia galacifolia—Oconee-bells
Smilacina racemosa—False Solomon's-seal
Steironema ciliatum—Fringed loosestrife
Streptopus roseus—Twisted stalk
Symplocarpus foetidus—Skunk-cabbage
Thalictrum dioicum—Early meadow-rue
TRILLIUM
UVULARIA—Bellwort. Merrybells
Vaccinium vitis-idaea—Cowberry
Veratrum viride—White-hellebore
Vernonia altissima—Tall ironweed
  V. noveboracensis—New York iron-
  weed

Wild Flowers
THAT GROW BEST IN DRY GROUND

Abronia species—Sand-verbena
Allium stellatum—Prairie onion
Ammophila breviligulata—American
  beachgrass
Arctostaphylos uva-ursi—Bearberry
Arenaria species—Sandwort
Artemisia stelleriana—Beach wormwood
Asclepias tuberosa—Butterfly-weed
Aster species
Baptisia species—False indigo
Callirhoe involucrata—Poppy-mallow
Cassia marilandica—Wild senna
CHRYSOPSIS—Golden-aster
Coreopsis grandiflora—Tickseed
Echinacea purpurea—Purple coneflower
Eustoma russellianum—Russell prairie-
  gentian
Gaillardia aristata—Blanket-flower
Geranium robertianum—Herb Robert.
  Red robin

Gilia rubra—Tree-cypress. Texas plume
Helenium autumnale—Yellow-star. Com-
  mon sneezeweed
HYPOXIS—Star-grass
Lathyrus maritimus—Seaside-pea.
  Beach-pea
Liatris species—Gayfeather. Blazing-star
Lupinus perennis—Wild lupine
Oenothera species—Evening-primrose
Opuntia compressa—Prickly-pear cactus
Penstemon species—Beard-tongue
Potentilla tridentata—Cinquefoil
Rudbeckia species—Black-eyed Susan.
  Coneflower
Saponaria species—Soapwort. Bouncing
  Bet
Silene caroliniana—Wild-pink. Catchfly
Viola pedata—Birdfoot violet
Yucca species—Adam's-needle. Soapweed

Wild Flowers
THAT GROW BEST IN SHADE

Anemonella thalictroides—Rue-anemone
Aplectrum hyemale—Putty-root
Aralia racemosa—American spikenard
ASARUM—Wild-ginger
Calopogon pulchellus—Grass-pink orchid
Caulophyllum thalictroides—Blue cohosh
Cimicifuga racemosa—Black snakeroot.
  Cohosh bugbane
CLINTONIA—Bead-lily. Queen-cup
Collinsonia canadensis—Citronella horse-
  balm
COPTIS—Goldthread
Cypripedium species—Lady's-slipper
DENTARIA—Toothwort
Dicentra species—Bleeding-heart. Dutch-
  man's-breeches
DODECATHEON—Shooting-star
Epigaea repens—Trailing arbutus
Galax aphylla
Gaultheria procumbens—Wintergreen.
  Checkerberry
Goodyera pubescens—Rattlesnake-
  plantain
  G. repens
HABENARIA—Fringed orchis. Rein orchis
HEPATICA—Liverleaf
Hydrastis canadensis—Goldenseal.
  Orange-root

Jeffersonia diphylla—Twinleaf
Linnaea borealis—Twinflower
Liparis liliifolia—Twayblade
  L. loeselii
LYCOPODIUM—Club-moss
MAIANTHEMUM—Wild-lily-of-the-
  valley
Mertensia virginica—Virginia bluebells
Mitchella repens—Partridge-berry. Twin-
  berry
Mitella diphylla—Mitrewort. Bishop's-cap
Monotropa species—Pinesap. Indian-pipe
Orchis spectabilis—Showy orchis
Phlox divaricata—Wild-sweet William
Podophyllum peltatum—May-apple
Pogonia ophioglossoides—Snakemouth.
  Rose pogonia
Polemonium reptans
Polygala paucifolia—Fringed milkwort.
  Gay-wings
POLYGONATUM—Solomon's seal
Pontederia cordata—Pickerel-weed
PYROLA—Shinleaf
Sanguinaria canadensis—Bloodroot
Shortia galacifolia—Oconee-bells
Smilacina species—False Solomon's-seal
Spiranthes cernua—Nodding ladies'-
  tresses
Streptopus roseus—Twisted stalk
Tiarella cordifolia—Foamflower

Trientalis borealis—Star-flower
TRILLIUM
UVULARIA—Bellwort. Merrybells
Vaccinium vitis-idaea—Cowberry
Viola species—Violet

Wild Flowers
THAT REQUIRE SUN

Althaea officinalis—Marsh-mallow
Anaphalis margaritacea
Arctostaphylos uva-ursi—Bearberry
Arenaria caroliniana—Sandwort
Artemisia stelleriana—Beach wormwood
Asclepias species—Milkweed
Aster species
Callirhoe involucrata—Poppy-mallow
CHRYSOPSIS—Golden-aster
Coreopsis species—Tickseed
Drosera rotundifolia—Sundew
Echinacea purpurea—Purple coneflower
Erigeron bellidifolius
Eupatorium species—Thoroughwort
Euphorbia corollata—Flowering spurge
Filipendula rubra—Queen-of-the-prairie
Gaillardia aristata—Blanket-flower
Helenium autumnale—Yellow-star
Helianthus species—Sunflower
HELIOPSIS
Hibiscus moscheutos—Swamp-mallow
Hypoxis hirsuta—Star-grass
Inula helenium—Elecampane
Iris species
Lathyrus maritimus—Seaside-pea
Liatris species—Gayfeather. Blazing-star
Lupinus perennis—Wild lupine
Lythrum salicaria—Purple loosestrife
Oenothera species—Evening-primrose
Phlox species
Potentilla tridentata—Cinquefoil
Rhexia virginica—Meadow-beauty
Rudbeckia hirta—Black-eyed Susan
Sagittaria latifolia—Arrowhead
Sanguisorba canadensis—Burnet
Sedum species—Stonecrop
Sidalcea species
SISYRINCHIUM—Blue-eyed-grass
SOLIDAGO—Goldenrod
Vernonia species—Ironweed
Viola pedata—Birdfoot violet
Zizania aquatica—Wild-rice

Index of Common Names

Adam's-needle: *Yucca*
African daisy: *Arctotis*
African daisy: *Lonas*
Alder: *Alnus*
Alkanet: *Anchusa*
Allegheny vine: *Adlumia*
Almond: *Prunus*
Alpine-azalea: *Loiseleuria*
Alpine pink: *Dianthus*
Alpine toadflax: *Linaria*
Alum-root: *Heuchera*
Amaryllis: *Hippeastrum*
Amazon-lily: *Eucharis*
Andromeda: *Pieris*
Angelica-tree: *Aralia*
Apple: *Malus*
Aralia: *Acanthopanax*
Arborvitae: *Thuja*
Arrowhead: *Sagittaria*
Ash: *Fraxinus*
Aspen: *Populus*
Atamasco-lily: *Zephyranthes*
Autumn-crocus: *Colchicum*
Avens: *Geum*
Azalea: *Rhododendron*

Baby-blue-eyes: *Nemophila*
Baby's-breath: *Gypsophila*
Bachelor's-button: *Centaurea*
Bald-cypress: *Taxodium*
Balloon-flower: *Platycodon*
Balloon-vine: *Cardiospermum*
Banana-shrub: *Michelia*
Barberry: *Berberis*
Barren-strawberry: *Waldsteinia*
Barrenwort: *Epimedium*
Basket-of-gold: *Aurinia*
Basswood: *Tilia*
Bay tree: *Laurus*
Bayberry: *Myrica*
Beach-pea: *Lathyrus*
Beach plum: *Prunus*
Beachgrass: *Ammophila*

Bean tree: *Catalpa*
Bearberry: *Arctostaphylos*
Beard-tongue: *Penstemon*
Bear's-breech: *Acanthus*
Beauty-berry: *Callicarpa*
Bee-balm: *Monarda*
Beech: *Fagus*
Beefwood: *Casuarina*
Bellflower: *Campanula*
Bells-of-Ireland: *Molucella*
Bergamot: *Monarda*
Black-calla: *Arum*
Black-eyed Susan: *Rudbeckia*
Black snakeroot: *Cimicifuga*
Blackberry-lily: *Belamcanda*
Black gum: *Nyssa*
Blackthorn: *Prunus*
Blanket-flower: *Gaillardia*
Blazing-star: *Liatris*
Blazing-star: *Mentzelia*
Bleeding-heart: *Dicentra*
Bleeding-heart-vine: *Clerodendrum*
Birch: *Betula*
Bishop's-cap: *Mitella*
Bishop's hat: *Epimedium*
Bishop's weed: *Aegopodium*
Bloodroot: *Sanguinaria*
Blue beech: *Carpinus*
Blue cohosh: *Caulophyllum*
Blue daisy: *Felicia*
Blue-eyed-grass: *Sisyrinchium*
Blue-eyed Mary: *Collinsia*
Blue laceflower: *Trachymene*
Blue sage: *Salvia*
Bluebeads: *Clintonia*
Bluebells: *Mertensia*
Bluebells-of-Scotland: *Campanula*
Bluebeard: *Caryopteris*
Blueberry: *Vaccinium*
Bluebonnet: *Lupinus*
Bluets: *Houstonia*
Bog-rosemary: *Andromeda*

Boneset: *Eupatorium*
Boston fern: *Nephrolepis*
Boston ivy: *Parthenocissus*
Bottle-brush: *Callistemon*
Bottle-brush: *Melaleuca*
Bottletree: *Brachychiton*
Bouncing Bet: *Saponaria*
Box: *Buxus*
Box huckleberry: *Gaylussacia*
Box sandmyrtle: *Leiophyllum*
Box-thorn: *Lycium*
Bracken: *Pteridium*
Brake: *Pteridium*
Bramble: *Rubus*
Broom: *Cytisus*
Broom: *Genista*
Buckeye: *Aesculus*
Buckthorn: *Rhamnus*
Buffalo-berry: *Shepherdia*
Bugbane: *Cimicifuga*
Bugleweed: *Ajuga*
Bugloss: *Anchusa*
Bunchberry dogwood: *Cornus*
Bush-clover: *Lespedeza*
Bush-honeysuckle: *Diervilla*
Busy Lizzie: *Impatiens*
Butcher's-broom: *Ruscus*
Buttercup: *Ranunculus*
Butterfly-flower: *Schizanthus*
Butterfly-pea: *Clitoria*
Butterfly-weed: *Asclepias*
Butterwort: *Pinguicula*
Button-bush: *Cephalanthus*

Cajeput tree: *Melaleuca*
Calamint: *Satureja*
California-bluebell: *Phacelia*
California-fuchsia: *Zauschneria*
California-poppy: *Eschscholtzia*
Calla-lily: *Zantedeschia*
Campion: *Lychnis*
Campion: *Silene*

Candytuft: *Iberis*
Canterbury-bells: *Campanula*
Cape-marigold: *Dimor-
photheca*
Cardinal flower: *Lobelia*
Carolina-jessamine:
Gelsemium
Cat-claw: *Doxantha*
Catchfly: *Lychnis*
Castor-bean: *Ricinus*
Cat's-ears: *Calochortus*
Celandine-poppy:
Stylophorum
Chalice-vine: *Solandra*
Chamomile: *Anthemis*
Chaste-tree: *Vitex*
Chestnut: *Castanea*
Cheddar pink: *Dianthus*
Cherry: *Prunus*
Chilean-bellflower: *Nolana*
Chiloe strawberry: *Fragaria*
China-aster: *Callistephus*
China-fir: *Cunninghamia*
China pink: *Dianthus*
Chinaberry: *Melia*
Chinese-forget-me-not:
Cynoglossum
Chinquapin: *Castanea*
Chokeberry: *Aronia*
Christ-thorn: *Paliurus*
Christmas-berry tree: *Schinus*
Christmas-rose: *Helleborus*
Cigarflower: *Cuphea*
Cinnamon fern: *Osmunda*
Cinnamon-vine: *Dioscorea*
Cinquefoil: *Potentilla*
Cliff-brake: *Pellaea*
Climbing fern: *Lygodium*
Climbing-lily: *Gloriosa*
Clock-vine: *Thunbergia*
Cockscomb: *Celosia*
Cockspur coral tree: *Erythrina*
Cockspur thorn: *Crataegus*
Coffeetree: *Gymnocladus*
Columbine: *Aquilegia*
Coneflower: *Echinacea*
Coneflower: *Rudbeckia*
Confederate-jasmine:
Trachelospermum
Cookoo-flower: *Lychnis*
Copper-tip: *Crocosmia*
Coral-bells: *Heuchera*
Coral-vine: *Antigonon*
Coralberry: *Symphoricarpos*
Cork tree: *Phellodendron*

Corkbush: *Euonymus*
Corn-lily: *Ixia*
Cornflower: *Centaurea*
Cotton gum: *Nyssa*
Cowberry: *Vaccinium*
Cowslip: *Caltha*
Cranberry bush: *Viburnum*
Cranesbill: *Geranium*
Crape-myrtle: *Lagerstroemia*
Creeping Jenny: *Lysimachia*
Creeping-zinnia: *Sanvitalia*
Crested-poppy: *Argemone*
Cross-vine: *Bignonia*
Crown imperial: *Fritillaria*
Crown-vetch: *Coronilla*
Cuckoo-pint: *Arum*
Cup-and-saucer vine: *Cobaea*
Cup-flower: *Nierembergia*
Currant: *Ribes*
Cypress: *Chamaecyparis*
Cypress: *Cupressus*

Dahlberg daisy: *Thymophylla*
Dawn-redwood: *Metasequoia*
Daylily: *Hemerocallis*
Desert-candle: *Eremurus*
Desert-willow: *Chilopsis*
Dewberry: *Rubus*
Dog-tooth-violet: *Erythro-
nium*
Dogwood: *Cornus*
Dovetree: *Davidia*
Dusty miller: *Centaurea*
Dutchman's-breeches: *Di-
centra*

Edelweiss: *Leontopodium*
Elder: *Sambucus*
Elephant's-ear: *Colocasia*
Elm: *Ulmus*
Empress tree: *Paulownia*
English daisy: *Bellis*
English ivy: *Hedera*
Evergreen candytuft: *Iberis*
Everlasting: *Anaphalis*
Everlasting: *Helipterum*

Falsecypress: *Chamaecyparis*
False Solomon's seal:
Smilacina
Feverfew: *Chrysanthemum*
Fig: *Ficus*
Filbert: *Corylus*
Fir: *Abies*
Firethorn: *Pyracantha*

Flowering-quince:
Chaenomeles
Foamflower: *Tiarella*
Forget-me-not: *Myosotis*
Four-o'clock: *Mirabilis*
Foxglove: *Digitalis*
Foxtail-lily: *Eremurus*
Fringetree: *Chionanthus*
Fumaria: *Corydalis*
Funkia: *Hosta*

Garland-flower: *Daphne*
Garden-heliotrope: *Valeriana*
Gayfeather: *Liatris*
Gasplant: *Dictamnus*
German-chamomile: *Mat-
ricaria*
Germander: *Teucrium*
Gill-over-the-ground: *Nepeta*
Globe-amaranth: *Gomphrena*
Globe-thistle: *Echinops*
Globeflower: *Trollius*
Gloriosa daisy: *Rudbeckia*
Glory-lily: *Gloriosa*
Glory-of-the-snow:
Chionodoxa
Glory-of-the-sun:
Leucocoryne
Golden-rain tree: *Koelreuteria*
Goldenglow: *Rudbeckia*
Goldenrod: *Solidago*
Goldthread: *Coptis*
Grape fern: *Botrychium*
Ground-ivy: *Nepeta*
Guernsey-lily: *Nerine*
Gum tree: *Eucalyptus*

Hackberry: *Celtis*
Hackmatack: *Larix*
Hardy-gloxinia: *Incarvillea*
Hardy-orange: *Poncirus*
Harebell: *Campanula*
Hart's-tongue fern: *Phyllitis*
Hawthorn: *Crataegus*
Hay-scented fern: *Dennstaed-
tia*
Hazelnut: *Corylus*
Heal-all: *Prunella*
Heath: *Erica*
Heather: *Calluna*
Heavenly-bamboo: *Nandina*
Hemlock: *Tsuga*
Hen and chickens: *Semper-
vivum*
Henbit dead nettle: *Lamium*

Herb Robert: *Geranium*
Hickory: *Carya*
Hinoki-cypress: *Chamaecyparis*
Holly: *Ilex*
Hollyhock: *Althaea*
Holy ghost: *Angelica*
Honesty: *Lunaria*
Honeysuckle: *Lonicera*
Hornbeam: *Carpinus*
Horse-chestnut: *Aesculus*
Houseleek: *Sempervivum*
Huckleberry: *Gaylussacia*
Hyacinth-bean: *Dolichos*

Immortelle: *Xeranthemum*
India-hawthorn: *Raphiolepis*
Indian-currant: *Symphoricarpos*
Indian-pipe: *Monotropa*
Indigo: *Baptisia*
Irish-heath: *Daboecia*
Irish-moss: *Sagina*
Ironweed: *Vernonia*
Ironwood: *Carpinus*
Ironwood: *Ostrya*
Ivy: *Hedera*

Jacob's ladder: *Polemonium*
Jack-in-the-pulpit: *Arisaema*
Japanese-quince: *Chaenomeles*
Jasmine: *Jasminum*
Jerusalem-artichoke: *Helianthus*
Jetbead: *Rhodotypos*
Joe-pyeweed: *Eupatorium*
Joseph's coat: *Amaranthus*
Juniper: *Juniperus*
Jujube: *Zizyphus*

Katsura tree: *Cercidiphyllum*
Kew broom: *Cytisus*
Kingfisher daisy: *Felicia*
Knotweed: *Polygonum*
Kudzu vine: *Pueraria*

Labrador-tea: *Ledum*
Lady fern: *Athyrium*
Lady's mantle: *Alchemilla*
Lady's slipper: *Cypripedium*
Lamb's-ears: *Stachys*
Larch: *Larix*
Lantern plant: *Physalis*
Larkspur: *Delphinium*
Lavender-cotton: *Santolina*

Lawn leaf: *Dichondra*
Lead plant: *Amorpha*
Leadwort: *Ceratostigma*
Leather-leaf: *Chamaedaphne*
Leatherwood: *Dirca*
Lemon-lily: *Hemerocallis*
Lemon-mint: *Monarda*
Lenten-rose: *Helleborus*
Leopard's-bane: *Doronicum*
Lilac: *Syringa*
Lily: *Lilium*
Lily-of-the-Nile: *Agapanthus*
Lily-of-the-valley: *Convallaria*
Lily-turf: *Liriope*
Lily-turf: *Ophiopogon*
Linden: *Tilia*
Lip fern: *Cheilanthes*
Live-forever: *Sedum*
Liverleaf: *Hepatica*
Locust: *Gleditsia*
Locust: *Robinia*
Loquat: *Eriobotrya*
Love-in-a-mist: *Nigella*
Lung-wort: *Pulmonaria*
Lupine: *Lupinus*

Madeira-vine: *Boussingaultia*
Maidenhair fern: *Adiantum*
Maidenhair tree: *Ginkgo*
Maltese-cross: *Lychnis*
Maple: *Acer*
Marigold: *Tagetes*
Mariposa-lily: *Calochortus*
Marjoram: *Origanum*
Marsh-mallow: *Althaea*
Marsh-marigold: *Caltha*
Marvel-of-Peru: *Mirabilis*
Matilija-poppy: *Romneya*
Matrimony vine: *Lycium*
May-apple: *Podophyllum*
Meadow-beauty: *Rhexia*
Meadow-foam: *Limnanthes*
Meadow-rue: *Thalictrum*
Meadow-saffron: *Colchicum*
Meadow-sweet: *Filipendula*
Medlar: *Mespilus*
Merrybells: *Uvularia*
Mescal-bean: *Sophora*
Mexican-orange: *Choisya*
Mexican-sunflower: *Tithonia*
Mignonette: *Reseda*
Mint: *Mentha*
Mitrewort: *Epimedium*
Moccasin-flower: *Cypripedium*

Mock-orange: *Philadelphus*
Money plant: *Lunaria*
Moneywort: *Lysimachia*
Monkey-flower: *Mimulus*
Monkshood: *Aconitum*
Moonflower: *Calonyction*
Morning-glory: *Ipomoea*
Mountain-andromeda: *Pieris*
Mountain-fringe: *Adlumia*
Mountain-laurel: *Kalmia*
Mulberry: *Morus*
Mullein: *Verbascum*
Myrtle: *Myrtus*
Myrtle: *Vinca*

Naked ladies: *Lycoris*
Nasturtium: *Tropaeolum*
New Jersey-tea: *Ceanothus*
Ninebark: *Physocarpus*

Oak: *Quercus*
Obedient plant: *Physostegia*
Oconee-bells: *Shortia*
Oleander: *Nerium*
Olive: *Olea*
Onion: *Allium*
Orchid tree: *Bauhinia*
Oregon-grape: *Mahonia*
Osage-orange: *Maclura*
Osier: *Salix*

Pagoda tree: *Sophora*
Pansy: *Viola*
Paper-mulberry: *Broussonetia*
Parasol-tree: *Firmiana*
Partridge-berry: *Mitchella*
Pasque-flower: *Anemone*
Passionflower: *Passiflora*
Pea-tree: *Caragana*
Pear: *Pyrus*
Pearl-bush: *Exochorda*
Pecan: *Carya*
Pepperbush: *Clethra*
Peppertree: *Schinus*
Periwinkle: *Vinca*
Persimmon: *Diospyros*
Pimpernel: *Anagallis*
Pine: *Pinus*
Pitcher-plant: *Sarracenia*
Plane tree: *Platanus*
Plantain-lily: *Hosta*
Plum: *Prunus*
Plum-yew: *Cephalotaxus*
Plumbago: *Ceratostigma*

Poinciana: *Delonix*
Pomegranate: *Punica*
Poplar: *Populus*
Poppy: *Papaver*
Possum-haw: *Ilex*
Pot-marigold: *Calendula*
Prairie-mallow: *Sidalcea*
Prickly-poppy: *Argemone*
Primrose: *Primula*
Primrose, evening: *Oenothera*
Privet: *Ligustrum*
Pussy-toes: *Antennaria*
Pussy willow: *Salix*
Putty-root: *Aplectrum*

Quaker ladies: *Houstonia*
Quince: *Cydonia*

Rain-lily: *Cooperia*
Rain-lily: *Zephyranthes*
Raspberry: *Rubus*
Rattlesnake-plantain:
  Goodyera
Red-hot-poker: *Kniphofia*
Rose-acacia: *Robinia*
Rock-cress: *Arabis*
Rock-purslane: *Calandrinia*
Rock-rose: *Cistus*
Rose-of-Sharon: *Hibiscus*
Rose-moss: *Portulaca*
Rosemary: *Rosmarinus*
Rue-anemone: *Anemonella*
Russell prairie-gentian: *Eustoma*
Russian-olive: *Elaeagnus*

St. John's-wort: *Hypericum*
Salt-bush: *Atriplex*
Salt tree: *Tamarix*
Sand-myrtle: *Leiophyllum*
Sand-verbena: *Abronia*
Scholar tree: *Sophora*
Sea-buckthorn: *Hippophae*
Sea-holly: *Eryngium*
Sea-lavender: *Limonium*
Sea-pink: *Armeria*
Sea-poppy: *Glaucium*
Seaside-pea: *Lathyrus*
Selfheal: *Prunella*
Serviceberry: *Amelanchier*
Shadblow: *Amelanchier*
She-oak: *Casuarina*
Sheep-laurel: *Kalmia*
Shinleaf: *Pyrola*
Shooting-star: *Dodecatheon*

Silk-vine: *Periploca*
Silk-tassel bush: *Garrya*
Silk-tree: *Albizia*
Silver-bell: *Halesia*
Silver-lace-vine: *Polygonum*
Skunk-cabbage: *Symplocarpus*
Smoketree: *Cotinus*
Snakeroot: *Eupatorium*
Snapdragon: *Antirrhinum*
Sneezewood: *Helenium*
Snow-in-summer: *Cerastium*
Snow-on-the-mountain:
  Euphorbia
Snowball: *Viburnum*
Snowbell: *Styrax*
Snowberry: *Symphoricarpos*
Snowberry: *Chiogenes*
Snowdrop: *Galanthus*
Snowdrop tree: *Halesia*
Snowflake: *Leucojum*
Soapwort: *Saponaria*
Society-garlic: *Tulbaghia*
Solomon's seal: *Polygonatum*
Sorrel tree: *Oxydendrum*
Sour-wood: *Oxydendrum*
Sour gum: *Nyssa*
Spanish-broom: *Spartium*
Speedwell: *Veronica*
Spicebush: *Lindera*
Spider flower: *Cleome*
Spider-lily: *Hymenocallis*
Spiderwort: *Tradescantia*
Spike-heath: *Bruckenthalia*
Spindle-tree: *Euonymus*
Spring-beauty: *Claytonia*
Spruce: *Picea*
Spring-beauty: *Claytonia*
Spring star-flower: *Brodiaea*
Squaw-carpet: *Ceanothus*
Squill: *Scilla*
Squirrel-corn: *Dicentra*
Stagger-bush: *Lyonia*
Star-flower: *Trientalis*
Star-grass: *Aletris*
Star-grass: *Hypoxis*
Star-jasmine: *Trachelospermum*
Star-of-Texas: *Xanthisma*
Statice: *Limonium*
Stock: *Mathiola*
Stonecress: *Aethionema*
Stonecrop: *Sedum*
Storax: *Styrax*
Strawberry: *Fragaria*

Strawberry-tree: *Arbutus*
Strawflower: *Helichrysum*
Sumac: *Rhus*
Summer-cypress: *Kochia*
Summer-hyacinth: *Galtonia*
Summer savory: *Satureja*
Sunflower: *Helianthus*
Sun-rose: *Helianthemum*
Swamp-mallow: *Hibiscus*
Swamp-pink: *Helonias*
Sweet-alyssum: *Lobularia*
Sweet-fern: *Comptonia*
Sweet-flag: *Acorus*
Sweet-gale: *Myrica*
Sweet gum: *Liquidambar*
Sweet-pea: *Lathyrus*
Sweet rocket: *Hesperis*
Sweet William: *Dianthus*
Sweet William-catchfly: *Silene*
Sweet woodruff: *Asperula*
Sweetbrier: *Rosa*
Sweet-shrub: *Calycanthus*

Tamarisk: *Tamarix*
Tea-tree: *Leptospermum*
Thornapple: *Crataegus*
Tobacco plant: *Nicotiana*
Tree-aster: *Olearia*
Tree-of-heaven: *Ailanthus*
Tree-mallow: *Lavatera*
Tritoma: *Kniphofia*
Trumpetcreeper: *Campsis*
Tuberose: *Polianthes*
Tulip-tree: *Liriodendron*
Tupelo gum: *Nyssa*
Turfing daisy: *Matricaria*

Umbrella-pine: *Sciadopitys*

Valerian: *Centranthus*
Valerian: *Valeriana*

Wallflower: *Cheiranthus*
Walnut: *Juglans*
Water-lily: *Nymphaea*
Wayfaring-tree: *Viburnum*
Wild-ginger: *Asarum*
Willow: *Salix*
Wind-flower: *Anemone*
Winter aconite: *Eranthis*
Winter-hazel: *Corylopsis*
Wintercreeper: *Euonymus*
Wintergreen: *Gaultheria*
Witch-hazel: *Hamamelis*
Yew: *Taxus*